THE WORK AND LIFE
OF DAVID GROVE

THE WORK AND LIFE OF DAVID GROVE

CLEAN LANGUAGE AND EMERGENT KNOWLEDGE

CAROL WILSON

Copyright © 2017 Carol Wilson

The moral right of the author has been asserted.

Apart from any fair dealing for the purposes of research or private study, or criticism or review, as permitted under the Copyright, Designs and Patents Act 1988, this publication may only be reproduced, stored or transmitted, in any form or by any means, with the prior permission in writing of the publishers, or in the case of reprographic reproduction in accordance with the terms of licences issued by the Copyright Licensing Agency. Enquiries concerning reproduction outside those terms should be sent to the publishers.

Matador
9 Priory Business Park,
Wistow Road, Kibworth Beauchamp,
Leicestershire. LE8 0RX
Tel: 0116 279 2299
Email: books@troubador.co.uk
Web: www.troubador.co.uk/matador
Twitter: @matadorbooks

ISBN 978 1785892 882

British Library Cataloguing in Publication Data.
A catalogue record for this book is available from the British Library.

Typeset in 11pt Gil Sans by Troubador Publishing Ltd, Leicester, UK

Matador is an imprint of Troubador Publishing Ltd

To Penny, James, Angela and all the dedicated practitioners of David Grove's Clean work, especially those who have contributed to this book.

CONTENTS

FOREWORD — xiii

INTRODUCTION — xvii

PART ONE: CLEAN LANGUAGE

CHAPTER ONE: THE PRINCIPLES OF CLEAN — 3
Metaphor — 4

CHAPTER TWO: TECHNIQUE — 11
Element 1: Position — 12
Element 2: The Questions — 13
Element 3: Reflecting Words Back — 17
Element 4: Tone and Pace — 19
Element 5: Syntax — 21
Element 6: Intuition — 23
Example of a Clean Language Session — 23

CHAPTER THREE: ASPECTS OF CLEAN LANGUAGE — 27
Body Language — 27
Structure of a Clean Language Session — 28
Clean Practice in Coaching — 32
How Clean Coaching Relates to Standard Coaching — 35
What Not to Do — 36
Negative Metaphors — 37
Redemptive Metaphors — 38
Clean Language at Work — 39
Clean Language by Telephone — 42

PART TWO: EMERGENT KNOWLEDGE

CHAPTER ONE: THEORY — 45
Clean Space — 45
Transition to Emergent Knowledge — 46
Map of a Client's World — 49

CHAPTER TWO: SMALL WORLD NETWORKS, CLEAN WORLDS & SIX DEGREES OF FREEDOM — 53

CHAPTER THREE: TECHNIQUES — 62
Structure of an Emergent Knowledge Session: — 65
- *Clean Start* — 65
- *Clean Process* — 67
- *Clean Finish* — 71
- *Clean Action Space* — 71

Clean Processes: — 72
- *Clean Pronouns* — 73
- *Clean Ancestry* — 74
- *Clean Networks* — 75
- *Clean Spinning* — 76
- *Clean Hieroglyphics* — 78
- *Clean Boundaries* — 79
- *Clean Time* — 81
- *Clean History of Goals* — 90
- *Clean Scanning* — 91
- *Clean Aid Including "Safety of Clean Language and EK"* — 93
- *Clean Scapes* — 98

CHAPTER FOUR: THE SENSES' CENSUS — 99
Introduction: Map of Your World — 99
Part I: Real World Questions to A — 100
- *Sense of A* — 100
- *Time of A* — 101
- *The Body Physical* — 102
- *The Body Parts* — 102

- Body Storage — 103
- Body Internal — 103
- Body Position — 104
- Body Movement — 104
- Body Metaphysical — 104
- Body of Speech — 105

Part II: Real World Questions to B — 107
Part III: Real World Questions to C — 108
Part IV: Real World Questions to D — 109

PART THREE: THE LIFE OF DAVID GROVE

CHAPTER ONE: BIOGRAPHY — 113

CHAPTER TWO: RECOLLECTIONS BY CO-PRACTITIONERS AND FRIENDS OF DAVID GROVE — 118

Rob McGavock — 118
Caitlin Walker — 128
Jennifer de Gandt — 146
Tania Korsak — 149
Philip Harland — 154
Lynne Burney — 156
Penny Tompkins and James Lawley — 159

PART FOUR: CASE HISTORIES BY DAVID GROVE'S PRACTITIONERS

KEIKO IZUMI — 171
Workshop with David Grove at the World Bank

CAITLIN WALKER — 178
1. Clean Sports Development in a University
2. Clean Team Building in a London Business School

IAN HALDANE AND DIANNE EMMERSON.   184
Clean Language and Clean Space Workshop for the Te Ihi Tu Programme

CAROL WILSON   193
1. Transformational Change through Metaphor delivered by Carol Wilson, Angela Dunbar and Wendy Oliver 2007 at the BBC
2. Project for Doctorate in Professional Studies: an Exploration of the Use of Clean Language and Emergent Knowledge Techniques by Corporate Coaches delivered by Carol Wilson 2011 at the BBC
3. Clean Language Session with a Business Executive

ANGELA DUNBAR   201
1. Clean Worlds Session delivered by David Grove
2. Clean Language Session Transcript

ADRIAN GOODALL   212
Clean Space Corporate Workshop

PART FIVE: TRANSCRIPTS OF DAVID GROVE'S SESSIONS AND WORKSHOPS

SESSION WITH PRIVATE CLIENT 28 MAY 2005   217

CLEAN PRONOUNS WORKSHOP AT THE THATCHED COTTAGE 2005   244

CLEAN HIEROGLYPHICS SESSION WITH DEBORAH HENLEY   249

GROUP SESSION BY PHONE 15 MARCH 2006 FEATURING CLEAN START AND CLEAN NETWORKS   282

SESSION WITH ANGELA DUNBAR: "I'M GETTING FITTER" FEATURING CLEAN BOUNDARIES   285

Contents

SESSION WITH PRIVATE CLIENT FEATURING
    CLEAN SPINNING 2005   295

SESSION WITH LYNN BULLOCK DECEMBER 2007   310

GROUP SESSION BY PHONE OCTOBER 2006 FEATURING
    CLEAN NETWORKS   337

PART SIX: LIST OF BOOKS AND WEBSITES

BOOKS AND ARTICLES ABOUT DAVID GROVE'S
    CLEAN WORK   349

BOOKS ABOUT THE SCIENCE OF EMERGENCE   352
Popular Culture Featuring the Science of Emergence   352
Websites   353

REFERENCES   354

FOREWORD

David Grove was a Character (with a capital C) who had a genius for innovating new ways to do therapy. He also had a remarkable generosity of spirit. This was exemplified in a metaphor he created while staying with us in London in 2002. One afternoon Caitlin Walker joined us in identifying metaphors for the role each of us wanted to play in the development of the clean community. David's metaphor for himself was a "launch pad" from which others could lift off to discover new and unexplored worlds. David had an 'open source' ethos. He never trademarked or registered Clean Language or any of his wonderful innovations. His suggestion to his students was always "take my work and make it your own".

Once we had won David over with, as he put it, "Penny's tenacious won't-take-no-for-an-answer style and James' inquiring, penetrating questions" he was completely supportive of our desire to produce a model of his work and to disseminate it to those who were interested. And it wasn't just us – the same was true of everyone whose heart he could see was touched by his work.

Remarkably little of David's prodigious output exists in published form since writing was not his forte. Among David's gifts were his voice, his powers of observation, his focussed attention, his memory, and his love of the nuances and rhythm of the spoken word – no doubt derived in part from his Māori heritage. (The Māori language was not translated into the written form until 1820, although the symbolic meanings embodied in carving, knots and weaving have a much longer history.)

Carol Wilson is imbued with a similar generosity of spirit and showed remarkable fortitude in supporting David. She not only let him stay in her beautiful English thatched cottage from which he ran all manner of impromptu and experimental workshops, she worked with him to systematise some of his ideas into teachable processes for coaches and other facilitators. Carol is one of the few people who managed to pin David down long enough to write about his work and to get it published. That is no mean feat when, as we know only too well, David never stood still for long. He developed ideas and processes at a pace that was hard to keep up with.

When David 'chased an idea' he pursued it with every cell in his body. For instance, David stayed with us in 2003 and the night before he was due to leave the country he picked a book off of our bookshelf and started reading it. "Nexus: Small Worlds & the Groundbreaking Science of Networks" was just the right book in the right place at the right time to stimulate David's latest pursuit, Clean Space. The next morning he hadn't finished the book and thoughtfully placed it back on the shelf before going to the airport. Imagine our surprise when two hours after leaving our home a taxi pulled up outside – containing David and all his luggage. He said he decided to miss the flight because he wanted to finish reading the book. He left his bags on the landing, and took the book to his room where he read it cover to cover – twice. He wouldn't even come down to join us for meals, so we took him food on a tray for the duration.

"The Work and Life of David Grove: Clean Language and Emergent Knowledge" is a significant contribution to the field. It includes Carol's work with David Grove between 2005 and 2007 and contains original transcripts of both his workshops and client sessions. Carol's inclusion of others' recollections and case histories adds richness and diversity. It reveals some pieces of the jigsaw of what David meant to those many, many lives he touched. And by not editing these contributors' descriptions she demonstrates a congruence with David's approach of preserving his clients' exact words, and respecting each person's subjective experience.

But Carol has done much more than than collate others' work.

Foreword

She has documented a large number of David's processes involving metaphor, Clean Language, Clean Space and those that come under the umbrella term, Emergent Knowledge. On top of that, her own cases studies show how she has applied Clean principles in real-world business situations.

We can think of no better way for Carol to honour David Grove's memory than to have produced this book.

We'll leave the last word to James Hillman, whose instruction for a life well-lived perfectly describes David Grove's contribution:

"All of us, each one of us, can and ought to give as much of himself as he possibly can – nay, to give more than he can, to exceed himself, to go beyond himself, to make himself irreplaceable."

Penny Tompkins and James Lawley, Waxahachie, Texas,
17 December 2014

INTRODUCTION

"David was a master at soliciting accurate information of which the client wasn't even cognizant previously. He had learned that not only do people carry information within the body, they carry it in the space around them as well. He could find all of the bits and pieces of a fragmented and dissociated client. He'd find them in cracks on the wall, behind things, up in the sky, behind them, in the carpet, in a mirror, through the window - the kind of places he'd find bits and pieces was endless. David went to very delicate and sacred places with clients. It could almost feel scary to a novice. It was literally word surgery and you knew it. You knew that the barest of bones of a person's emotional life were laid out on the table, and trusted that he would always manage to tidy things up in a safe way and/or bring healing to the dynamic at play."

— Rob McGavock 2010

A year or so before his death, I received a call from David Grove. It was his custom to travel around the world, staying with various practitioners, of whom I was one, who could help develop his work. He said he was planning to spend some time in France, and suggested he hire a houseboat, and that perhaps I would like to come out for two weeks to complete the book we planned to write together. Aware of my love of boats, he was proposing the optimum surroundings to tempt me to take time out of my busy schedule and finish our book. We chatted about the possibility but made no plans – Grove's own calendar depended on where his lively mind would take him at any particular moment and which people or theories he had come across that stimulated new ideas.

So I continued my life and work, incorporating Clean Language and Emergent Knowledge wherever possible, and wondered from time to time when we would be able to finish the book. It never happened: the next communication I received about Grove was that he had died, suddenly, of a heart attack.

Grove pioneered the technique of Clean Language while working as a therapist with victims of trauma during the 1980s. He discovered that clients (and in this book I use the word 'client' to represent patient, coachee, or whoever is on the receiving end of the process) would often speak in metaphor to describe their experiences and that the most effective way of resolving traumatic memories was to honour and develop these metaphors by asking open questions, or reflecting back the client's exact words:

> "I noticed, if I didn't force people when they were talking, they would naturally start using metaphor to describe their experience."
> - David Grove (Tompkins & Lawley 1995)

This was at odds with the prevailing principles of conventional therapy, which encouraged patients to talk in depth about their trauma. Grove's technique asked questions of the metaphors themselves, or repeated back the exact words used by the client. He called the process 'Clean' because it did not interfere with or contaminate the client's own experience; it put clients in control of their own healing process.

Grove eventually developed this linguistic work into spatial techniques, where clients physically move to other positions. Initially called Clean Space, it became Emergent Knowledge, based on the science of Emergence, Milgram's theory of Six Degrees of Separation and Chaos Theory. Words, even when limited to the client's own, inevitably carry the risk of association with the baggage carried by the conscious mind, like past disappointments, limiting assumptions and fear of failure. The spatial systems of Emergent Knowledge left even the words behind in order to tap into the whole, pristine self of the client.

When people talk in 'real world' language (non-metaphor), they are speaking from the conscious mind, which is clouded by all kinds of baggage – fear, past failure, and agendas which have been implanted by, for instance, parents or teachers over the years. When people express their thoughts in metaphors they are communicating directly with what Jung termed their 'unconscious' minds. So if the facilitator directs questions to the metaphors, then he or she is enabling the client to explore the 'whole self' rather than being blocked by conscious limitations. This 'whole self' includes Jung's 'unconscious mind' and David Grove sometimes called it 'intuition'. All three descriptions are used interchangeably throughout this book. Clean processes are specifically designed to reach this whole self.

This formed the basis of twentieth century psychologist Jung's work. He prefaces his autobiography, which is largely an account of the symbols which appeared in his dreams, contained within sparse information about the events of his life, (Jung 1961) by stating:

> "Recollection of the outward events of my life has largely faded or disappeared. But my encounters with the 'other' reality, my bouts with the unconscious, are indelibly engraved upon my memory. In that realm there has always been wealth in abundance, and everything else has lost importance by comparison. I can understand myself in the light of inner happenings. It is these that make up the singularity of my life, and with these my autobiography deals."

However, there is one key difference between Jung's work and Grove's: Grove placed no importance whatsoever on interpreting the symbols which appeared. He maintained that merely identifying the symbols and watching them unfold was sufficient to alleviate the traumas they represented. Jung however believed that interpretation was not only crucial, but a duty of the therapist towards his patients (Jung 1961):

> "It is equally a grave mistake to think that it is enough to gain some understanding of the images and that knowledge can here make a halt. Insight into them must be converted into an ethical obligation. Not to do so is to fall prey to the power principle, and this produces dangerous effects which are destructive not only to others but even to the knower. The images of the unconscious place a great responsibility upon a man. Failure to understand them, or a shirking of ethical responsibility, deprives him of his wholeness and imposes a painful fragmentariness on his life."

The potential difficulty with this obligation to interpret the symbols is that issues are often presented in symbols either because they represent traumas which are too painful or damaging for the person to face, or arise from a situation which occurred at a young age, before the person had words. Jung assisted his patients in recalling and describing their dreams, and then he interpreted the symbols for them, diagnosing their origin. The first process is in line with coaching principles, the second is not. Coaches do not diagnose their coachees' problems and these principles hold particularly true in David Grove's Clean work. This demonstrates the shift in attitude which occurred in the second half of the twentieth century across all areas of life, including psychology, work and personal development, which encouraged people to start taking responsibility for themselves, and to look towards the future with a positive, solution focused approach.

In normal conversation, we talk with our conscious minds, and the result may be clouded by the baggage mentioned above, or agendas imposed on us by others such as parents or influences from our early lives. A question which is effective in terms of developing the recipient invites the whole self to answer, reaching parts which may be obscured or blocked from the conscious self.

Many people have a sense of the person they were 'born to be', and that there is a 'life's path' they are 'meant' to be on. There are times when people feel that they are living in a way that is true to that self and on that path; they might say 'I was born to do this' or 'This was meant to be'. At other times, people feel that their actions are out of alignment and that they are not living according to their values or making the most of their talents; they might use phrases like 'I'm not firing on all cylinders', or 'I'm stuck in a rut'.

Grove maintained that a healthy embryo is conceived as a pristine being, with innate qualities and talents. Unfortunately life has a way of distorting and obscuring these, and this can begin even in the womb, during a difficult pregnancy or birth, in childhood, or later in life. The causes can be major or minor traumas, physical or mental pain, limiting influences about what the person should, can't or must do, exposure to negative emotions such as fear and anger, and many other setbacks. These incidents can modify the systems of our internal landscape, or psychescape, creating barriers that obscure some of our innate knowledge from view. Clean processes help to rediscover and reintegrate these lost pieces of knowledge, providing new energy and resources to the client.

I have collated all the work that Grove and I did together in this book. The ideas, opinions and examples are purely David Grove's, except where I have stated otherwise. Being a fast typist, I was able to take down his lectures and sessions word for word. At other times I recorded sessions and training modules. The quotes reproduced throughout this book are Grove's actual words rather than a paraphrase. Occasionally, this includes minor grammatical errors, repetition or non-sequiturs, but Grove had a uniquely poetic cadence to his speech and in order to preserve that I have left these passages unedited.

However, due to his rich vocabulary and the dense meaning

incorporated in his speech, sometimes Grove's statements are not that easy to understand. One of the roles I played at our seminars was to stop him if something was too obscure and either demand an explanation, if I had not understood, or a paraphrase for the participants if they seemed confused. When working one to one, I insisted he explained every word and principle. He liked this and said that being forced to go over things more than once enabled him to obtain more depth of understanding and expand his theories – in fact, I was putting him through something akin to the iterative questioning process described in the Emergent Knowledge section of this book.

The purpose of this book, in particular the section on Emergent Knowledge where most of our work together occurred, is to bring Grove's unique discoveries to the world in their original state wherever possible. Where I am quoting the interpretations or accounts of myself or other practitioners who worked with him, I have made that clear.

David Grove was a man of contradictions, many things to many people and not overly concerned that he sometimes contradicted himself. He worked with different practitioners throughout his life and encouraged them to contribute to his work. He once explained this approach to me by describing it as a trunk with various branches, each branch being cultivated by his work with a different practitioner. My branch was the application of Clean Language and Emergent Knowledge in coaching, which we christened 'Clean Coaching', and it came about because of the growing number of coaches drawn to Clean Language and attending Grovian sessions. He said he valued each branch equally and was emphatic that none of the branches constituted the trunk.

The reason that it is safe for coaches to use Clean processes after the relatively short amount of training they usually undertake is because Clean work is 100% client led. Therapy is often diagnostic and prescriptive to a greater or lesser degree. This is anathema to Clean processes, where all decisions are

Introduction

made by the client's own intuition – a safer guide even that the conscious mind. If Clean principles are adhered to, the client's own unconscious self will dictate how far and where to go in terms of exploring the psyche. So, where a conventional therapist could unwittingly increase a trauma, a Clean practitioner cannot do so provided he or she follows the guidelines.

A principle Grove held dear was that his work was open source. He refused to lay claim to anything in the form of copyrights or trademarks and insisted that his purpose was to discover the knowledge and release it into the world. There have been moves by some of the practitioners he worked with to 'own' certain pieces of work that he created with them. Whereas I am the copyright owner of this particular book, the knowledge shared in it is entirely open source and belongs to no-one.

My personal approach is to regard all the various areas of Grove's work as having value, whether or not I was involved, and at whatever stage of his life they appeared. Grove himself had a tendency to dismiss what had gone before and value only the piece of work in which he was currently engaged - but that evaluation might change every day! I faced the challenge of having created manuals for courses which would be out of date by the time we delivered the training several weeks later. But I considered them as none the less valuable for that.

This book attempts to cast some light on Grove and his work from several perspectives:

1. Part I is a description of the process of Clean Language itself.
2. Part II similarly describes Emergent Knowledge.
3. Part III provides a biography of Grove and some personal accounts from key practitioners with whom he worked.
4. Part IV is a collection of case histories from Grove's leading practitioners, describing sessions they have delivered using Clean Language and Emergent Knowledge.

5. Part V provides full transcripts of actual sessions and workshops delivered by Grove, recorded or taken down by myself or other practitioners.
6. At the end you will find a list of references, recommended books and websites, a glossary and an index.

I believe that in years to come, as Grove's Clean principles and practitioners increase throughout the world, future generations will be curious to know what kind of a man Grove was, how his volume of work assembled itself, who were its main proponents and how they worked. This book attempts to provide a few small guiding lights on all of these topics, and to identify the various pathways available for further research.

Grove's work continues to expand all over the world, through workshops, practitioners, books and conferences. There are strong Clean groups in the US, Australia, New Zealand and France as well as the UK.

PART ONE
CLEAN LANGUAGE

"What a Clean question does is arrest both time and space. In Clean Language, we drop down in between the lines of the semantic and linguistic carrier, to the subtext that sits underneath. Clean Language lassoes a word and drops it into this space. So we enlarge the space so that we can create the client's language in metaphor, or memory, or behaviour, or coughs and splutters – any kind of communication. Then what happens is we gather that information in this different language of metaphors and symbols. Clean Language has to create the metascape – like a landscape that is a representation of a client's internal experience."

– David Grove 2005

Chapter One

The Principles of Clean

Clean Language is a process which uses metaphor and neutral questioning to ease emotional blocks and resulting limiting behaviour patterns. Unlike the guided visualisations widely used in psychotherapy and healing processes, the key to Clean Language is that practitioners are led entirely by their clients, through asking questions which will elicit metaphors and develop them with the least possible influence from the practitioner. The techniques are useful in human interaction in general, in the workplace and outside, as well as formal use in therapy, coaching and related fields.

Below is an example created by Angela Dunbar of several ways of conducting a conversation, which highlight the difference between a Clean style and every day communication. Imagine a friend who says he is *'feeling a bit down'*. You want to be as helpful as possible. What might you say?

"Is it because your wife left you?" This could be an obvious assumption and may be right, but it does not encourage your friend to explore and draw upon his own knowledge and understanding.

"What are you unhappy about?" Now you are assuming that *'a bit down'* means 'unhappy'. Do you know more than he does about his feelings?

"What could you do to stop being unhappy?" Now your assumption is that he wants to stop feeling this way, and that stopping is the thing to do. You may be right in the long term, but at this point in time all he may want is to share and explore his sadness.

"How could you cheer yourself up?" This approach assumes that cheering up is possible and that it is the preferred outcome.

Imagine asking this question:

"And you are feeling a bit down. And when you are feeling a bit down, is there anything else about feeling a 'bit down'?"

This is a 'Clean' question because it honours the speaker's words, so that he:

- *will feel listened to, understood and not judged;*
- *has the opportunity to explore ideas and feelings before rushing to a short term solution;*
- *can take the responsibility of deciding on the best course of action instead of relying on outside advice.*

Metaphor

The word 'metaphor' comes from the Greek 'metapherin' meaning 'to carry something across' or 'transfer'. Metaphors could be seen as systematic thought structures containing information about a person's thoughts, feelings and psychological make-up, and were defined by Lakoff and Johnson's (Lakoff and Johnson 1980) as *"understanding and experiencing one kind of thing in terms of another"*.

Metaphors are an inherent part of our daily life, both in our waking and sleeping states. We use them consciously to convey a feeling, description or situation. Unconsciously, during sleep, our dreams string together metaphors and symbols, some of which are easily attributable and others so obscure that they remain a mystery. Metaphors we often use include:

- *A millstone round my neck*
- *Flat as a pancake*
- *I'm freezing*

- *I'm boiling*
- *Throw some light on*

Less obvious metaphors are:

- *What's your view?*
- *I'm under pressure*
- *I can't get through to you*
- *I'm in a relationship*

Metaphor has played a significant part in therapy and self development for many years, contributing to Jungian therapy, NLP, Transpersonal Psychology, Psycho Synthesis, and ancient healing rituals.

Looking within a person's symbolic 'landscape' for meaning is not new. Carl Jung explains the importance of the unconscious mind in the following way (Jung 1964):

> *"Man, as we realise if we reflect for a moment, never perceives anything fully or comprehends completely…*
>
> *No matter what instruments he uses, he reaches the edge of certainty beyond which conscious knowledge cannot pass…*
>
> *As a general rule, the unconscious aspect of any event is revealed to us in dreams, where it appears not as a rational thought but as a symbolic image."*
>
> – Jung, Man and his Symbols (Chapter One)

The unconscious takes note of all events and experiences, and will store this information in forms and symbols that may be somewhat obscure to our conscious minds. Jung was convinced that by analysing those symbols we have access to a much wider and more comprehensive understanding of ourselves, our relationships and the wider world around us.

A symbol might be taken from a client's dream and consciously developed during a session. Jung believed that the subconscious did not have words and communicated with the conscious mind through symbols. A symbol might be an object, a word, a living being or a scene.

It is not uncommon to dream of someone we know, but find that in the dream they are behaving uncharacteristically, or portraying a relationship with us which is different to the relationship we have with that person in real life. This is the subconscious mind using the person as a symbol, in order to portray something that might be entirely different.

For instance, I knew a woman who had recurring dreams about a famous actor. She eventually recognised that the dream related to her emotional state during a traumatic relationship with a man with a name that rhymed with the actor's. Yet her previous lover did not appear at all in the dream as himself, and the actor of the dream did not display any of the lover's characteristics. The unconscious mind had latched onto a symbol as a way of examining the trauma in an attempt to resolve it.

At the end of her course of Jungian therapy, another woman told me she dreamed of a new hairpiece being fitted onto her own hair by a shop assistant called Amanda. There was a sense of urgency as the shop was about to close. The therapist suggested that the hairpiece represented the new self-knowledge that the client had gained during therapy being integrated to her previous knowledge and said that the word 'amanda' is Latin for 'love'. The client had never studied Latin, did not know anyone called Amanda, and was not aware of the Latin meaning. She felt that the explanation fitted, and that the sense of urgency due to 'closing time' in the dream related to the fact that she felt this would be her final session before the therapist had suggested it.

There is a key difference here to Clean techniques; in Clean, practitioners do not place their own interpretations on the symbols and do not ask their clients to either. One of Grove's key breakthroughs was the discovery that it does not matter whether the symbols are identified by the conscious mind; what brings about the healing process is the exploration of them. In fact, to go one stage further, it can be pivotal to the healing process that the symbols are not identified. If a man has suffered a trauma so intense that the mind will not allow him to remember it, being asked to interpret the symbols that represent it will place him in a 'Catch 22' situation and may put a stop to the healing process altogether. Clean enables people to explore their pain through metaphor and to go straight through it and out the other side, without ever having to identify what caused the pain in the first place.

Returning again to the history of metaphor in psychology, psychologist James Hillman worked with what he termed the "imaginal world" (Hillman 1989). The client might be asked to imagine a meadow or a house. Each client's meadow would be specific to that person, and by exploring the meadow the client could develop at a deeper level than he or she might through real life exploration. This gives a nod in the direction of Clean, in that after the introduction of Hillman's metaphor, the client's own symbols can be developed.

David Grove moved on from this point in that a Clean process does not involve suggesting a meadow or any other scenario, but asks the client to describe whatever comes to mind. Whether that turns out to be a metaphor about surroundings, people, self or others, or even no metaphor at all but a discussion in the 'real world' is immaterial to the effectiveness of the process. What is crucial is that the client is encouraged to talk without any outside influences.

Blocks, fears and phobias are often the result of traumatic experience when we were too young, or too damaged to recall them. In real terms, the trauma may or may not have been serious; it could have arisen simply from being frightened by something relatively insignificant at a young age, or equally from something as serious as child abuse. It is possible that the trauma might be a result of a difficult birth or something that happened to the mother while the child was in the womb. The intensity of the trauma does not necessarily relate to the severity of the cause.

What happens is that a protective framework is set up by the psyche, for example as a shield against the sound of parents fighting with each other when the child is too young to understand what is happening. Years later, this defensive mechanism may be triggered by unrelated events, perhaps by aggression in a business meeting, or fear of loss in a relationship, and the adult will revert to behaviour dictated by the trauma's framework. Although this may now be inappropriate, it is still functioning. More seriously, the framework will be using up a part of our energy and resources, rendering them unavailable to us. There are plenty of metaphors around relating to this, like 'feeling as if a part of me is missing', and particularly in a healing context, 'becoming whole again'. There is a famous story in the bible of Jesus healing a man and saying: "Behold, thou art made whole" (John 5:14). In fact earlier on in this chapter I first typed 'peace of mind' as '*piece* of mind', which was curiously apt as metaphor in healing is a process of reclaiming a piece of one's 'mind', or psyche or emotional make up.

> *"If a trauma has extensive roots, the whole thing must be identified for a true healing to take place."*
> – Rob McGavock (Grove & McGavock 1998)

Clean processes can dismantle such frameworks and allow people to access new energy and abilities. For example, Clean is highly effective in alleviating the fear of public speaking, social shyness, fear of authority and uncontrollable anger, as well as helping concentration and alleviating stress. It is a healing process which will home in on where it is most needed; the metaphors which will come into people's minds develop, as if they are watching a film, and may result in improved function and capacity in areas different to the ones that they originally entered the process for:

Traumatic Memory

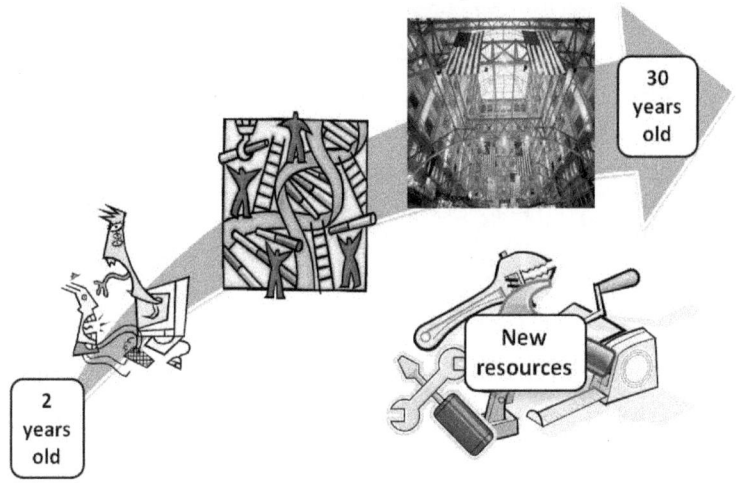

Another case might be where a child is subjected to abuse. This may generate a need to escape one's own body, isolating the trauma in a part of the psyche which becomes 'dissociated' or separated from the conscious mind. Sometimes the information about the trauma can be contained somatically in a part of the body, or in a gesture and, arguably, in a physical illness. An example of this would be a client's foot tapping in response to a question. A Clean response would be to ask, "And what does that foot know?" The question is directed at the foot which has signalled that it represents a part of the psyche that contains information. A more conventional question, such as "Why are you tapping your foot?" would go to the client's conscious mind and the answer would be unlikely to access the knowledge hidden in the client's unconscious mind, or 'whole self'.

Clean principles treat the client's psyche as a system and, if one part of that system changes, it will affect all the other parts. After experiencing deep shifts during a session, people are often beset by a strong desire to sleep, in order to allow the psyche to work through the realignment. Sometimes a session has to stop immediately after a powerful symbol has emerged, because the mind will simply not move on until the new landscape has settled.

Dreams and metaphors have been used for thousands of years to aid healing processes. Jung himself was regarded as an expert in diagnosing illnesses from the metaphors appearing in patients' dreams. More recently, many therapists are exploring techniques of healing through metaphor.

Chapter Two

Technique

"If the person has relevant information inside them, a Clean Question will go straight to that place, not because of the content but because of the way of delivery. All the rhythm and extra words like 'and' and 'so', help to enhance the activity of whatever the active word is."

— David Grove 2005

David Grove identified a series of questions which would least influence his clients while on their metaphorical journey. According to Tompkins and Lawley (Lawley & Tompkins 2000), who shadowed Grove's sessions over a period of years, he used only nine questions at least 80% of the time and coupled this questioning with repeating back the client's exact words. There is a strong parallel here with the coaching principle of being on the client's agenda rather than that of the coach.

There are six elements to the effective construction and delivery of Clean Language:

1. Position
2. The questions
3. Reflecting words back
4. Tone and pace
5. Syntax
6. Intuition

The second element, 'the questions', is crucial and without it the procedure will not be Clean. The third renders it much more effective and elements 1, 4 and 5 are essential to be truly Clean. However, the experience is still likely to bear results even if they are not incorporated, for example in a business meeting where it might feel strange to use the unfamiliar syntax of Clean Language, to slow the tone and pace or to ask people to change their positions. About the sixth, you have no choice – all Clean facilitators and, in particular, their clients have to rely upon intuition.

Element 1: Position

The position of the client and the facilitator can affect the client's ability to access his or her internal resources. The session should always start with clients being asked where they would like to sit and where they would like the facilitator to be. Having learned this Clean technique, I always start standard coaching sessions in this way, sometimes to the surprise of a corporate manager. However, if one enters a room full of empty chairs around a table, one always has a sense of where to sit. People will (usually unconsciously) choose a seat which matches their own psychological map, from where they will be able to think and perform more comfortably.

In a Clean session it is even more important, as the correct positions will allow the client to access inner blocks and resources without any interference.

> "So when you are setting up, you think about what is the Clean space for that client. If you ask a client to find a space that they feel most comfortable in, then you help make space be the holder of their information. If you are working one to one you invite them: 'Where would you like me to sit?' They

will give you the right angle. What that means is that you are then not there, because they will clear you out of their space. Their psychescape or mindset is here [indicating a space]. You are out, but there is a window which will let your questions go nicely through. If you are here, or here [indicating spaces], they will be well defended and they just won't hear you the same way.

If they are calling you because they have got this big problem and you leave them sat there [indicating], this space here [indicating] will have all the big problems in it and you are going to be up against it before you start. [If you ask them to choose the positions] then, when you ask the Clean question, you are not dragging them away from having just yelled at the kids. You've given them a Clean Start."

– David Grove 2005

Element 2: The Questions

Having identified that his clients fared better when allowed to explore their own metaphors, Grove set about working out ways which would encourage them to do this. He used only a small selection of questions over and over again. These were identified through the observation of hundreds of sessions by Penny Tompkins and James Lawley, two therapists who witnessed Grove's work in the 1990s. (Lawley & Tompkins 2004). They estimated that he used the same set of questions for approximately 80% of the time, as well as reflecting back the client's words.

Clean Language Questions

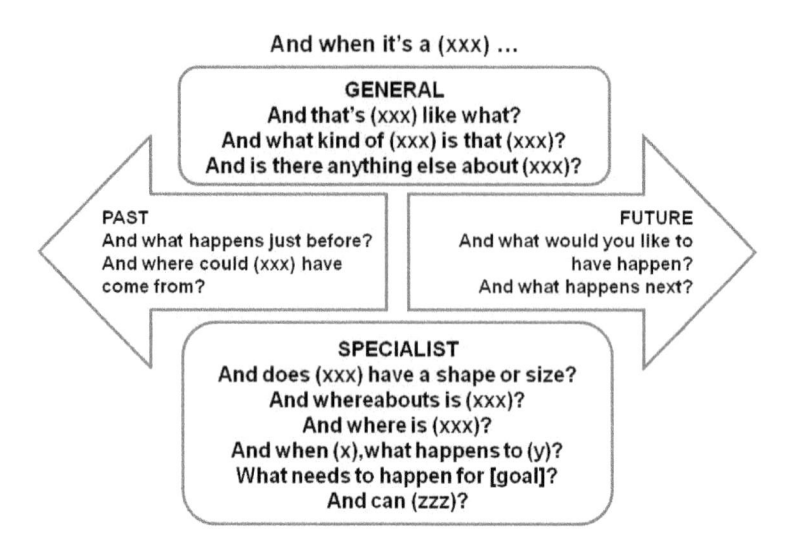

And when it's a (xxx) …

GENERAL
And that's (xxx) like what?
And what kind of (xxx) is that (xxx)?
And is there anything else about (xxx)?

PAST
And what happens just before?
And where could (xxx) have come from?

FUTURE
And what would you like to have happen?
And what happens next?

SPECIALIST
And does (xxx) have a shape or size?
And whereabouts is (xxx)?
And where is (xxx)?
And when (x), what happens to (y)?
What needs to happen for [goal]?
And can (zzz)?

These questions are likely to elicit a metaphor:

- *"And that's (xxx) like what?"*
- *"And does (xxx) have a shape or size?"*
- *These questions explore the metaphors:*
- *"And what kind of (xxx) is that (xxx)?"*
- *"And whereabouts is (xxx)?"*
- *"And is there anything else about (xxx)?"*

This question examines the past in terms of the pathway to the issue:

"And what happens just before?"

This question examines the past in terms the source of the issue, or identifies a resource which may help:

"And where could (xxx) have come from?"

This question is solution focused, moving the client's attention forward. It should only be used after a metaphor has been explored:

"And then what happens?"

This question explores connections between different symbols:

"And when (xxx) what happens to (yyy)?"

Note the order of the second question above: "And does (xxx) have a shape or size?" In conventional speech we might be more likely to say 'size or shape'. However, Grove intuitively felt that saying 'shape or size' landed with the recipient at a deeper level, partly because of the sound of the words and partly because of the refreshingly unexpected order. The following extract is taken from a workshop we ran in 2005, where participants were creating drawings of where questions 'landed' in their bodies:

Grove: *The 'shape or the size' goes below the line. I have spent fifteen years trying to come up with anything better. For example, take 'so does it have a size or a shape?' I'm going to flip those two around and you just draw what the difference is between these:*
'And does it have a size or a shape?'
'And does it have a shape or a size?'
What's the difference in the drawing between the shapedness of those two questions? Anything feel different?
Student: *Shape is a bit longer at the end and size is more staccato.*
Grove: *Which one felt better?*
Student: *Shape or a size felt better.*

Grove's definition of Clean was all about the experience of the client:

> "Here's a definition of Clean Language: if it feels right to the receiver of the information then that's what makes it Clean. If it doesn't feel right then it's not Clean for that person.
>
> If the person has relevant information inside them, a Clean Question will go straight to that place, not because of the content but because of the way of delivery.
>
> All the rhythm and extra words like 'and' and 'so', help to enhance the activity of whatever the active word is."
>
> – David Grove 2005

Other questions may be asked if they relate directly to a statement from the client. For example:

Client: *The birds are chasing me.*
Facilitator: *And when the birds are chasing you, how many birds are chasing?*

Because the client has implied a number, it is Clean to ask what that number might be.

The questions loosely adhere to the framework above, in terms of when each is asked. The principles of being Clean require that certain questions are asked only when the client has introduced the concept. For example, *'And does it have a shape or a size'* would be asked only when the client has implied that there is an 'it'. Similarly, the statement *'I feel fear'*, labels 'fear' as an object, so a question about the size or location of the object 'fear' could be asked:

- *And whereabouts is fear?*
- *And does fear have a shape or a size?*

However, if the client says *'I am afraid'* a more appropriate Clean response would be:

- *And when 'afraid', what kind of 'afraid' could that 'afraid' be?*

It is best not to use the word 'you' if avoidable, because this tends to elicit a conscious 'real-world' response from the client. The sentence above would be delivered with an emphasis and pause around the first 'afraid'. This is clearer than trying to repeat the client's exact words, *"And when 'I am afraid', what kind of afraid is that afraid?"*, which might cause confusion about to whom 'I' refers, the client or facilitator.

Sometimes clients do not readily talk in metaphor. While it is acceptable to ask for a metaphor, perhaps to explain the process, there is no value in forcing this; metaphors are presented by the unconscious mind at the appropriate time, so a consciously formulated metaphor will not carry any information which is not already available by having a normal conversation. If this happens, it is best to continue using the Clean questions even if the client is talking in 'real world' terms. Listen carefully for a metaphor and develop one if it appears.

> *"How do we get questions to go to the clients' experience? The narrative has a movement from the beginning of what the client says to the end. Most likely, once they have told you the story, it is unlikely that will make any difference. In 'The Rime of the Ancient Mariner', the mariner was compelled to stop a wedding guest and tell a story, then he had to tell the story again. The 'tyranny of the narrative' makes you sit and listen."*
> – David Grove 2005

Element 3: Reflecting words back

In Clean Language only the client's own words are reflected back. There is no paraphrasing or inserting the facilitator's words, for example:

Client: *I'm on a river in a boat rushing towards a waterfall.*

Facilitator: *And when you're* **on a river in a boat rushing towards a waterfall** *is there anything else about that?*

OR:

Facilitator: *And you're on a river in a boat rushing towards a waterfall. And is there anything else about* **river, boat** *and* **waterfall**?

It is imperative in Clean to repeat back the words exactly as they have been spoken and in the same order. In Clean, we never clarify by rephrasing words or phrases, as you might do in coaching or normal conversation. This honours people's way of expressing their experience and avoids contamination from the facilitator.

Where clients use too many words to repeat back, for instance while they are describing a metaphor which they find particularly powerful, the Clean Facilitator may rephrase what had been said but only with a selection of the client's exact words:
Example (client's words are highlighted):

Client: *It is a forest. A thick, dark forest.*
Facilitator: *And what kind of a* **forest** *is a* **forest** *that is* **thick** *and* **dark**?
Client: *It's very shady, with sun above dappling through the trees. There's a sound of birdsong and it's very peaceful. There's water running, a river. Quite a wide river.*
Facilitator: *And is there anything else about* **a wide river** *that runs through* **a forest** *which is* **thick, dark** *and* **peaceful** *with* **birdsong**?

OR:

Facilitator: *And when it's* **a thick, dark** *and* **peaceful forest** *with* **water running** *and* **birdsong**, *whereabouts is that* **forest**?

The facilitator chooses the words which seem to have the most resonance for the client, always including the last keyword/s spoken. If the client uses too many words to repeat back, the facilitator selects those words which seem to contain the most significance for the client.

Element 4: Tone and pace

Clean Language questions are paced about one third slower than questions delivered in normal speech. The rhythm is created by pauses at certain places which Grove called 'response inviting gaps'. These gaps allow the client time and space to process the question in the head or in the body, in real time, without having to wait until the end of the question to begin to make sense of it.

Grove discovered that questions spoken in a normal voice tend to go to the conscious mind and therefore be answered by the conscious mind, eliciting no new or hidden knowledge and carrying the baggage of everyday life and past experience. However, questions delivered in a Clean way head for the unconscious mind, which is where Clean processes do their work, and are answered by the client's intuition, or whole self.

During a workshop I asked a participant to draw a representation of her body, and mark where the questions I asked her landed. Overleaf is the picture she drew.

The large dot in the forehead is the place that a coaching question spoken in an everyday voice landed. Then I asked her a Clean question, phrased slowly and in a measured way. The arrows began to proliferate from the centre of the chest, hands and head, spreading out in all directions, and the dotted line surrounded the whole body.

This image was characteristic of all the pictures drawn by the participants during this workshop, and during the workshops I co-delivered with Grove when the students drew similar maps. The questions delivered in a normal voice tended to land in the head, while the Clean questions landed in or around the body.

A similar exercise which Grove delivered was to ask people to draw the shapes of sounds, an exercise he learned from Vilayanur Ramachandran at California University. First he asked the participants to draw the sound 'booba', prounouncing it long and slow as in 'boooooobaaaaaaaa', and then the short, sharp 'zak'. 'Booba' tended to elicit a rounded drawing, whereas 'zak' usually had some points in the drawing.

So a Clean practitioner would deliver the words slowly, and with pauses where marked. The [hesitation] marked below is shorter than the [pause] and is used to give a slight emphasis to a word which seems to have been powerful for or resonated with the client:

Facilitator: *And when there's* [hesitation] *mud underfoot and it's* [hesitation] *slimy* [pause] *is there anything else* [hesitation] *about* [hesitation] *that?*

> "You feel a Clean question in your body rather than your head. A Clean question doesn't go in through a person's ears. If you want to go in through the ears, then you talk at this pace (quite fast). You need to slow it down to two to three times slower than your normal speaking voice, and it has a rhythmic feel.
>
> If the person has relevant information inside them, a Clean Question will go straight to that place, not because of the content but because of the way of delivery.
>
> All the rhythm and extra words like 'and' and 'so', help to enhance the activity of whatever the active word is.
>
> Some of it is in the words. Some of it is also in the type of syncopation that's inherent in the rhythm and it needs to have a rhythm that is poly-rhythmic in it so that although you seem to be saying the same words over and over again the rhythm pattern is different that lies underneath.
>
> What makes that stuff go in are the acoustical parameters of it, those together with the words. There's usually only one active ingredient in it – all the rest is just packaging. If you're given medication you're never given the full active ingredient of a drug; it is always cut and surrounded by inert substances and that helps to enhance the effectiveness of it. In homeopathy, of course, it's suffused until apparently there are no molecules there.
>
> – David Grove 2005

Element 5: Syntax

Clean Language questions often start with 'And' and occasionally 'So'. 'And' is a conjunction which joins the facilitator into the client's current reality. Whether the client is day dreaming or deep in thought, 'and' joins the facilitator's question to wherever the client is focussed.

> "A Clean Language question is a question that feels right to you that you can answer easily. A Clean Language question takes you to places you hadn't thought you were going to go."
> – David Grove 2005

Tacking a conjunction on to the front makes the question kinder and less invasive. The client is less likely to become defensive. It is part of the principle of reflecting back someone's words, giving a sense of continuation from what he or she has just said. The source of this part of Clean Language illustrates Grove's ability to home in on useful tools regardless of external appearances. During one workshop, he described how watching seventies TV dog trainer Barbara Woodhouse talking to dogs helped him to understand the significance of rhythm in words. He was talking about the word 'and' and the slight hesitation after it, which had the effect of putting an emphasis on the 'd':

> "Now all this I got from Barbara Woodhouse, the dog trainer. That's how I learnt to put together the polysyllabic rhythming [sic] of [Clean Language] and I figured that if she could talk to those mutts that have never been trained before, and they are heeling beside her in 30 seconds, then something's up. Because of the sounding and the emphasis on the words, like that 'd' in 'and', is that it is too long for you to hear it, so you have to drop it into some other space."
> – David Grove 2005

Clean Language questions are often closed, eg:

Is there anything else about that?

Phrasing this question as an open one, for example, *'What else is there?'* would not be Clean, as it implies that there must be something else.

Element 6: Intuition

Clean Language enables clients to access their intuition. This might also be referred to as the unconscious (Jung's term) or subconscious mind, or the whole self. It is the place where we can find knowledge which may have been hidden or closed off from us throughout our lives, releasing new resources and energy as it comes back into the main psyche system.

> *"Let your intuition be your guide."*
> – David Grove 2004

In Clean Language, both facilitator and client should follow the client's intuition.

Example of a Clean Language session

The Clean Language questions developed by Grove are listed below with some sample answers to explain their context. Bold text shows how the client's words are reflected back. Notice how the conversation has a beginning, setting the goal, a middle where the current situation and the goal are explored, and an end which ties the process down to action, all of which are similar to the structure of a standard coaching session.

Start: **Purpose:**

Facilitator	And what would you like to have happen?	To find out what the client wants
Client:	I'd like to be more focused	

Middle:

Facilitator:	And what kind of **focused** is that **focused**? *Or:* And that's **focused** like what? *Or:* And does **focused** have a shape or size?	To elicit a metaphor
Client:	Like an eagle soaring and swooping down on its prey	
Facilitator:	And is there anything else about **an eagle soaring and swooping down on its prey?**	To focus attention
Client:	It has smooth shiny feathers	
Facilitator:	And whereabouts is **an eagle** with **smooth shiny feathers?**	To develop awareness
Client:	It's soaring way above my head	
Facilitator:	And what happens just before **it's soaring way above your head?**	To expand attention
Client:	It takes off from inside my heart	
Facilitator:	And when **it takes off from inside your heart and is soaring way above your head,** what happens next?	To expand attention
Client:	I can think more clearly	
Facilitator:	And when you **can think more clearly,** that's like what?	To elicit a metaphor

Client:	Like a shiny new computer working fast	
Facilitator:	And whereabouts is **a shiny new computer working fast?**	To develop awareness
Client:	In my head	
Facilitator:	Where could **computer** have come from?	Identifying a possible resource
Client:	From my effort, preparation, studying	
Facilitator:	And is there a relationship between **a shiny new computer working fast in your head** and **an eagle soaring?**	To develop awareness
Client:	They work together	
Facilitator:	And when **computer** is **working fast** what happens to **eagle?**	To develop awareness
Client:	Eagle is happier and flies higher	
Facilitator:	What needs to happen for **computer** to be **working fast?**	To find out how the goal can be reached
Client	I need to spend more time on preparation.	
Facilitator	And can you **spend more time on preparation?**	
Client	Yes I can	If answer is no, ask more questions

The questions will not necessarily be asked in the order above. Notice that the client quoted above goes in and out of metaphor. Some people stay in metaphor all through the combination and others never go into metaphor – the technique still works and it is not necessary to force a metaphor. If asked for a metaphor, the client is likely to oblige but it will be a construction of the conscious mind and therefore will not carry the hidden knowledge that Clean Language is intended to unearth. The unconscious mind will speak in whatever symbols will serve it best, whether they be real world language or metaphor.

During a Clean session, metaphors often evolve of their own accord to a place featuring calm, positive symbols, indicating that the person will have worked through some anxiety on an unconscious level and will be less troubled in future. People are often surprised at the number of changes which occur on many levels after such a session; for instance they may find it easier to speak up at meetings, or to flirt, or to sleep through the night, when the original reason for the session was about something quite different. This is the unconscious mind at work – changing one element has sent a wave of changes through the whole system.

Questions about the past, the future and the relationship between the symbols can be brought in:

- *When the facilitator and the client have a clearly defined metaphor with an identifiable location*
- *When the client has discovered a new resource (often in the form of a new symbol)*
- *When a spontaneous change has occurred in the metaphorical map.*

CHAPTER THREE

Aspects of Clean Language

Body Language

Grove did not limit his questioning and reflecting to the client's words alone. Sounds, signals and body language were taken notice of. Often people make gestures with or instead of their words, like a sweeping hand movement. Asking the next question, Grove would reflect back the same movement, sometimes with words and sometimes without:

Client: *There's an eagle swooping above* [making swooping movement with hand]
Facilitator: *And when there's an eagle swooping above* [making same swooping movement] *what happens next?*

I once saw Grove working at a seminar with someone whose foot started to jiggle during the questioning. He asked "What does the foot know?" and received a detailed answer.

An additional component to the process is drawing. This works extremely well for some people and not at all for others; it is a matter of personal preference. While asking the Clean Language questions, the facilitator can ask the client to draw each answer as well as or instead of speaking it. This is explored in depth in 'The Senses' Census' on page 99 which Grove devised during our work in 2005.

During a Clean Language session, the client may enter a trance state to some degree and often feels the desire to do nothing but sleep afterwards. Grove believed that this is because everything in our unconscious minds is related, so if a significant change has taken place, it reverberates throughout the whole psyche system. The brain then wants the body to shut down while all the relevant changes are made throughout.

The process seems nothing short of miraculous and I have sometimes had to bring a session to a halt after working with metaphor for ten or twenty minutes, because of the profound effect on the client and his or her need to wait until all is unconsciously rearranged before exploring further. People sometimes find after a Clean Language session that emotional reactions which they were subjected to regularly before the session, such as irrational fear or uncontrollable spurts of anger, have simply stopped happening, with no conscious effort.

Clean processes take place at the most fundamental level of consciousness; if we take the analogy of a person going through life as a train running on tracks, then if other interventions seek to adapt or fix the train, Clean changes the very tracks upon which it runs.

Structure of a Clean Language session

There are various ways of starting and running a Clean Language session. Some suggestions are offered below, but these can be varied in any way provided it is in line with Clean principles.

Starting a Session

Before even sitting down it is Clean to ask the client where he or she would like to sit. Have you noticed that if you walk into a room full of empty chairs, you know instinctively where to place yourself? Grove believed that how and where we choose to place ourselves physically reflects our mental layout. So if clients are allowed to choose their own position, their intuition will guide them to the place where the session will be the most productive. This extends further to the relationship between the place where the practitioner is in relation to the client:

- "And where would you like to be?"
- "And where would you like me?"

Clean shares the solution-focused approach of coaching in starting the session by identifying the desired outcome of the client:

- "And what would you like to have happen?"

The client will normally reply by stating a goal or a problem. Sometimes clients reply to questions that were not asked – usually this is because they are replying to the questions they need to hear, rather than the ones the facilitator has chosen to ask. In a situation like this, it is important to follow the client, who in turn will follow his or her intuition, rather than return to the original question. Whatever words the client uses will have been very specifically chosen by the unconscious mind.

Another way of approaching Clean Language and Emergent Knowledge is to introduce the processes in the middle of another type of session, say coaching, counselling or therapy. This may be triggered by one of the following occurrences:

- *When the client uses a descriptive metaphor*
- *When the client says that he or she is stuck in some repeating pattern of behaviour*

One way to introduce the techniques into a session is simply to offer them:

- *'I have a technique of working with metaphors which may help here. Would you like to try it?'*

- *"I have a technique which may be helpful here that involves moving to different places in the room. Would you like to try it?"*

Notice that in each case, the client's permission is sought. This creates a clear boundary between the session that the client has agreed to, and the new type of session that is about to happen. It is important to state this boundary openly because the client will probably become aware on some level that a different technique is being used, and may become fearful or suspicious.

Ending a session

The client's journey will take as long as it takes – there might be some revelationary, 'light-bulb' moments where profound and long-lasting changes take place, or not much evident change at all. The responsibility for this does not lie with the practitioner – people will move as far as they need to.

The practitioner's responsibility is to manage the time, so that the client is not left in the middle of a powerful metaphor, particularly if there are some negative symbols present. During a demonstration by a trainer, a colleague of mine became transfixed with the image of a snake attached to her cheek. Because of the constrictions of time, as this was a demonstration, she was left in this state and said that the metaphorical snake remained metaphorically attached for three days afterwards. This is an extreme example, but it underlines the need to ensure that clients are left in a comfortable place by the end of a session.

It is advisable to bring a client out of metaphor when ten to 20% of the time remains. This can be done by:

1. Moving towards more action-oriented language:
    - *"What needs to happen for xxxx"* (Checking out conditions for change)
    - *"And can xxxx?"* (Checking out capabilities)

2. Or highlighting that the session is nearing its end:
    - *And as we are bringing this session to an end, what do you know now about all of that?*
    - *And what difference does that knowing make?*
    - *And do you need to say anything more to bring this session comfortably to a close?*

This seems to send a message to the client's unconscious mind, which is in control of the process, to prepare the client for the end of the session. I have noticed that, even in ordinary coaching sessions, if we are doing a two hour session, the client will reach some kind of destination (eg an insight, new knowledge, knowing how to solve a problem) near the end of that time. If we have one hour, it will happen within one hour. If I am doing a ten minute public demonstration, it happens within ten minutes and, on one occasion, when participants had only two minutes each way to coach each other during a training session, they found the same result: a breakthrough within only two minutes!

The key to this is always to keep the client aware of the time; so declaring how long the session will be at the beginning, and keeping track as time passes, so that you can let the client know whereabouts you are on the time frame whenever it seems useful. This would probably be only towards the end, but occasionally, where there is a choice of direction, it can help in the middle of a session.

3. Or suggesting assignments or exercises:
    - Physicalising ('acting out' a part of a metaphor)
    - Looking up significant words to discover their meaning / source
    - Drawing the metaphor landscape (or finding an existing picture)
    - 'Real world' action planning based on conditions identified. 'Real world' means actions like *'contact my colleague on Tuesday'*, as opposed to metaphors.

Clean Practice in Coaching

Many people sense that they have a 'real me', which is not always the one they show to the world. They may feel that this 'real me' is not good enough, or too bright, too strong, and they are afraid to shine; or a sense of duty has been bred into them, how they should behave, what they should think. I once heard a client exclaim, *"It was my mother who married him, not me!"* as she realised, during a Clean session, that her whole life had been lived according to her over-controlling mother's agenda, not her own.

People often have a sense that there is a 'path' or 'life's purpose', a calling they could be following, if they could only identify it. Clean processes help people uncover these vague senses and eliminate what is not necessary or no longer of use to them.

Through working with Clean, I have become more aware of picking up on these symbols or labels during coaching sessions or every day conversations. They are like gifts from the person's unconscious mind, as if it is saying *'you may be talking about schedules but this is what really needs to be examined'*. Whenever one crops up I stop and ask it some questions, for example:

1. Someone might use a word like *'recognition'*:

"What I want is **recognition** for what I'm doing at work. The **recognition** of the hours I am putting in."

As soon as I word like this repeated twice I will ask a question like:

"And what does **recognition** mean to you?"

This is not phrased in a purely Clean way, because that might sound odd in the middle of a coaching conversation, and anything that sounds odd might make the coachee uncomfortable. However, it follows Clean Principles, which can be applied in any situation.

2. At other times, a coachee might use an obvious metaphor, like:

"It's as if I'm on an **express train**."

This is another 'gift' and the coaching should stop here and explore what is being offered:

"What kind of **express train**?"

The responses may continue in metaphors, which should be explored until a sense of completion or new insight is reached. Then the coaching can resume in its normal way.

3. Sometimes the label is not an obvious metaphor. On one occasion, I heard a client refer to herself in the third person. She (name changed) said:

"**Sally** will pass her exams and **Sally** will get **her** promotion."

So I asked:

*"What kind of a **Sally** is that **Sally** that will pass her exams and get her promotion?"*

As she described this 'Sally' she became visibly more confident and energized.

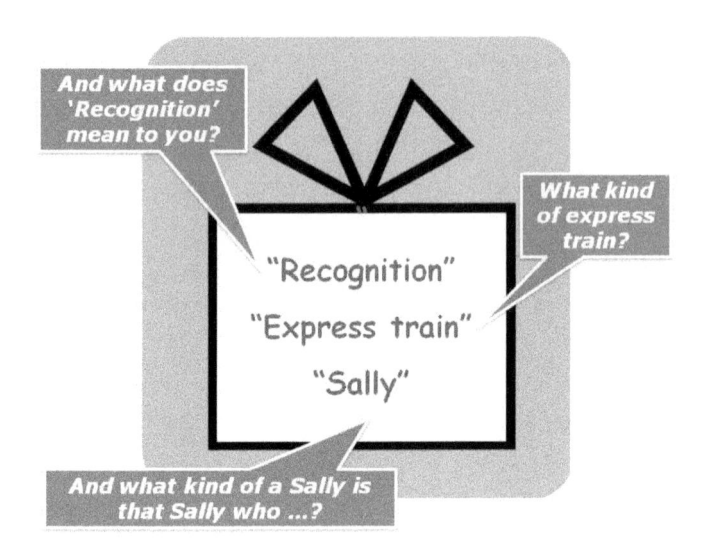

> **And what does 'Recognition' mean to you?**
>
> **What kind of express train?**
>
> "Recognition"
> "Express train"
> "Sally"
>
> **And what kind of a Sally is that Sally who ...?**

Someone may be coached about a situation that cannot be changed, particularly in times of financial cuts and recession. Conversations which explore symbols and metaphors help alleviate pressure when no action can be taken, enabling the person to feel more comfortable and manage the situation more effectively.

It is not advisable to insert a formal Clean Language process into a session without the client's permission, in the same way that coaching someone without permission can feel awkward or invasive. The coach could say:

'I know a process using metaphors which might help here; would you like to try it?'

There is no need to explain all the background and

technicalities, but a boundary should be established between the use of this technique and what the coach regularly does with this coachee.

How Clean Coaching Relates to Standard Coaching

In standard coaching:

- the coach asks questions of the client which are answered from the perspective of the client's current reality;
- the client sets goals from his or her current perspective, which goals are sometimes aimed at stepping outside that perspective;
- the coach focusses non-judgementally on the client's agenda;
- the process is wholly client led within the client's current values.

In Clean Coaching:

- the coach asks questions of facets of the client's reality, not of the client;
- the client sets goals from a perspective which is already outside the boundaries of his or her current one;
- the coach focusses non-judgementally on the client's agenda;
- the coach facilitates the client in creating a pathway forward by tapping into previously inaccessible talents and abilities;
- the process is led by the client's pristine self without influence from habits, phobias or repeating behaviour patterns.

What Not to Do

Before encountering Grove's work, I had already discovered the power of metaphor in my coaching sessions. A conversation might go as follows:

Client: *My fear is like green bile: it's everywhere – on the walls, floors, ceiling.*
Facilitator: *Can you see a door you could go through to get out?*

Do you see the un-Clean response? In my desire to help I have created a resource from my own metaphoric landscape.

A Clean question might be:

Facilitator: *Is there anything else about green bile that is on the walls, floors and ceiling?*

This allows the client to develop his own metaphorical landscape and reach a new level of understanding about the fear. As the session progresses, the client will often create a device to provide a way out, but it may not be the door I suggested. In the client's own subconscious, a door may hold a completely different connotation than in mine and could even be a negative symbol, for example as a child he may have been locked behind a door as a punishment. During Clean Language sessions, people enter a deeper level of consciousness where they are vulnerable to suggestion. Therefore inserting a symbol which to them is negative, may have quite a traumatic effect.

What might happen in the above session if the client is left to his naturally occurring symbols, is that a hand might reach in or a platform appear; equally the green bile might transmute into something more benign, like molten gold, a valuable substance, or clear water through which he can swim to safety.

If the facilitator stays with the questions listed on page 14 using the Clean syntax and style of delivery described in Chapter Two and reflecting back the client's words, it will not be difficult to remain completely detached. Clean practitioners soon lose the habit of inputting new symbols or interpreting those of the client.

Negative Metaphors

A client's negative metaphors need to be honoured, like any other metaphor, but not developed too far. Usually, when examined, positive symbols begin to appear and the landscape changes. Sometimes a helpful symbol appears, for example, a door leading out of an oppressive space.

As soon as positive symbols appear, the coach should start to examine that positive symbol, for example:

Client: There's a goblin. It's disgusting and it's attached to my leg.
Facilitator: And is there anything else about a goblin that is disgusting and attached to your leg?
Client: It won't let me be.
Facilitator: And what kind of 'be' is that 'be'?
Client: Light and warm, singing.
Facilitator: And what kind of singing is singing, when light and warm?

It is impossible to force positive symbols to appear. However, if time is short, it is important to ensure that the client is left in a more comfortable place than with a goblin attached to his or her leg. This image might remain with the client for days afterwards.

Some questions which might quickly move someone into a more comfortable psychological place, without contaminating the experience, are:

- *And is there a space that would like you to go to it?*
- *And what kind of you were you before the snake was winding itself around your neck?*
- *And what is outside of the snake?*
- *Is there another space you could go to that also knows about the snake?*

The final question is an 'adjacent' question, and its purpose is to help the client to feel more comfortable, without suppressing the new knowledge which has emerged in the symbol of the snake.

Although clients may sometimes stray into deep psychological territory, as long as the principles of Clean are followed their own unconscious minds, or intuition, will be in control. Both client and coach can trust that intuition not to lead the client into any situation that may be harmful. This is the value of Clean processes and why it is possible for people with little training to use them with clients.

Redemptive Metaphors

Sometimes it is necessary to pull the client back through time, not only through the client's history but back to ancestral generations, to a powerful healing metaphor which exists *prior to the history* of the trauma that began in a particular problem domain.

> *"Often the symptomology is not biographical to the client's lifetime but rather originates from out of their lineage. A traumatic experience that took place generations and/or cultures before the life of the client can be passed on through the generations to manifest in the client's life, and then it continues to be passed on in one way or another by them."*
>
> — David Grove

Once discovered and developed the redemptive metaphor is invited to go back to the time before the trauma, to bring about a healing. This process is explained in full in the article "Problem Domains and Non-Traumatic Resolution Through Metaphor Therapy" (Grove & McGavock 1998).

Clean Language at Work

Although Grove designed Clean Language in order to help trauma patients, it can also add value in terms of clear thinking and communication in any situation, particularly at work. For example, take this conversation:

Report:	I'd like to introduce a coaching programme.
Boss:	What kind of a coaching programme?
Report:	So that our leaders will manage in a coaching style.
Boss:	What kind of leaders?
Report:	The team leaders.
Boss:	Is there anything else about the team leaders?
Report:	They want to coach but think they don't have time.

The boss could instead have advised what type of programme to introduce, a suggestion which may have been unsuitable for the leaders in question and their particular challenges. Notice how much time has been saved by taking the Clean approach.

To ensure the conversation sounds normal, the rules of Clean Language have been relaxed. For example, a strictly Clean response to the second statement would have been *'And what kind of leaders are those leaders?'*

Imagine a similar conversation taking place in a sales situation. Jenny, a leadership consultant, has secured a meeting with Simon, the Head of Learning & Development at her targeted organisation. Many consultants might come armed with a

PowerPoint presentation, and start the meeting by opening the laptop and talking about what they have to offer for the next fifteen minutes. The problem with this is that, although Jenny may indeed have the skills that the organisation requires, she may not have chosen to describe the ones that are most relevant to the buyer's current situation. Instead, a Clean conversation might go like this:

Buyer	We want to introduce a coaching programme.
Consultant	What kind of a coaching programme?
Buyer	To enable our managers to coach their staff.
Consultant	What kind of managers?
Buyer	The senior level managers.
Consultant	Is there anything else about the senior level managers?
Buyer	They are under pressure and think they don't have time to coach.
Consultant	I have a testimonial from a previous executive who attended one of our courses, saying that he can now do in twenty minutes what used to take him four hours; would it be useful to you to show that to your managers?

The conversation above has quickly informed Jenny of where the organisation needs help, and which of the offerings in her toolbox will be the most useful to dwell on. Simon, the buyer, will come away feeling that Jenny is completely in tune with the organisation and understands its needs. Notice how Jenny has incorporated the principles of Clean Language without using the formal syntax.

It is possible that Simon might introduce a metaphor at some point. Where people use metaphors in normal conversation – whether at work or at home – rapport and understanding can be enhanced by questioning that metaphor and, in particular, not introducing a different one. This can be done casually without the other person feeling that any kind of process is being followed:

Buyer	*That would be very helpful. If we win the managers buy in for this programme it will all be plain sailing.*
Consultant	*What will it be like when it is plain sailing?*
Buyer	*Amazing! The place will be full of energy, people working as a team. My job will certainly be a lot easier.*
Consultant	*What else needs to happen for it to be plain sailing?*
Buyer	*Another problem is that we have spent a fortune sending managers on courses which they like, but when they get back to the workplace they don't use the skills.*
Consultant	*That's a common problem. We get round that by dividing the training into two sections, at least a month apart, and having them practise the skills in between. That ensures the skills become embedded and the managers use them in the workplace.*

Notice how Jenny has picked up on the metaphor 'plain sailing'. When people provide such a metaphor it is usually a container for feelings, thoughts and values which are important to them, and draw on their background, culture, influences and aspirations. Whereas it would be impossible to learn these diverse influences in the space of a short meeting, following the metaphors will acknowledge them and build a sense of familiarity between the two people.

In this case, exploring the metaphor produced a spurt of enthusiasm and vision in the buyer. This was helped by framing the question about the future, a coaching technique known to raise energy and motivation. Again, the conversation reached a point where a specific need was stated by the buyer, enabling our consultant to introduce one of her key offerings at a time when it would be most welcome.

When using Clean techniques in sessions, the guidelines which David Grove spent many years identifying should be followed exactly, using the questions on page 14 and, in particular, the slow, rhythmic cadence of Clean Language. However, in a work or conversational situation, the techniques and principles of Clean can be dipped in and out of, as and where appropriate.

Clean Language by Telephone

People are sometimes sceptical to hear that Clean sessions can be delivered successfully by telephone, particularly the spatial techniques of Emergent Knowledge described in the next section. However, the nature of Clean means that it is not necessary for the facilitator to know or understand the client's metaphor, whether it be a picture in the client's head or a different place in the room. The questions are asked solely for the benefit of the client's own knowledge, rather than for the facilitator to learn or assume anything from the words or positions – and this includes the body language of the client.

Although it would be impossible, in a telephone call, to notice the 'jiggling foot' described on page 27 there would most likely be a verbal signal as well – a hesitation, difference in tone, a grunt or cough, which could be asked about, for example: *"What does 'uh' know?"*

I introduced Grove to telephone training and sessions in 2005 and it became his preferred medium for delivery, partly because of the ill-health which beset him when he travelled. Our own courses and sessions are currently successfully delivered by editor Angela Dunbar almost entirely by telephone and webinar.

PART TWO

EMERGENT KNOWLEDGE

"An Emergent solution is one that is evidenced by a natural state of being in which mind, body, soul and spirit are of one accord, allowing the unexpressed shadow side of knowledge to have equal congress with the socially acceptable expression of the problem. When completed, an Emergent Knowledge solution has a natural and congruent fit for the client and does not require the physiology of effort, such as practice, reinforcement or dint of will to maintain the solution."

– David Grove 2004

"Emergent Knowledge is an information centered process developed as a theory of self-discovery, to facilitate an individual's journey into the inner landscapes of mind, body and soul. This information contains knowledge which, when drawn on, provides a solution to whatever problems have been identified. This knowledge or wisdom resides in the inner world of the individual and can be used to resolve life's challenges or problems."

– David Grove 2005

CHAPTER ONE

Theory

Clean Space

By the early part of this century, Grove's work had progressed away from linguistic techniques and into spatial ones, which he originally termed "Clean Space". Whereas Clean Language explored the psyche through questions and reflecting words back, Clean Space explored it by asking people to move to different positions in the room (or sometimes outside of it).

Have you ever been stuck for a solution and felt the need to go out for a walk 'to clear your head'? Do you identify with the phrase 'a change is as good as a rest'? Have you found that moving into another environment seems to refresh your mind and give you new ideas? Have you noticed that when you walk into an empty room which is laid out with chairs for a meeting, you have a sense of where you want to sit?

Grove tapped into all of these tendencies when he devised Clean Space. It treats physical space as the landscape of the psyche; therefore when one moves to another part of the room, it is like moving to another area of the mind, where it is possible to discover different knowledge, skills and attributes from those in the previous location.

The statements used are as Clean as the linguistic questions, for example:

- *What would you like to have happen?*
- *Find a space that represents your goal and move to it.*

- *Write down your goal or a representation of it on a post-it, or select an object which represents your goal, and position it in the appropriate place.*

When asked these questions, people usually know exactly where to move to in order to uncover some new knowledge. This is because the knowledge already exists inside them but they have somehow lost access to it.

Grove did not spend long in Clean Space. It formed the ground for his final work in Emergent Knowledge and the Six degrees of Freedom which we explore in this section.

Transition to Emergent Knowledge

David Grove's Emergent Knowledge (to which he gave the symbol ΣK) was influenced by a variety of sources, including the science of Emergence, Chaos Theory and Milgram's Six Degrees of Separation. I believe ΣK came about because Clean Language is inevitably tainted sometimes by the baggage that the words hold for each individual, drawing people back to 'real world' conscious thinking. Spatial work allowed the client to leave the undertones that words carry behind and communicate more directly with the hidden, or unconscious mind.

Emergence (Strogatz 2003) is the theory underlying:

- How ant colonies are formed in a logical way, placing the rubbish far away from the food. It was once thought that there must be a 'leader' ant, communicating to the others the master plan, but it is now understood that the ants as a collective constantly exchange signals with each other and decisions emerge from this process.
- How human cities are formed: all over the world through the ages, in some cases our cities have emerged without any

particular leadership, but always with the rubbish ending up away from the food supply.
- How Google works: Google consists of copies of all of the world's websites stored in a vast network of computers. When a question is entered, a process is triggered whereby the question is put to all of the websites in the network. Iterative questions (repetitive questions which are the same or similar) produce more results from some websites than others, and this is linked not only to the information on the website but the standing that website has among other websites. For example, if a website has a Google rating of 1/10 and the URL is then featured on the BBC website, which has a very high Google rating of 9/10, the status of the original website will be raised to a higher figure. It will then appear nearer the top of the list that Google produces when asked about content which matches the topics on the website. Grove theorised that putting similar iterative questions to the psyche would produce results in the same way, encouraging the most significant answers to surface more easily.

During his work in Clean Space, Grove began to notice that it was not necessary to download all the information in a metaphor. Some Clean practitioners regret this, because the process of downloading metaphors is enjoyable and even blissful at times, for the client and uplifting for the facilitator. However, Grove was a ruthless economist with process and said that the 'feel-good' factor resulted from the emotion that accompanied the re-discovery of parts of the self that may have been veiled for many years. He believed that what mattered was the re-integration of those parts and that this should be accomplished in the least possible time. He found that once a metaphor was identified, exploration by means of two to three questions was as effective in the reintegration process as an extended examination, and that delving deeper into the metaphor was not necessary.

Grove was influenced by sampling theory in this hypothesis:

"In sampling theory, if you take a sine wave and you want to take the information in that wave and transport it somewhere else, the minimum amount of pieces of information required to pick up from one place and to be able to faithfully reproduce the original information in another place is 2.3. In the same way, if we ask approximately 2-3 questions we can create a sufficient amount of information in a metaphoric landscape so that it can be an accurate representation of the meaning of what the client was trying to convey in words. This could extend to asking one question or four questions.

If you keep asking questions around the same metaphor, you will get deeper into it. The more information you get, the harder it will be to move on. This is why on average we only ask 2-3 questions maximum on each metaphor. If you ask more you will create a larger emotional dwelling spot, a memory will have been invoked and the person will have been gripped by that feeling." – David Grove 2005

Below is Grove's diagram which maps out theory of Emergent Knowledge. It places the client as being at A, the client's goal at B, and the space in between as C, C being the place where we are likely to find all kinds of resistance built up from habits, memories, previous unsuccessful experiences, fear and the other hurdles which stop us in our tracks. We will also find resources in C which the client may have lost the use of, but which can now be rediscovered and utilised to reach the goal. The facilitator is marked as *f*, outside of the process altogether. Emergent Knowledge is represented by the symbol ΣK, and the arrows show the areas where knowledge can emerge from.

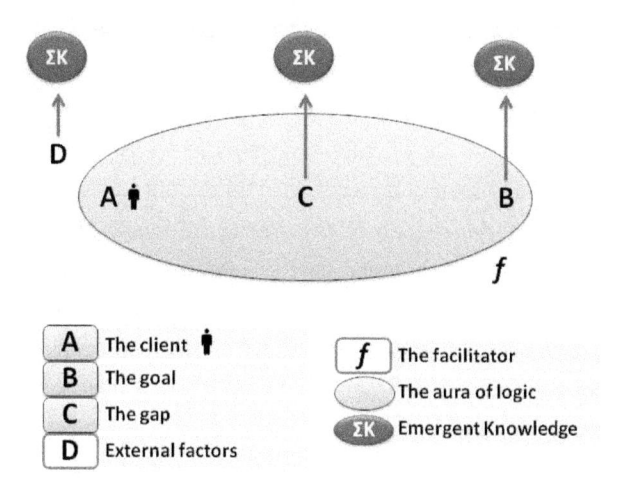

Map of a client's world

A	The client
B	The goal
C	The gap
D	External factors

f	The facilitator
	The aura of logic
ΣK	Emergent Knowledge

The client starts in position A.

- Position B is the object, what A wants to achieve
- C is the space between A and B, the journey. Whoever the client is at A, and whatever the goal at B, there must be something in between, otherwise they would be in the same place. This is the space of C, which contains obstacles and resources which can be uncovered through Emergent Knowledge.
- D is the space that lies outside of the boundary of A, B and C and represents external factors that are beyond the control of A
- The facilitator is in the space of f, which is outside of the client's process and content. Grove said: "As the coach, you must stay in the territory of 'f'. If you are going into surgery, you don't want to have a relationship with the surgeon."
- ΣK is Emergent Knowledge, which evolves from any space except A. This is because at A, the client is thinking with the conscious mind and will not be able to reach the type of self-knowledge emerged by the process, which is from the unconscious or intuitive mind

"Emergence creates boundary conditions by laying the problem out in space, and engages the individual's intuition as the primary guide to finding a solution. The facilitator stands outside of this process and does not add, comment, discuss or analyse any of the client's content. The facilitator is engaged at the operating systems level, asking a series of questions several times over, independent of the content offered by the replies of the client. Emergent Knowledge holds that the expression that is inherent in the nature of the problem also contains everything that is necessary for its solution. Conventional knowledge moves you from A to B and is goal oriented: Emergent Knowledge changes both the nature of the person at A and the nature at the problem or goal at B, such that, to a new world order, getting from A to B is irrelevant."

– David Grove 2005

At the end of 2004, following Grove's instructions, I drew the three dimensional map of a client's world shown below. He was trying to capture the broad compass of EK, but never felt he achieved this (during his work with me) and reverted to the flat version shown above.

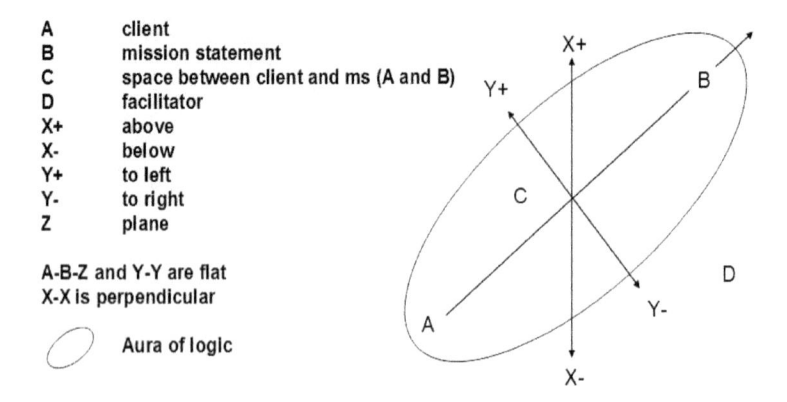

A	client
B	mission statement
C	space between client and ms (A and B)
D	facilitator
X+	above
X-	below
Y+	to left
Y-	to right
Z	plane

A-B-Z and Y-Y are flat
X-X is perpendicular

◯ Aura of logic

In the three-dimensional diagram 'B' stands for 'mission statement', a term Grove used to represent what the client wanted.

> "You are born with your own mission statement, but it usually gets knocked out before the age of six. Often we end up living the mission statement someone else forced upon us, a parent perhaps. A possible question to ask is 'were you born with that mission statement or did someone give it to you?'"

The facilitator is denoted by 'D', instead of the later 'F', when D would become 'external factors' outside of the client's world, which itself was termed 'the aura of logic'. The diagram is intended to represent the client's world not as flat but with a third spatial dimension of height – depth.

Grove advocated against asking the A-B plane for information – it holds the defining of the problem. Once the facilitator gets drawn into the narrative, he or she becomes part of the system and cannot help. Grove termed this *"the tyranny of the narrative"*. XY and Z hold a different kind of information, and Grove advised that the facilitator should ask what is in space C, between the client A and the mission statement B. This should be explored briefly using Clean Language, particularly regarding size and shape; find out where the boundaries are; ask what is beyond the boundary, up, down and to the sides.

Although Grove abandoned his new diagram, I am reproducing it because it reminds us that Grove's spatial work was not two but three dimensional. Clients would be encouraged not only to walk around the room but to use all of the space around them, including above and below. He obtained an eight foot tall fairground gyro chair in which his clients could respond to questions by demanding to be turned in any direction including upside down. The contraption was towed behind his car from one end of the UK to the other and eventually he acquired two more gyro chairs, in France and the USA respectively.

It is often the case that the goal itself is redefined during the questioning process or, as Grove said, *"getting from A to B is irrelevant"*. I once watched him conduct a two and a half hour session (reproduced on page 249) which started with the client being asked to write a representation of her life's purpose on a post-it note. She wrote a phrase which she said had been her goal for as long as she could remember. At the end of the session, Grove referred back to the original post it. She picked it up, screwed it up and threw it away. "Oh, that doesn't matter anymore," she said.

CHAPTER TWO

Small World Networks, Clean Worlds and Six Degrees of Freedom

One of the key aspects of Emergent Knowledge is its connection with the small worlds networks theories originally developed by a Hungarian author, Frigyes Karinthy (1929), and which, particularly in respect of the rise of social networking, has captured the attention of scientists and mathematicians through the years, including Michael Gurevich (1961) Manfred Kochen, (1973), Stanley Milgram (1978), Benoit Mandelbrot, John Guare, and Guglielmo Marconi. This eventually became known as the Six Degrees of Separation theory, which states that everyone in the world is separated by a maximum of six connections and that they may not be the obvious links; it is sometimes by the weakest and most obscure connections that the strongest contacts are made.

To illustrate the theory, imagine that John, a student at Newcastle University, wants to interview the Mayor of New York in connection with his thesis. Writing or telephoning Bloomberg's office direct is not likely to result in any more than a form letter of reply. However, if John approaches a fellow student who is American, who has a cousin living in New York, that cousin may know someone who knows someone who works in the Mayor's office. Through these indirect links, John is more likely to make a useful contact with his target. This illustrates the Six Degrees of Separation theory.

Experiments have been conducted which prove the theory

along with others that disprove it; however, its relevance to Emergent Knowledge lies not in its accuracy, but in the similarity spotted by Grove with the way that the human psyche works, through connections between what seem like insignificant links rather than obvious paths. He devised his own Six degrees of Freedom model from Milgram's theory. If the client, at A, is stuck, then asking that client directly how to get to the goal at B is not likely to reduce the 'stuckness'. However, the spatial questions of Emergent Knowledge allow the client's unconscious mind to make necessary but less obvious connections, working through internal blocks and uncovering hidden resources.

Small World Networks

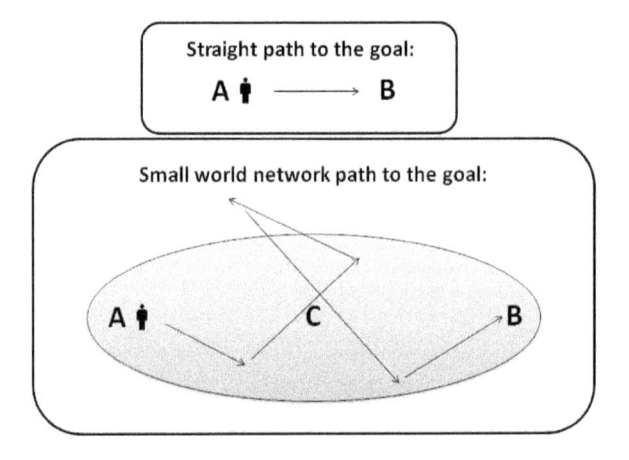

Straight path to the goal:

A ⭢ B

Small world network path to the goal:

A   C   B

Notice how the network path sometimes doubles back on itself and goes outside of the 'aura of logic'.

The key to the linkages are the weak ties between the logical steps that one would normally take to find an answer; these weak ties are like short cuts to the solution. For example if there are fifty points on a circle, you would imagine you have to go through each point to complete the circuit, but if there are a number of weak links in the circle where one vaguely knows another, then all of a sudden you can jump to a place where you only have two more points to reach the end instead of forty.

> "Clean Worlds [the name Grove gave to Emergent Knowledge at this stage of his work] is based on stochastic principle. The word 'stochastic' derives from archery and means learning from the first shot for the second shot. A stochastic system takes into account previous history. In Clean Worlds we need to get the history of the mission statement. For a disassociated part to come back, there has to be a point of contact."
>
> – David Grove 2004

Grove found that it takes an average of six similar questions to achieve a result. By the fourth question there was what David called "a wobble" in which things began to shake up and transform.

> "It's one of the things that happens when you're doing this process. Sometimes if it's a very emotional body thing your body is going to heat up, and you can't think what's going on. And when it's more cognitive, then you'll often get really confused because your cognition is beginning to come apart and deconstruct. It can only re-build again once you get to the fifth and sixth space. Also one of the nice uses is that it's not just a head thing. Your body is actually involved.
>
> Number 4 is what I call The Wobble. What happens with The Wobble is it deconstructs what went on before. It appears to support 1, 2 and 3. If you wait long enough it wobbles and starts to undo everything you held was true the first three times. If you keep going and do 5, something happens, and at 6 something new is born. When you hit The Wobble, other parts of the body are saying 'I don't want to do this'. The process allows for the ambiguity of part of you wants to, and part of you doesn't. This is giving value to those

parts that don't subscribe. The pressure builds up through 1, 2 and 3, leads to a better wobble at 4, and leads to a good 5 and 6."

— David Grove 2006

In Emergent Knowledge remarks or gestures made in passing are picked up on and explored. Often they delivered rich veins of new knowledge which catapulted the client into new territory – rather like landing on a ladder in Snakes and Ladders can take you straight up to the top of the board. Fortunately there are no links in Clean like the snakes that take you back down again!

> *"This type of network is created by weak links such as some offhand or obscure remark which, if picked up on and explored, can take a client to the 'sweet spot' of a new perspective, and a solution which might not appear if the most obvious line of enquiry were followed. The key is for the facilitator to use simple iterations [repetitive questions] over and over again in order to guide the process until a network solution occurs. Iterative questions are often similar rather than exactly the same, and the difference may be in a word or two, or even a change in the tone of voice.*
>
> *If the client's issue can be thought of metaphorically as an egg type problem, then conventional knowledge processes look for an egg type solution. The application of the Emergent Knowledge system creates a non-ordered, non-linear small world network of seemingly unrelated, irrelevant, red herring type data points that coalesce at a sweet spot, in which the mantle of a non-scaling, profound knowledge experience changes the very core of the client. In this moment emerges a new world order solution, one which confers the wisdom of a chicken's cosmology rather than that of the egg. Hence, Emergence creates opportunities to solve egg type problems with chicken type solutions.*

If we think for a moment about the types of problems or issues that clients are going to tell you as what we might call egg type problems, if you are an egg in an egg world, then every problem that will get created in this problem domain will also be an egg problem. So the first egg problem is:

'I am really cold.'

You solve that by putting the egg in a warm place in the sun. But the sun keeps getting hotter: another problem:

'I'm too hot.'

You put the egg in the shade, then it's under a tree, which is fine for the shade but the tree has got heavy fruit and now the egg is scared something will drop and break it. So that's the next egg problem. You could solve it by putting the egg up in a tree; then the fruit problem is solved, but if the wind blows the egg is scared it will fall out of the tree and break. You could find a nice warm cave – problem solved! But now it's lonely. You end up coaching a series of egg type problems – if you solve one you get another and another and another.

So I want to get a solution that lies outside of this egg type problem world, outside of the problem domain, the small world of A B and C. For example:

"So what kind of egg was that egg before it was an egg?"
"It was a hen."

I want to find a solution that will solve an egg type problem but with a different cosmology, so this is a question of how do you re-source? If I pull back from the egg to a different type of space, through a question like "What kind of egg was that egg before it was an egg?" well, it was a hen. So that question pulls you out of an egg type world into a chicken type world. So out in this space of D is a solution type that is a chicken. By then introducing chicken solutions for egg problems, all of a sudden the egg problems are completely different from the chicken's. So the chicken type solution simply comes in, sits down on the egg – it's all over! It turns the egg, it's the right temperature – all the conditions are completely right for the egg.

We get a different cosmological order of solution, for example, a hen likes to be up in a tree, doesn't get cold, fluffs up feathers, doesn't need looking after because can scratch a living itself. Once I find the hen, then what I am looking for is to bring the chicken type solution into the egg problem domain. So a solution that the hen can bring is very different to the solution the egg wants.

So part of the notion of the world view that your client is first going to introduce, that we might term the 'initial starting conditions', is that they will set goals. And those goals are likely to be goals that are constrained by these egg type problems. And you can solve them but there is an awful lot of work to do. So part of what the philosophical emphasis of Clean Coaching is defining, is where the domain is placed for the initial starting conditions that your client is going to give you, and looking for ways of finding information that lies outside those particular boundary conditions.

This is what we will find in the space of D. The information that lies outside these boundary conditions is likely to provide very different solutions from the ones we might find between the space of A to B.

Another way of thinking about this would be like a box of tissues [David picked up a box of tissues lying nearby]. There's an egg shaped world already there [indicating the oval in the centre of the pack] so A would be at this end and the goal is to get to there, and here's the stuff that is in between, which essentially you've got to coach [indicating the tissues extruding from the centre hole]. It's all folded in there and this little plastic barrier here [the oval has a plastic slit].

This space out here [indicating the box itself] would represent the D shape, and it's a completely different space because it's rectangular. And so by carefully placing both A B and C, it allows the client to expand their consciousness into that space, so instead of that being contained and tightly folded up like the tissues in this tissue box, they are able to expand.

Our initial starting conditions are really important. We want to start with where the client is and define what these boundary conditions are, knowing that we can create questions and information which will enable the client to move into a solution type space. One of the key things is that you cannot create a solution in the problem space. When you have a problem space, it's the space that has the information that holds the problem. The solution space is another one.

I found this out rather personally a couple of years ago when one of my colleagues said I had bad posture. I have all my life. The colleague worked for several hours trying to get me to stand up straight and it never happened. No matter what, I could never do it. After a bit of time one of them said, 'I am going to correct your posture.' In that moment I realised I could never be corrected in the same space. So I said, 'Now ask me "Is there a space that knows about correcting the posture?"'

In that moment my shoes (because I didn't have anything to do with this), my shoes pulled me back across the room. I stopped, she adjusted my posture and it stayed for the first time. It has pretty much stayed – I didn't believe it myself – I kept going to a chiropractor to see if it was true. So the problem space is not the solution space."

– David Grove 2005

Part of David Grove's intention in the work we did together was to identify method and form in his practices so that they could be taught as frameworks to support trainees who did not have the opportunity to work with Grove himself, and who had not been trained in therapy.

Grove was open to all types of input and learning and quickly discarded anything that he did not consider useful. He questioned me thoroughly to understand the guidelines and frameworks of coaching, and integrated some of those rules into our work. For example, he liked the structure of the GROW model (Whitmore 2009), which shows some similarities to the shape of his Clean sessions:

Goal — What do you want? What is happening now? — Reality — What could you do? — Options — What will you do? — Will — **GROW**

I introduced him to the standard method of coach training, which invites participants to elicit their own self-directed learning by watching a demonstration, offering the learning points themselves rather than being lectured to by the trainer, and then practising together, all interspersed with questions and discussions. Grove took to this approach and adopted it in our training. It particularly suited him, as the process helped him to explore and come up with new ideas as much as it helped any participant to do so.

I noticed that Grove absorbed useful tools from all types of influences, from eminent psychologists to Barbara Woodhouse, the dog training TV celebrity, which I have described more fully on page 22. He was fascinated by her intonations in commands like 'sit**tt**!', with its emphasis on the 't', and he used examples like this to illustrate the power inherent in the way words are delivered, not just their meaning.

This is described in the quote on page 22.

CHAPTER THREE

Techniques

During the spring and summer of 2005, I helped Grove to develop Emergent Knowledge and translate the techniques into a series of exercises in order to create a training course which could be delivered to coaches and other practitioners.

All the exercises employ the Six degrees of Freedom process described on page 54, where the Clean facilitator asks similar questions approximately six times. These questioning routines allow the system of the client's psyche to change, which in turn allows all of the client's information to network together.

On the following pages the complete set of processes which Grove created while working with me are described in full:

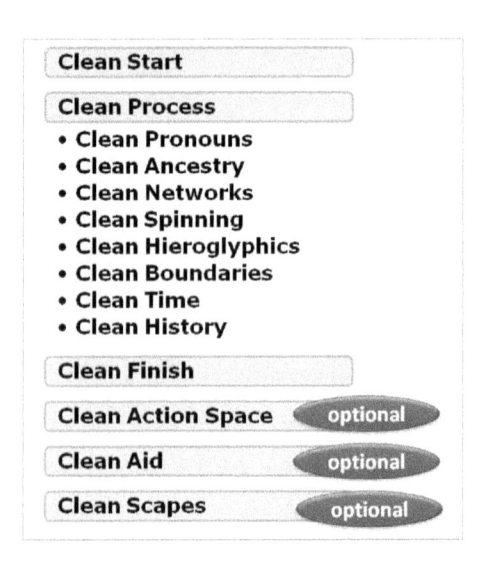

- **Clean Start**
- **Clean Process**
  - Clean Pronouns
  - Clean Ancestry
  - Clean Networks
  - Clean Spinning
  - Clean Hieroglyphics
  - Clean Boundaries
  - Clean Time
  - Clean History
- **Clean Finish**
- **Clean Action Space** *(optional)*
- **Clean Aid** *(optional)*
- **Clean Scapes** *(optional)*

Techniques

At the time Grove divided the above processes into two types:

1. **Knowledge Exercises**
   The Knowledge Exercises were defined as a process which explores a client's epistemology (an academic term meaning 'how you know what you know'). Knowledge Exercises unfold or lay out into space the material that was already there and create a map of what the client holds in their metaphorical spaces. The Knowledge Exercises were identified as Clean Start, Pronouns, Hieroglyphics, Time, History, Action Space, Aid and Scapes

2. **Operants**
   An Operant was defined as a process which enters the *Map of a Client's World* illustrated below, and enables the client to change it. Operants act like portals which can take the client – and the facilitator – into the client's inner psychescape. Clean Networks and Spinning were described as Operants.

The theory behind the classification does not add anything in practice to the efficacy of the processes, and there are times when a Knowledge Exercise can act as an Operant and vice versa, so in order to avoid confusing the reader I have not alluded to these categories again in this book.

The references to A, B, C and D on the following pages relate to the *Map of a Client's World* explained on page 64 and reproduced below:

Map of a Client's World

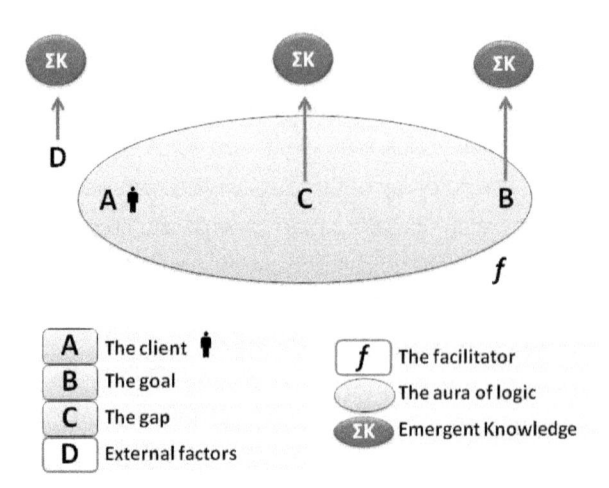

A	The client
B	The goal
C	The gap
D	External factors

f	The facilitator
	The aura of logic
ΣK	Emergent Knowledge

The client starts in position A.

- Position B is the object, what A wants to achieve.
- C is the space between A and B, the journey. Whoever the client is at A, and whatever the goal at B, there must be something in between, otherwise they would be in the same place. This is the space of C, which contains obstacles and resources which can be uncovered through Emergent Knowledge.
- D is the space that lies outside of the boundary of A, B and C and represents external factors that are beyond the control of A.
- The facilitator is in the space of f, which is outside of the client's process and content.
- ΣK is Emergent Knowledge, which evolves from any space except A. This is because at A, the client is thinking with the conscious mind and will not be able to reach the type of self-knowledge emerged by the process, which is from the unconscious or intuitive mind.

"Lightning operates by coming down into step leaders which are 50 metres long. You get a zig and then you get a zag. What happens is the lightning hovers fifty metres above the earth then you get a tracer, which means that some point of some object actually leaps up from the earth and touches the lightning; the lightning never strikes the earth. So this little tracer leaps up fifty metres and connects with the lightning and then it's grounded – and that's what creates the lightning strike."

– David Grove 2005.

What David meant by this comment is that during Emergent Knowledge processes, something deep inside the client's psyche may leap up like the lightning conductor, to connect with the conscious world.

Structure of an Emergent Knowledge Session

Clean Start

Purpose of the process: To ensure that the client and the goal are in the best places from which to emerge knowledge. All of the ΣK processes in this section will begin with this set up exercise, except for Clean Pronouns which can be run as a stand-alone exercise, or as part of a session.

Who is being coached: A (the client).

The exact terminology of this question can be varied according to what the coach intuitively feels suits the coach and the client. Ask the client:
> What is your goal/mission statement/purpose in life/desired outcome?
> or

What would you like to work on during this session?
or
What would you like to have happen?

For the purposes of this section, I will refer to what the client has said he or she wants to achieve as [goal]. Other words in square brackets represent the words the client has used.

Write or draw [goal] on a piece of paper or find an object that represents [goal] and place it in a space that feels right to you.

Client places object.

Where would you be in relation to [goal]? In front, beside, behind, in another room? Is the distance right between you and [goal]?

Then ask the following questions at least six times, in any order and until client is sure the space is right:

Are you in the right space?
Are you at the right height?
Are you facing the right direction?
Are you the right amount of distance from [goal]?

Then ask these questions at least six times in any order and until client is sure the space is right:

Is [goal] in the right space?
Is [goal] at the right height?
Is [goal] facing the right direction?
Is the distance right between you and [goal]?

Once the Clean Start questions have been completed, there is no need to repeat them unless the client wishes to move [goal], in which case the set up process should be run again to ensure that both client and [goal] are in the right spaces.

Clean Process

The facilitator will then choose a process to work with or try several (described over the following pages). These, or similar Clean Language questions can be used within each process, as appropriate, to focus on the client's words, writings, drawings or gestures. Their purpose is to emerge knowledge by downloading the information contained therein.

Eventually, Grove dispensed with exploring the metaphors altogether and clients were simply asked to change position in order to acquire new self-knowledge. He had come to the conclusion that facilitators and clients liked working with metaphor because of the heightened emotional experience which is usually triggered by the experience. Eventually he came to regard this as 'dirty' in itself, and decided that the cleanest way of working was simply to focus on position and leave the content behind.

However, I have included the methods for exploring metaphor in the following descriptions of ΣK techniques, because they provide a rich store of exercises for facilitators to use with their clients, and because I believe they have intrinsic worth.

Grove had a tendency to dismiss parts of his work which had gone before, and value only the method he happened to be working on in the moment. Yet it seems to me that all his ways of working, going right back to the early explorations with metaphor in the 1980s, remain effective. I view the later techniques as expanding the earlier ones rather than replacing them. In spite of his occasional dismissal of his previous work, Grove would draw on it when appropriate, from time to time.

Exploring metaphors is a meaningful and enjoyable process to clients. Not enough research has been done to evaluate which of the methods is most effective, and it is probably the case that different amounts of exploration of metaphors suit different clients. There is also something to be said for giving clients an enjoyable experience, so I believe that it is acceptable for facilitators to experiment and decide how much of the metaphors to explore using their own intuition.

> *And when it's [a long hard climb] is there anything else about [a long hard climb]?*
> *And whereabouts is [a long hard climb] that is [very difficult]?*
> *And what kind of 'you' is the 'you' in that [goal]?*
> *And is there anything else about a 'you' that is [hard working]?*
> *And what kind of space is a space that's [successful] when it's [hard working]?*
> *And it's a [circle]. (repeat gestures if there are any).*
> *And how big is that [circle]?*
> *And is there anything else about a [circle] that's [as wide as the room]?*
> *And when [it can see you] what does [it] know?*
> *And how old is that letter [C]?*
> *Is there anything else about [7]?*
> *And when there's an [ant squiggling around], what does [ant] know?**
> *And what does that [thing] know?*
> *And what does that [foot] know (when client starts tapping foot)?*

* The reference to an 'ant' is included because I once witnessed a real ant crawl across the piece of paper on which the client had written her [goal], during her session with Grove. Because she mentioned it, Grove respected it as a symbol in the session and asked questions of it. New knowledge about the client emerged in her answers. This demonstrates that anything raised by the client may contain information to be decoded. David called those 'real-life' things in the space around the client (such as this ant) 'co-inspiring' items, recognising that they might become part of the coaching process.

Useful signs for a facilitator to look for are:

Scaling:

> "When you are born you are pristine – everything is scaled right. The mission statement then will be different to all the others. Something usually happens – going to school, death, etc, that changes the scale.
>
> If a parent gets angry, even if they make it up the next day, the anger may have become encoded in the child – there is a part of the child that does not move past the anger.
>
> When things are disassociated they tend to be out of scale. When things are back in scale, you know the disassociated part has healed."
>
> – David Grove 2005

I saw an example of this when watching Grove work with a participant in the training room: the participant said that in the space of C (referring to the diagram on page 64), there was a gulf and a gorge. As he said the words he made a sweeping movement with his hand to illustrate the gulf and the gorge:

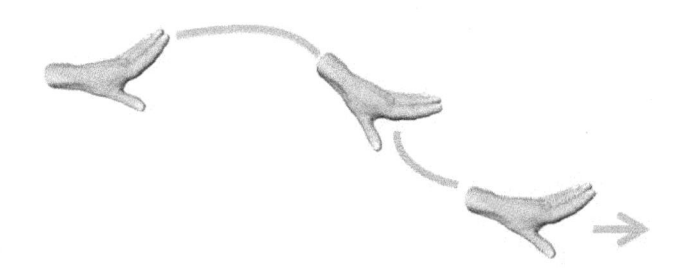

After going back through his mission statements he remembered that, at the age of three, his father used to make him jump off a diving board. He said he had been stuck there ever since, in the terror of that moment – the child never resurfaced. The hand movement and the words '*gulf and gorge*' were metaphors for that traumatising dive.

Extremities

> "During a time of trauma, for example during child abuse where the child can't move, the child has to get out of its body but can't. Sometimes they disappear into their extremities. The client's foot might start tapping, or their fingers moving. Look for movement in hands and feet – talk to the finger or the toe. Ask what it knows. Compulsive washing of hands can arise from this."
>
> – David Grove 2005

Stripping Down

The facilitator can strip off the adjectives, for example:

Facilitator: Where did that come from?
Client: A baby
Facilitator: And what kind of baby could that baby be?
Client: An unwanted baby
Facilitator: And what kind of unwanted could that unwanted be?
Client: Unwanted by parents
Facilitator: Where did you come from before you were unwanted?

In the example above, given by David Grove during a training session in 2005, the facilitator pulls off '*parents*', focusing on '*unwanted*', which is the thing that is around that baby. The facilitator puts the '*I*' back in, with the final question.

Techniques

Clean Finish

These questions help to bring the session to a comfortable close:

> And what do you know about that ... [goal] ... now?
> And is there anything else you know about that [goal]?
>
> Find a space that knows about that ... [goal] ... now.
> And what do you know from that ... space ... there?
>
> Is there a space that wants you to go to it?
> And what do you know from that ... space ... there ... now?

Clean Action Space

Purpose of the process: To tie the new knowledge and energy into tangible changes which help the client move forward.

Who is being coached: A, (the client).

The action space can happen at the end of every session, whichever processes have been used, or at the end of every process. It is optional and depends on where the client leads as the facilitator follows. You could ask the Clean Action questions in the middle of a session, if there seems to be an action that needs to be noted. Action Space is where the coach ties the client down to action so that any newly emerged knowledge, sense of wellbeing or energy will lead to tangible and measurable changes.

> Is there a space that knows about what action you want to take?
> [Client moves to the space]
> What's the first action that you know that you could do from this space?

What's the second action?
Is there a third action?

Ask for around six actions, and tie each action down to specific commitments:

How will you do that?
When will you do that?
Is there anything else you would like to do?

The client may have freed up a great deal of energy during the session, and may be impatient to try out the new system which he or she senses has emerged inside. This is the time to channel that new energy into specific actions.

The content of the action is entirely up to the client. Never suggest actions, nor challenge or encourage the client to set any.

Clean Processes

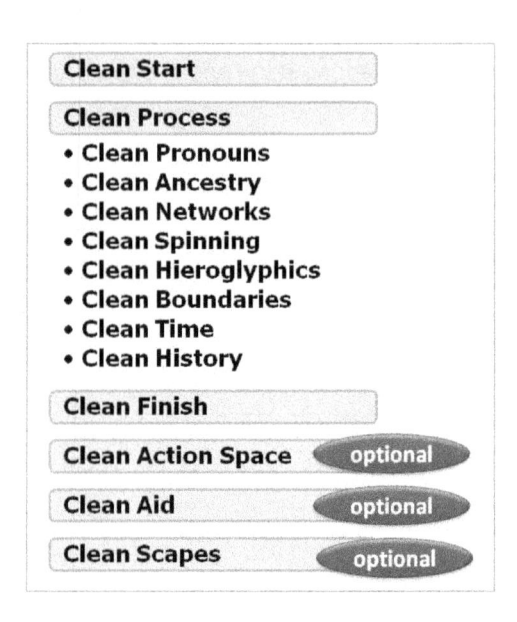

Clean Start

Clean Process
- **Clean Pronouns**
- **Clean Ancestry**
- **Clean Networks**
- **Clean Spinning**
- **Clean Hieroglyphics**
- **Clean Boundaries**
- **Clean Time**
- **Clean History**

Clean Finish

Clean Action Space *optional*

Clean Aid *optional*

Clean Scapes *optional*

Clean Pronouns

Purpose of the process: For the client to understand that there is more than one self that may respond in any situation. The different forms of the questions address these different selves, some of which may be parts of the client's psychological system which have become disassociated at some point in their lives. At each point we are downloading information then moving on, like surfing the internet, clicking on websites and downloading some of the information there. Some clients will find it helpful to draw the positions on a body map.

This exercise can be run as stand-alone or as part of a session.

Who is being coached: A (the client)

1. **Ask about 'I':**
   When you say 'I', whereabouts is your 'I'? Is it in your head, your body or outside?
   Can you draw a body map and mark where your 'I' is on the map?

   Ask these developing questions:

   And when I is [in your head], does it have a shape or a size?
   And when it's [egg-shaped], is there anything else about an I that is [egg-shaped]?

2. **Ask about 'me':**
   When you say 'me' whereabouts is your 'me'?

   Ask client to draw and then ask the developing questions above.

3. **Ask about 'you':**
   When someone says 'you' to you, where does the 'you' go to?

   Ask client to draw and then ask the developing questions above.

4. **Ask about 'myself'**
   When you say 'myself', where could your 'myself' be?

   Ask client to draw and then ask the developing questions above.

To round off this process, ask some Emergent knowledge questions which could be addressed to the client or other part of the system, for example:

*Find a space that knows about the 'you' that is [energetic]
What do you know from that space there?* (See Clean Networks on the next page for this question)
*What do you know now?
Is there anything else about an I that is [powerful and integrated]?*

The words in square brackets represent the client's words reflected back.

Clean Ancestry

Purpose of the process: This exercise is about finding out what is attached to the client and how it is attached.

Who is being coached: A (the client)

Techniques

Whereabouts is your mother?
[Client answer, eg 'in my backbone]
Whereabouts is her mother?
[Client answer]
Whereabouts is her mother?
[Client answer]
Whereabouts is your mother's family when she's [in your backbone]?
[Client answer, eg 'in a cage. My head is outside the cage.']
How old is the head outside the cage?
[Client answer, eg 'six']
The same exercise can be carried out for the paternal lineage.

Clean Networks

Purpose of the process: as we move through life we accumulate layers of knowledge. Some layers become separated or cut off, through time, or circumstances, or disturbing experiences. When the client physically moves to a different space, knowledge can be accessed which had seemed to be lost.

Who is being coached: the whole system, A B C D.

1. **Clean Start** (See page 21) check all page numbers in this section

2. **Start to emerge knowledge.** Remember the importance of rhythm in your questions, indicated by '...' for a pause.

   And what do you know from that... space... there?
   And when it's [client's answer], is there a space that knows about [client's answer]?
   [client moves to the space]

And what do you know from that… space… there?
And is there anything else about [client's answer]?
And is there a space that knows about [client's answer]?

These questions can be continued for a long period of time, or curtailed according to the time available. If you need to bring this exercise to a close, the time to do so is when the client appears to have reached new insight. New insights tend to occur roughly every six questions (see Small World Networks on page 53).

3. **Ask some developing questions** (see Clean Process on page 67). If the client describes a metaphor after having moved to a particular space, and it seems there may be some significant content in that space, download the information before moving on by asking questions like the developing questions described on page 61, for example:

And what kind of space is a space that's […] when it's […]?
And it's a [circle]. (repeat gestures if there are any).
And how big is that [circle]?
And is there anything else about a [circle] that's [as wide as the room]?

4. **Clean Finish** (see page 71).

Clean Spinning

Purpose of the process: To emerge knowledge which may be uncovered when the client faces different directions.

Who is being coached: the whole system, A B C D.

Techniques

1. **Clean Start** (See page 65)

2. **Start to emerge knowledge.** Remember the importance of rhythm in your questions, indicated by '...' for a pause.
   And what do you know from that... space... there?

3. **Ask some developing questions** (see Clean Process on page 67). Remember to use the client's exact words:

   And when it's [a sunny field] is there anything else about [a sunny field]?
   And does [a sunny field] that is [green and lush] have a shape or a size?

4. **Emerge knowledge by spinning.** The client can turn in any direction he or she chooses at any time:

   Turn to a different direction and find out what you know from that direction.

   Repeat these questions as many times as the client is emerging knowledge. This could last for a short time or for a whole session:

   Turn again. And what do you know from that ... direction?
   Keep turning. And what do you know from that ... direction ... there?

   If a metaphor arises which seems to carry some significance, ask two or three developing questions. Do this only occasionally, to keep the client moving forward, not on every turn:
   And is there anything else that you know from that... space... there?

And is there anything else about [a forest] that's [green]?

Then move on by turning the client again.

If the client turns to face the [goal] again, ask:

And what do you know about that… [goal]… now?

5. **Clean Finish** (see page 71).

Clean Hieroglyphics

Purpose of the process: To find the origin of the words which have been written down. Each of the letters in the spaces has a history to it.

Who is being coached: B, the [goal].

1. **Clean Start** (See page 65)

2. **Start to emerge knowledge** by asking about the letters and the space around them.

   What do you notice about the letters of the words that are on [goal]?
   Is there any letter that looks different?
   And what does that letter [C] know?
   Are there any other interesting letters?
   And what does that letter [A] know?
   And what does the [yellow space] know?
   Is there anything else interesting about the letters or the spaces between the letters?

3. Ask some developing questions (see Clean Process on page 67) during the process, wherever you feel there is a metaphor worth developing. Remember to use the client's exact words.

4. **Clean Finish** (see page 71).

Clean Boundaries

Purpose of the process: To explore what is around and outside of B, the [goal]. The exercise tends to re-scale things that might be out of proportion in the client's perception, ie problems may become smaller and goals may become bigger and more important. This exercise can be carried out by asking the client to draw the boundaries, as in the sample script below, or to describe the boundaries if the client prefers that to drawing.

Clean Boundary questions are particularly useful when a client mentions some type of boundary, or space that surrounds them, while doing another exercise. The key is to explore what the boundary is made of and whether there are other spaces and boundaries outside of it.

Another version is to explore the space inside, and what is inside that space, and that space etc.

Who is being coached: B, the [goal] and D, the external factors.

Clean Start (See page 65)

1. **Start to emerge knowledge** by asking questions to discover a boundary and the space around it. The word 'edge' can be used instead of 'boundary' if it seems more natural.

    What kind of space is the space around [xxx]?

And is there anything else about that space?
And does that space have a shape or a size?
And how far does that space go?
And what kind of boundary or edge does [xxx] have?
And is there anything else about that boundary?

When the client is drawing or writing:

As you answer that question, place that boundary or edge on that [statement/drawing].
And when you have that boundary or edge around that [xxx], what kind of space is the space that is around that boundary of that [xxx]?

2. **Ask this first space some developing questions** (see Clean Process on page 67).

How big is that space and what are the qualities of that space?
And what kind of space is that space?
And is there anything else about that space?

Then explore the space and boundaries again:

And how far does that space go?
And what kind of boundary or edge does that space have?

At this stage there will be the original boundary around the statement, the space around that boundary and the next boundary, which has just been identified.

Let the client know that the original statement can be redrawn or rescaled if it feels appropriate.

3. **Repeat steps 2 and 3** to uncover more spaces, to

maximum of five to seven spaces, as long as knowledge is emerging. Download the information from each new space identified, by asking about two to three questions about it, for example:

And what does the boundary that is outside of the space that is around your statement know?
And what does that outer edge know?
[ask client to place these on the drawing or statement if there is one, and continue to do this throughout the rest of the exercise]
And what does the space between those two boundaries know?
What does that space know?

And what does that edge or boundary know that is around that statement?
What does that boundary know?
And what does that [xxx] know now? [where xxx is a drawing or statement]

Clean Finish (see page 71)

Clean Time

Purpose of the process: to re-align or re-scale the client's internal time signature to match that of his or her current reality.

Some people's experiences are folded into space. They store experience and information somatically (in their body) such as in their heart, in their guts, or their hands. They may also store information spatially, externally, so that their eyes look off into space to retrieve that information before they can speak about it.

Other people have information which is folded into time:

clues to this are found in their language which is peppered with phrases that have a time signature or time code embedded in the metaphors or speech patterns they use, for example:

> I'll be with you in a tic
> I can't remember when that happened
> I remember it like it was yesterday
> I didn't get enough time
> There is just not enough time in my day
> I haven't another minute to spare

For these people, experiences are folded and entrapped within their metaphorical landscapes, which distorts their perception of time. This internal perceptual time is overlaid and imprinted upon current everyday reality. Hence they may always be in a rush like the mad hatter or they are completely oblivious and in a much slower world of their own which, again, bears little reference to present day time reality.

The purpose of coaching a client's perceptual relationship to time is to re-align or re-scale the internal time signature to match that of the current reality, and the trigger for this exercise is when the facilitator hears a client making references to time, like the ones listed above.

Time is generally organised in two different manners. The person moves through space and, as they do that, time moves by them. The alternative is that they remain in one place and time itself moves. For example:

1. I have to keep moving. I've got so much to do and so little time to do it in.
2. I'm really stuck. I don't know what to do. And life just seems to be passing me by.

Who is being coached: the whole system, A B C D.

Techniques

Major issues in setting goals can sometimes be resolved simply by changing the internal perceptual organisation of a person's time signature to one that matches his or her present day life; the ΣK practitioner can help clients to iron out their wrinkles in time. Part of it has to do with laying out the client's history and how his or her sense of past, present and future has organised itself.

Clean Start (See page 65)

1. **Emerge knowledge about past time:**
   a. **Location:**
   Find a space that knows about how you organise time and your relationship with it.

   From that space, whereabouts is your past? Is your past in front of you, is it behind you, is it to the side of you, is it below or above you, or is it inside of you? Whereabouts is your past?

   Spatially, where were you born, where is your childhood, where are your teenage years, your twenties, thirties etc, [Repeat up until where is yesterday?]

   Now draw out a map of your past with all these significant ages or events that happened to you. Notice which parts of your past are in different places, for example what years may be in front of you rather than behind.

   b. **Name:**
   What kind of time could this time be and what would you call it?

   c. **Knowledge:**
   What does this time that is in the past called [xxx] know?

What does this time that is in the past called [xxx] know about you in the space that you are in now?

What do you know from the space that you are in now about this time in the past called [xxx]?

How does this time that is in the past called [xxx] help you to reach your current [goal]?

How does this time that is in your past called [xxx] prevent you from reaching your current [goal]?

What kind of [goal] would this time that is in your past like you to have now?

What would this time that is in the past called [xxx] like to have happen?

How might this knowledge that is in the time that is in the past called [xxx] change you?

How might this knowledge that is in the time that is in the past called [xxx] change what you might do?

How might this knowledge change [goal]?

How might this knowledge change the people the places or the things that are around you?

2. **Emerge knowledge about present time:**
   a. **Location**

   And whereabouts is your present?

   And what kind of space does your present occupy? Is it behind you, in front of you, to the side of you, or inside you?

   Make a map of where your present is in respect to your past.

   b. **Name**

   What kind of time is your present time or now time?

   What name would you call it?

   c. **Knowledge**

   What does this time in the present know?

   What does this time in the present know about you in the

space that you are in now?
What do you know from the space that you are in now about this time that is in your past from the space that you ?
How does this time that is in your past do to help reaching your current [goal]?
How does this time that is in your past prevent you from reaching your current [goal]?
What kind of [goal] would this time that is in your past like you to have now?
What would this time that is in your past like to have happen?
How might this knowledge change you and what you do?
How might this knowledge change your [goal]?
How might this knowledge change the people the places or the things that are around you?

What does your time that is in the present know?
What does your time that is in the present or the now know about you in the space that you are in?
What is your relationship to time that is in your present?
How does the time that is your present time help or hinder your [goal]?

What does this time that is in the present called [xxx] know?
What does this time that is in the present called [xxx] know about you in the space that you are in now?
What do you know from the space that you are in now about this time in the present called [xxx]?
How does this time that is in the present called [xxx] help you
- to reach your current [goal]?
- in your life now?
- with this [xxx] problem?

How does this time that is in your present called [xxx]
- prevent you from reaching your current [goal]?

- *influence your life now?*
- *support this [xxx] problem?*

What kind of
- *[goal] would this time that is in your present called [xxx] like you to have now?*
- *influence in your life now would this time that is in your present called [xxx] like you to have?*
- *support for this xxx problem could this time that is in your present called [xxx] like you to have now?*

What would this time that is in the present called [xxx] like to have happen?

How might this knowledge that is in the time that is in the present called [xxx]
- *change you?*
- *change a particular feeling or emotion that is inside a specific part of your body?*
- *change a particular thought or words in your mind?*
- *change what you might do?*
- *change your [goal]?*
- *change the people the places or the things that are around you?*

3. **Emerge Knowledge about future time**
   Ask similar questions to the ones detailed above, regarding the location, name and knowledge about the future.

4. **Clean Finish** (see page 71)
   Grove expanded this exercise with the following sets of questions:

   The 'before you were you' time zone

Do you have a sense of time:
- *before you were born?*
- *from whence you came?*
- *of being who you were before you are who you are now?*

Do you have a sense that you came into this world at the wrong time?
Make a map.

The 'ancestral' time zone

Do you have a sense of time that:
- *belongs to your ancestral lineage?*
- *this time comes from your mother's ancestry?*
- *this comes from your father's ancestry?*

What shape does this ancestral time zone have and where is it located?
Make a map.

The 'historical' time zone

Do you have a sense of time that belongs to history?
Do you have a sense of which people and which history and which land belongs in this time zone?
Map the shape and position of this time zone.

The 'before time was time' time zone

Do you have a sense of time in which there is no time?

The 'mind body spirit' time zone

Do you have a sense of time that is held in your body?

Map out the different senses of time that are inside your body

Do you have a sense of spiritual time?
Is it inside you, outside of you?
Map that time.

Do you have a sense of time that is a soul time?
Is it inside you, outside you?
Map that time.

Do you have a sense of time that is in your mind?
Is it inside your mind, is it outside of your mind?
Map that time.

The 'lost' time zone

Do you have a sense of time:
- *that is not your own?*
- *that belongs to someone else?*
- *that is shared?*
- *that is your time?*
- *that is others' time?*

Do you have a sense:
- *of lost time?*
- *of being out of time?*

Overlay 1: Prior timescape

What kind of time was your time before it was this current time? How old were you when you had a sense of time that was different from the time that you have now?
Whereabouts were you when you last had a sense of time that was before the sense of time you have now?

How were you different at that time than you are now?
What was the event that changed the sense of time you had before this one that caused that sense of time to change into your current sense of time?
Draw a map of the timescape that was your previous sense of time with past, present and future.
What kind of [goal]s were your [goal]s at this time from this timescape and how do they differ and what is the difference between the [goal]s from this time compared to the [goal]s from your current time?

Overlay 2: Where do you spend your time?

Where do you spend most of your time and what time do you seem to live in the most?
And what age could you be when you live in that time or when you spend time in that time?

Overlay 3: Endgame

Which of these time zones help you towards your [goal]?
Which hinder you?
Do these time zones have different [goal]s to yours and what are they?
Which of these times want the [goal] that you want?
Which of these times don't?
What people, what places, what things and what events help you to live in or spend time in these different time zones?

Because you spend time in these spaces, there are consequences. How does this relate to your [goal]s?

This will probably be co-related to the area that the client has sketched out. Clients can populate where they live.

Clean History of Goals

Purpose of the process: To emerge knowledge which may have been lost when the client was deflected from his or her life's congruent purpose.

Who is being coached: the whole system, A B C D.

1. **Clean Start** (See page 65)

2. **Start to emerge knowledge** by finding the source of the [goal]s:

    Find the source of the [goal] by asking some of the questions below until there are no more prior [goal]s:

    What was your [goal] before this [goal]?
    Whereabouts could it be?

    Information is constrained by certain ages. Find out where things are stored and connect with the date:

    How old might [...] be?
    What might [age] be wearing?
    If you are here, whereabouts were you born?

    Sometimes people place previous [goals], or indicate that they were born, in front of where they are standing instead of behind. That means their life has got turned around. The positions might zig zag.

    Explore the [goals] all the way back to where the client was born and possibly before, to get back to the point before events changed the client's mission statement.

Techniques

From time to time, using your intuition to decide when something is worth exploring, ask developing questions about [last goal], such as:

What kind of a [...] is that [...]?
Is there anything else about [...] when [...]?
Does it have a shape or a size?

The client may find it helpful to draw Clean Scapes while doing this exercise, or to plot the positions using post-its.

3. **Clean Finish** (see page 71).

Clean Scanning

Purpose of the process: to ensure that the client is experiencing the exercise that will be most beneficial.

Certain processes will work better than others with different clients and at different times. It is not always possible to know which one to select with any accuracy, so Grove created 'Clean Scanning' in order to trial a few questions from each process to see which is the most productive.

Clean Scanning is not a process in itself, but a measure to bear in mind after the facilitator has chosen an exercise to work with. It is not part of the procedure but 'meta' or outside of it. The purpose is to ensure that the process is the right one for this person in this particular experience.

For example, the facilitator might choose to start with Clean Spinning. If no productive information is coming up after the client has been asked to change direction approximately six times, then it is best to abandon this process and choose another one. There is no need to inform the client – the facilitator can simply switch to another line of questioning.

Similarly, if Clean Networks has been selected, the facilitator will be asking the client to go to another space. If the client can immediately fulfil that request, it means that Clean Networks is working for the client. If, after asking around six times, the client either finds it difficult to know where to move to, or the space moved to does not yield information which complies with the criteria of the checklist above, then Clean Networks is probably not a productive process to use with this client.

The way to identify whether a process is working is by asking oneself these questions:

1. **What is the density of information?** If the process is useful to the client, new information will be emerging. If not much is coming through after a few questions have been asked, then move on.

2. **What is the ease of the answer?** If the client is repeatedly finding it hard to answer your questions, the process you have chosen to use is probably not working. Do not confuse this with times when the client finds it hard to speak because of the complexity of information arising.

3. **What is the level of productive engagement?** How absorbed is your client in the process? If it is not attracting their intense concentration, it is time to try another.

The facilitator's decision on which process to use will be informed by a combination of intuition and responses from the client. For instance, the client may have mentioned that he or she is always short of time. This can be taken as a prompt to run the Clean Time Exercise. If the Senses' Census questionnaire (on page 99) has been completed, it may be apparent that there are different 'I's and 'me's working against each other, in which case it may be helpful to run the Clean Pronouns exercise. Similar pointers may arise when

Emergent Knowledge is incorporated into another type of session altogether, such as coaching, in which case one of the processes can be introduced for say ten or twenty minutes, in order to deal with one particular stumbling block.

Clean Aid

Purpose of the process: There may be times when the client seems to be going to a psychological level which is deeper than you feel you are qualified to explore, crossing the boundary into therapy. Equally, your client may appear to be sinking or stuck in a negative space or metaphor. There are some simple techniques to use in cases like these and it is essential to move the client out of a negative space by the end of the session.

1. Ask the space to move the client:

   Is there a space which would like you to go to it?
   And what do you know from that... space... there?

2. You can also ask a question to switch negative to positive:
   And what would you like to have happen?
   Find a space that knows about [what client would like to have happen]

3. **The reality check.** When the client is going to a deeper place than you are comfortable you can handle, these questions will help to bring the client back to a conscious, or 'real world' level. They can also be used to start and/or end a session:

   What do you want now?
   Where are you at with it now?

What are your current options?
What are you doing about it at the moment?

See also the advice on how to deal with negative metaphors, on page 37.

Grove was keenly aware of the boundaries between therapy and coaching, and took a process which explores the 'inner child' out of the Clean Coaching curriculum because it tended to take clients to places which coaches are not qualified to deal with. A signal that a client may be approaching such an area includes statements about a child, or words like 'long ago'. When clients seem to be moving into metaphors which represent their childhood, the coach should question a safer area which the client has recently mentioned, or use the Clean Aid questions. The client will still be able to acquire help through accessing the unconscious mind, but in a safer way than through direct contact with their 'inner child'.

During a training conference call in 2005, Grove had this to say about the caution required when working with the 'inner child':

> *"'How old could you be when you feel scared?' is easier to answer than 'How old could scared be?' You are as likely to get an answer. Go for the 'I' pronoun. The more you land on that 'scared' word, the greater you are going to get the scared feeling within the person. For example, if the person says 'I am six and I am scared', if you go 'What could scared be wearing?' rather than 'What could six be wearing?' you will get a lot deeper feelings than on the word 'I'. If you have a client who says 'I feel scared', and you can hear that they don't really want to be in the scared space, you could add this: 'And how old could you be just before you felt scared?' You are adding a slight pulling back to the feeling, which would be the equivalent linguistically of asking the question 'How big is the space that's around*

you when you feel scared?' [The reply might be] 'It's a really tight space.' And then you ask the question 'So what kind of space is a space on the outside of [a really tight space]? It's really open. What you have done is enlarged the space out by asking a space question. On the other one you have pulled back time linguistically, which is an equivalent. 'How old could you be just before you were scared?' indexes time back a bit and you get the age, but you don't get the worst scared."

– David Grove 2005

About safety of Clean Language and Emergent Knowledge

During a training session in August 2005, Grove was asked a question about the boundaries of practising Clean techniques with friends and family. His reply encompassed the whole question of safety, and what he termed the 'removed-ness' of Clean Language and 'double removed-ness' of Emergent Knowledge:

"Once you start using the space and those [Emergent Knowledge] questions, there is a degree of removed-ness, that if you have the content, then you get the narrative. If you just get the metaphors, which you do with Clean Language, then you are one removed from the content. When we are using the space stuff, we are two removed from the content. That's what builds in safety – the space acts as a container, therefore has the sense of holding the client's information in a space that feels it truly belongs to them, provided you have good Clean questions, because these questions don't break that space boundary you have created.

All these questions [below] are 'dirty' questions, because you invade the sanctity of the person's experience by inviting yourself in there, so that the only real communication that can happen after that is that they share the A B and C space with you instead of being right out there:

'Tell me how you feel?'
'What's that like for you?'
'Tell me more about what's happened.'
'How do you feel about that?'

My personal view is that it can be quite a lot of fun working with space with close friends and loved ones. You can set a caveat to begin with: 'If there is anything that I ask that doesn't feel right in any way, then let me know. And if there are any questions that you don't want to respond to, I want you to make sure that you do not respond. If there are questions that don't feel right, let me know and I will find one that does.' That way you feed the control of the experience to that person. They know the boundary and conditions you have put around which cede control to them.

This runs counter-intuitive to normal counselling theory, which is that the counsellor sits down and a major part is to build rapport and trust with the person so they trust you. My take on that is that it is a bunch of malarkey. The only reason you want to build trust is because you are going to ask them questions which [require that] the person has to trust you, because those questions are going to hurt them as they answer them. If you don't ask questions that require the person to trust you with the information that they are giving you, then that is automatically built in without trying to develop it.

In traditional therapy it is called the 'transference' and 'counter transference' which takes place with the client, and it is important to build that [in traditional therapy] because you are in the middle of ABC. But in Clean questions you are not in the middle. So that when they [the client] step into this other world, they are marvelling at this hallucinatory 3D reality that is going on in front of their eyes. Part of the power of the 'and' is because it lets you [the practitioner] join into that experience rather than distracting them away. That's part of the safety."

This comment was made by David during a demonstration during a training course:

"He is going back to A. Notice a degradation in the boundary conditions — it's now temporary. Notice I am not trying to break out the boundary. What would be unclean of me is to put my model of the world — you should have more space, more's better — then I would be coaching to try and get that barrier down. That barrier has protected him from the turmoil that's out there for a long time. But there is information that is in that barrier.

Part of what we're learning in the system is to navigate through it. Be disciplined and learn to deal with the elements of information there. I must be as much a coach of the boundary and barrier as I am to the space there. Because if I put a question in and try to break that barrier down, there is knowledge and information in that barrier that has protected him all these years. That's why this is very delicate and illustrates the notion of being a coach and treating all the information that is in there equally."

— David Grove 2005

Clean Scapes

Purpose of the process: To download the client's information and provide clarity.

Clean Scapes are drawings which clients can be asked to do

during any exercise or operant. Some people find it easier to emerge knowledge through drawing, others prefer language, or spatial movement, or choosing outside objects. You should follow the client's preference if any emerges.

For example:

In Clean Pronouns, the client can be asked to draw a body map and plot the places where the 'I', 'Me' etc are. The client must always draw their own body map and not be presented with one.

In Clean Time, clients can draw maps of their time and where it is in relation to the themselves.

In Clean Networks, the coach can plot the movements on a sheet of paper and give it to the client at the end of the session.

CHAPTER FOUR

The Senses' Census

David Grove created this detailed questionnaire for clients to fill in on paper or online. Most clients would find the questionnaire in its entirety too lengthy to complete at one sitting. You can make up a shorter version or give it to the client in sections throughout the coaching series. Some people like filling in questionnaires and others do not; therefore, adjust the use of the questionnaire according to the client's preferences. The questions work equally well when asked orally. Make it clear that it is necessary to answer only questions which seem relevant.

Introduction: Map of Your World

A	The client
B	The goal
C	The gap
D	External factors

f	The facilitator
	The aura of logic
ΣK	Emergent Knowledge

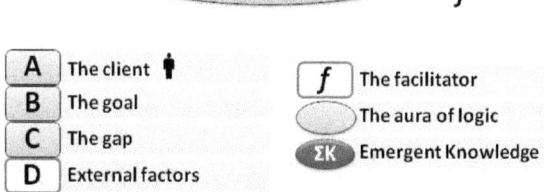

99

You start in position A.

- Position B is the object, what you, at A, want to achieve
- C is the space between A and B, the journey
- D is the space that lies outside of the boundary of A, B and C and represents external factors that are beyond the control of you at A
- The facilitator is in the space of f, which is outside of your process and content.
- ΣK is Emergent Knowledge, which evolves from any space except A. This is because at A, one is thinking with the conscious mind and will not be able to reach the type of self-knowledge emerged by the process, which is from the unconscious or intuitive mind

Part I: Real World Questions to A

Answer only the questions you feel are relevant to you. An answer of 'I don't know' is of equal value to the answer that you do know. This is because an 'I don't know' can indicate a piece of the puzzle that is missing, which will be explored during the Emergent Knowledge Cycle.

Sense of A

What is your sense of:
- Who you are right here today?
- How would you describe yourself?
- Who you were before you were the 'you' you are today?

What were the defining events that shaped your life to be who you are?

The Senses' Census

What is your sense of a time when you were 'a pristine you', i.e. you fitted the world you were in?

Can you remember that moment and draw the experience, or have you never been pristine and never felt you belonged in this/your life or that not all of you has arrived in this life?

Looking back over your life, what shape does your life history have? What metaphor or image best describes your life history from when you were born to who you are today?

Draw a map of your life? Would it be defined by:
- *Your ages?*
- *The places you lived?*
- *The things that happened to you?*
- *Dates on the calendar?*

Time of A

What is your sense of time?

Where is:
- Your past?
- Your present?
- Your future?

Locate each of the above spatially and outline them on a map.

How much of your past is in front of you, what ages are they and how much is behind you?

Do you have a 'time signature' that describes your relationship to time, eg:

- I'll be back in **two ticks**   [Time Reference
- I'm so busy I can't fit enough in my **day**   is *Italicised*]

List all your most common time signatures:

The body physical

What is your sense of your body?

Draw a body map, describe the physical attributes of your body and place these attributes on your map

What is your sense of the age of your physical body?

What has your sense of your physical body done to contribute to who you are today?

What has your sense of your body done to hinder who you are today?

What was the previous sense of your physical body before it was the one you have now?

The body parts

Draw a body map. Define and place on the map the descriptions of each of your body parts and what contribution each has made to who you are today:

Example body parts:

Brain	Shoulder	Back	Torso
Eyes	Chest	Hands	Fingers

Mouth	Arms	Legs	Feet
Reproductive organs			

Is there a difference between the age you are today and your sense of the age of your [fingers]? (Repeat for the parts of the body you have identified).

Body storage

Identify the answers to these questions and label them on your body map.

What parts of your body have a sense of:

- Holding or storing memories of your past? (eg hands)
- Belonging to someone else? (eg father's hands)
- Being controlled by someone else?
- Not belonging to you?
- Being out of your control?
- Being lost or missing?

Body internal

What information do you have a sense of that is held and stored in the different places inside your body?

Name the internal spaces of your body, then describe and draw them on a new body map (eg mind, heart, kidneys)

Do you have a sense of space that is in your [heart] and what is held or stored in that space? – repeat for the spaces you have named

Body position

Describe the different body positions that you have today which feel most comfortable, eg is there a particular way you sit, stand or fold your arms?

Do you have a sense of the age you feel when your body is in [that] position?

What kind of body postures support who you are today?

What kind of body postures hinder who you are today?

Map those postures and the age of the postures.

In what places or situations do you hold these body positions?

Body movement

What movements does your body or body parts make?

Do you have a sense of an age that is held in that movement?

What familiar body tics or gestures do you have?

Do you have a sense that they do not belong to you but to someone else?

Draw and describe that movement and whose movement it might be or who must be in the space on the other side of that movement.

Body metaphysical

Locate the position and spatial dimensions of the following and draw on a body map:

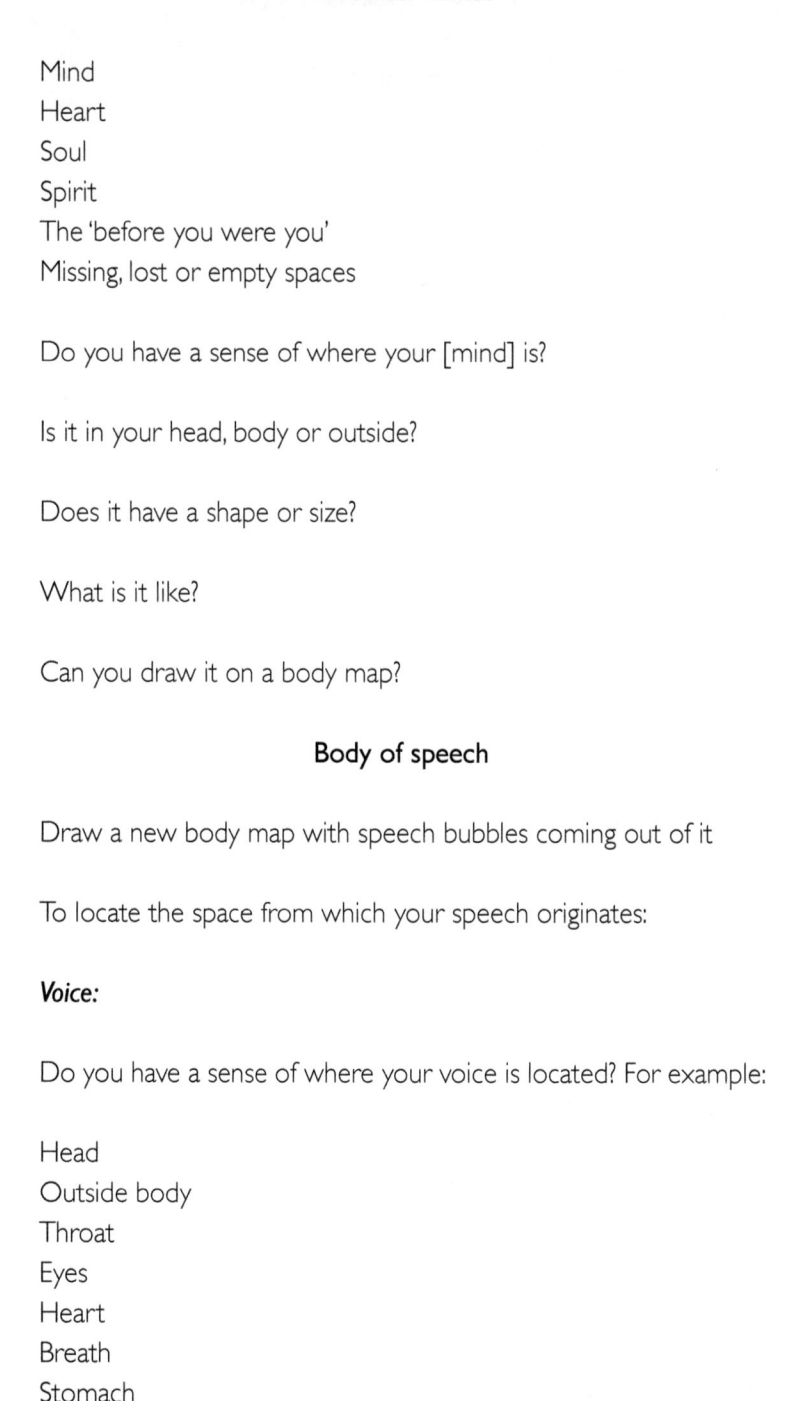

Mind
Heart
Soul
Spirit
The 'before you were you'
Missing, lost or empty spaces

Do you have a sense of where your [mind] is?

Is it in your head, body or outside?

Does it have a shape or size?

What is it like?

Can you draw it on a body map?

Body of speech

Draw a new body map with speech bubbles coming out of it

To locate the space from which your speech originates:

Voice:

Do you have a sense of where your voice is located? For example:

Head
Outside body
Throat
Eyes
Heart
Breath
Stomach

How many different voices do you have?

How old is each voice?

What voice is lost and not heard?

Words:

Where do your words come from?

Which words are your words?

Which belong to someone else?

What do your words do when you speak them?

What effect do your words have when they go out to someone else?

Sounds:

What are the most common sounds you make? For example:

Sighs
Coughs
Clicks
Ers and ums
Silence

Spell the sounds or draw a representation of the sounds

Do you have a sense of how old each sound is?

Do you have a sense of silence or quietness?

Where is it located?

How old could the silence be?

Part II: Real World Questions to B

What is your goal, desired outcome, or purpose in life?

How many different [goal]s do you have?

Is there an object or objects that best represent your [goal]s?

Is there a statement you can write down that represents your [goal]?

Can you make a map of a space that is big enough to hold your [goal]s?

Locate each [goal] on the [goal] space map

Do you have a sense of the age you were when you first created that [goal]?

Where did the [goal] come from before it was yours?

At what moment in time and in what place did the [goal] become yours?

What kind of boundary is around that [goal]?

Create another [goal] space map of the [goal] you had before this one.

How old were you when you had that [goal]?

What was the source of that [goal]?

Where were you when you got that [goal]?

Who gave you that [goal]?

Part III: Real World Questions to C

Draw a map of the space that separates you from your [goal].

What are the things on your map that support you reaching your [goal]?

What are the things between you and your [goal] that prevent you from reaching your [goal]?

Do you have a sense of how old each of those objects is?

Is there a metaphor or image which best represents the landscape through which you may have to travel to reach your [goal]?

How many objects are there in that landscape that represent the things that support you?

Is there an age at which those objects first occurred?

How much of the space on that map is occupied by your past which, instead of being behind you, is now in front?

What kind of boundary is around the outside edge of the map of your space?

Part IV: Real World Questions to D

The space outside the map represents unknown and unforeseen events that could support, hinder or completely change the nature of you at A, your [goal] at B and the map of the journey you have described at C.

Can you list or draw a representation of events that would change the map of your journey from A to B. What people, places or things could influence you, your journey and your [goal]?

＃ PART THREE

THE LIFE OF DAVID GROVE

CHAPTER ONE

Biography

David Grove was born in Tauranga, New Zealand on December 1st 1950 of European (his father) and Ngati Hikairo (his Maori mother) ancestry. David took great inspiration from his Whakapapa (Maori genealogy) and ancestral teaching. He graduated from the New Zealand Universities of Canterbury, where he completed a BSc and Otago, where he obtained a post graduate degree in business administration, before taking a masters in Counselling at the State University of Minnesota in the USA. There he studied Ericksonian and family therapy, and published a book with Basil Panzer called *"Resolving Traumatic Memories"* (1989 Irvington).

His work focused on the development of linguistically-based techniques that enabled therapists to access information contained in primary process language forms, and the facilitation of experiential change in non-cognitive learning. He then developed work and competency-based training for mental health professionals, counsellors and therapists, which is extensively known throughout both the United Kingdom and United States, and was approved by the American Psychological Association (APA) for Continuing Education for Psychologists.

David was renowned for learning from all aspects of life; systems theory, physics, ancient Greece, aviation, the web and populist culture. He could synthesise these ideas into his work and emerge with innovative new processes.

David came from Kawhia on the west coast of North Island,

a seaside harbour, and had a lifelong love of all things nautical. He first married Marilyn Pare, whom he met around the age of 19 in New Zealand. At that time Marilyn was involved with the Salvation Army while David worked on different projects related to business recovery. He had a flare for working with struggling businesses. He was not interested in the detail, but had great ideas which worked when put into operation.

David then moved to Los Angeles with Marilyn to work as a zoologist. He held a variety of jobs at the time, including as a guide on the whale watch programmes in Southern California, trading in lifeboats from the Queen Mary, and importing top of the range cars like Bentleys and Rolls Royces from the UK. David's long time friend John Mote recalls him as having an entrepreneurial streak for buying and selling things.

This first marriage broke up in LA and he returned to New Zealand to live with the Motes. It was around this time that his spiritual exploration began. He was examining concepts and looking at where ideas and thoughts come from, and struggling to understand the break-up of his marriage.

Grove was invited to join the London Phobic Trust as a Consulting Psychologist and he organised the International Symposium on Stress and Anxiety Disorders in 1985. His work included presentations on imagery at training seminars for the UK Society for Ericksonian Hypnosis.

In the late 1980s David organised a conference in London with RD Laing, who was instrumental in setting up a retreat centre with him in Eldon, Missouri. Between 1991 and 2000 David focused on the development of this retreat and another the Lake District, Cumbria, UK. These centres provided training programs and week-long healing retreats for therapists and psychologists.

David's second marriage was to Cei Davis. In 1993 he met Penny Tompkins and James Lawley, whose detailed study of his work is described on page 159.

Among other practitioners he worked closely with Philip

Harland and Caitlin Walker whose work with him is described on pages 154 and 128 respectively.

In 2004 with John Mote's assistance David wrote a programme called Te Hno Nga Ki Te Ora to assist people to understand the life force that influences the decisions people make. This is more complex in the Maori community, where there is a responsibility to the ancestors and wider family, and the stories that are part of one's life. The stresses of recognising and adhering to those responsibilities in a modern society create a lot of tension. David was trying to develop a programme teaching people how to use metaphors to react with their inner life. One of the issues for the Maori in New Zealand is mental health. There is a high incidence of mental illness in Maori communities. David called the project "In search of your mind's life" and it is still running at the time of writing. John Mote wrote and recorded many transcripts of David's work which are still in his possession today.

My own experience of David Grove, during our work together in 2005 and later years, was that he had little interest in making a name for himself or even in making a living; he was entirely focused on developing healing processes. Living a peripatetic existence, he developed and facilitated many competency-based training programmes, books and healing retreats for thousands of therapists and mental health professionals from introductory, to advanced and masters levels in the UK, USA, Ireland and New Zealand including:

- Healing the Wounded Child Within
- Resolving Traumatic Memories (book & training program)
- Healing Retreats in Kawhia & Warkworth
- Resolving Feelings of Anger, Guilt and Shame
- Clean Language
- Therapeutic Metaphors
- Metaphors to Heal By

- Personal Journeys
- Emergent Knowledge
-

His seminars were based on his own original work around resolving traumatic memories and healing the wounded child within, which sometimes encompassed physical healing. Workshops were always unpredictable because his insatiable curiosity took the lead over any advertised programme, but the results were invariably precise, original and often spellbinding.

While being dedicated to his work, and not suffering anyone or anything to stand in the way of it, Grove could be a mischievous magician and was held in indulgent affection by all who knew him because the gentle genie showed up in kind gestures, like the infinite, painstaking, psychological help that was on offer to all comers, a shop for the soul that never closed. At his funeral, James Lawley gave the following eulogy:

Was David Grove a Great Man?

If greatness is determined by the number of stories told about you,
then David Grove, you were a great man.

If greatness is determined by creativity and inventiveness,
then David Grove, you were a great man.

If greatness is determined by the number of people whose lives are touched and in whose memories you reside,
then David Grove, you were a great man.

If greatness is determined by generosity of spirit and the amount of knowledge given away,
then David Grove, you were a great man.

*If greatness is determined by compassion for the pain
and suffering the human spirit can endure,
then David Grove, you were a great man.
If greatness is determined by one's optimism and
expectation that people can heal and transform their lives,
then David Grove, you were a great man.*

*And, if greatness is determined by taking the path never
travelled before with courage and dignity, knowing there is a
price to pay to yourself and to your loved ones,
then David Grove, you were truly a great man.*

Excerpt from James Lawley's tribute at David's funeral
service 21 Jan 2008)

David Grove was buried at Pyes Pa Cemetery Tauranga.

Psychologist Ernest Rossi has frequently been credited with the following tribute to Grove, and he recently confirmed to me that it is an authentic quote and gave permission for it to be included in this book:

"A gentle genie has escaped from the lamp. His name is David Grove and his magic, Clean Language."

– Ernest Rossi

Ernest Lawrence Rossi, Ph.D. is a Diplomate in Clinical Psychology and the recipient of three Lifetime Achievement Awards For Outstanding Contributions to the Field of Psychotherapy: He is a Jungian Analyst, the Science Editor of Psychological Perspectives and the author, co-author and editor of more than 40 professional books and more than 170 peer reviewed scientific papers in the areas of neuroscience, psychotherapy, dreams, and therapeutic hypnosis that have been translated into a dozen languages.

CHAPTER TWO

Recollections by Co-Practitioners and Friends of David Grove

The following accounts have been contributed by the many friends, colleagues, fellow practitioners and followers who knew David Grove during the past thirty or more years. Their purpose is to paint a broader picture of the character of inventor of Clean Language and to provide a pathway for future researchers.

Rob McGavock
Caitlin Walker
Jennifer de Gandt
Tania Corsack
Philip Harland
Lynne Burney
Penny Tompkins and James Lawley

Rob McGavock

Rob McGavock is a Licensed Professional Counselor who resides in Columbia, Missouri, USA. He acquired his degree from the University of Missouri in Counseling Psychology. During the course of his career he has worked as a therapist and group facilitator at several psychiatric hospitals and several alcohol and drug rehab hospitals. He has designed two intensive outpatient programs and he has been a speaker on various topics through the years. He has also conducted a private practice. Rob had the privilege of living within sixty miles of David's Eldon, Missouri Retreat where he observed David's work for many hours. He counted David as a best friend and mentor. Rob currently works for an Employee Assistance Program that is owned and operated by a local hospital. He is a therapist, presenter, and a consultant regarding employee relation concerns to companies that contract with them. He is married to Brenda McGavock, PhD, a Clinical Psychologist in private practice who was also a close friend of David Grove. They have two daughters and two grandchildren at the time of this writing.

Recollections of life with David Grove
August 3, 2011

I knew David since the early nineties. I remember reading a brochure that my wife, a clinical psychologist, gave me about his retreat work. His retreat centre was located close to Eldon, MO in rural Missouri about 60 miles south of Columbia MO where I live. David and his wife, Cei Davies, had bought a big home with acreage for clients/professionals from all over the world to come and do personal work and to learn his theories and methods. David had been travelling and living in an RV *[Recreational Vehicle, the American term for a Motor vehicle equipped with living space]* for years doing seminars around the USA.

Eldon was to be the location for his work in progress, which was to develop his theories and methods for resolving psychological/emotional trauma. People who came were his very willing guinea pigs. He was working there with some very heavy duty cases in which people had experienced serious sexual, physical, and emotional abuse. He never shied from any case that came to him. Many of the people who came were wounded professionals from various healing disciplines. Professionals would also send their toughest cases to him. People would come and stay for a week or two and he would hold sessions all day and sometimes into the night, usually with the whole group present. Once finished he'd say, "Okay, you're done for now and (pointing to someone else) you're next." His mental acuity and energy were phenomenal when he was focused in his work. He would conduct therapy eight to ten hours per day, six to seven days or more in a row. He'd use his voice inflection to create a trance-like state in which information was more easily accessed. People observing in the room would drop off to sleep sometimes as a result.

As a therapist I had been most interested in learning better methods for working with trauma cases without re-traumatizing people. The information on the brochure was well written and highly intriguing to me so I called and arranged to go for a visit. Little did I know that David would have such long-standing positive impact on my both my professional and personal life. I felt lucky to have, quite possibly the world's greatest therapist and theorist living so close to me in the middle of nowhere, rural Missouri. He liked the idea of being so remote in mid-America so as to create an inward journey before even arriving in Eldon. The closest international airports were Kansas City and St. Louis, about three hours away by car.

My visit to meet David began a long mentor/therapist/best friend relationship that lasted until his death and still affects my work in quite positive ways. I am a Licensed Professional Counsellor (masters degree level), licensed to conduct therapy for clients. I work for a major hospital in the area that owns and operates an Employee Assistance Program. We contract with companies that wish to provide counselling, managerial consulting, and training to their employees. We also do critical incident stress debriefings. My wife Brenda, who would also become a close friend and helper/support to David, is a PhD clinical psychologist in private practice here in Columbia, MO. Together we would host numerous workshops in which David would conduct client therapy and training for professionals. We hosted his last yearly Intensive Workshop, which was always a catch all of new information and ideas for the year, at our home in Columbia. This all came about rather quickly on a whim when he was once visiting. Brenda sent out an e-mail and we were not optimistic about getting a sizeable group together so fast. Were we ever wrong. Within weeks it quickly filled with people eager to work with and learn from David again. People always seemed to flock when he'd appear on the radar. I suppose we'll never know how many people David has impacted and where all they hail from around the world.

David was a masterful therapist whose ego or transference never interfered with or contaminated his work. I observed hundreds of hours of his work with clients and professionals. Being close by, David and Cei graciously accepted me at their retreats and I would try to help out in any way I could. Cei was not only a masterful therapist herself, she was a great cook and she worked quite hard at making guests comfortable.

David's metaphor therapy was fascinating and effective for people and it completely honoured the integrity of their own life experience. He would elicit healing by developing metaphors from the client that were a perfect fit because they originated with them. David also designed questions that would pull people back in time generationally. He would then discover a pristine *redemptive metaphor* that he would wash forward through their life experience, healing various contributing issues along the way and the issue that was first presented. He would often have people draw their metaphors to make them more concrete and stimulated to be of assistance. This had quite a nice healing effect and it also became a brilliant visual record of the work being done.

David had a phenomenal memory. He would remember exactly where he left off with a client that hadn't seen him for years. He never took notes. He would jokingly say that he didn't care anything for the people, he just wanted their metaphors. This wasn't true, David had a heart of gold. He would never impose his own ideas or his metaphors on clients. He was very careful not to do so. This was the hallmark of his *Clean Language* concept and approach, that so captivated the interest of many professionals around the world.

David and Cei developed a certification course in metaphor therapy complete with manuals carefully illustrated with many wonderful drawings by Cei. It had to have taken her many painstaking hours to do so. He produced video training tapes as well for the course which continue to be fascinating to view.

As far as challenges, I would say that David let no dust settle on him. He could be difficult to keep up with. The world was literally his home. He would blast off to various parts of the world on a whim to continue working with professionals and clients who would eagerly invite him to come. I travelled with David numerous times and it could be a wonderful but nerve wracking experience. David had a way of disappearing right when the plane was boarding. I would look way down the concourse and here he would come a running, just making it before the boarding door closed. He actually missed some flights.

I spent several weeks in the UK with him at an Intensive in the Lake District. It was absolutely fabulous. He looked at metaphor through music, acting, and poetry at that Intensive. Willy Russell, the famous playwright (*Educating Rita*) and composer, was a friend of David's and attended, a casting director came, and contemporary UK poet Adrian Henry who did poetry readings. Steve Joliffe who played briefly with Tangerine Dream played music for us as well. What an experience it was.

On another three week trip with David to France to Jennifer DeGandt's lovely retreat in Normandy David was developing his more recent 'Power of Six' methods. He was also using his gyro chair (he bought a gyro chair from a guy who charged for rides. It was so big it was on a trailer).

The theory of 'Power of Six' was that if one would take a difficult client experience through six consecutive steps asking the same question such as: What's the first thing you know about _____?, What's the second thing you know about _____? the third thing — and so on six times, the problem would transform with a resolution. By the fourth question there was what David called "a wobble" in which things began to shake up and transform. The sixth rendition was "a rising out of the ashes", the Phoenix of a resolution. I saw it work for clients and experienced it myself.

Once, Brenda, David, and I were on a walk on a farm property near our home when Brenda stumbled. The fall seemed to trigger some emotion and frustration for her. David told her to stay on the ground and then started the 'Power of Six' process with her immediately. By the time he was done (fairly quickly) she had resolved the anxiety that was feeding the emotion that was triggered by the stumble. That's how things roll with David sometimes. There could be spontaneous combustion at any moment.

To top things off at the retreat in France he might strap a person into his gyro chair and turn them every which way <u>and</u> upside down which would yield different information as he asked questions due to the different angles a person was placed in. Sometimes it worked without David asking much more than "*What do you know now?*"

David was a master at soliciting accurate information of which client wasn't even cognizant previously. He had learned that not only do people carry information within the body, they carry it in the space around them as well. He could find all of the bits and pieces of a fragmented and dissociated client. He'd find them in cracks on the wall, behind things, up in the sky, behind them, in the carpet, in a mirror, through the window — the kind of places he could find bits and pieces was endless. David went to very delicate and sacred places with clients. It could almost feel scary to a novice. It was literally word surgery and you knew it. You knew that the barest of bones of a person's emotional life were laid out on the table, and trusted that he would always manage to tidy things up in a safe way and/or bring healing to the dynamic at play.

UK author Philip Harland was at the Normandy retreat and has written quite a good book on the 'Power of Six' method. I'm sure Philip understands only too well how difficult David could be to pin down for information. David certainly entrusted Philip to pull it all together which he has done beautifully. While in Normandy David worked me over on the gyro chair and I felt it really transformed some material that he had been working to help me resolve for years. I joked for years with David that I would patiently wait until he got good enough to help me, and he did not disappoint.

Another challenge for professionals learning David's methods and theories was that he would readily discard previous methods he had developed in favour of new ideas. This would occur just when people were beginning to grasp the magnitude and nuances of his methods and putting them to practice. This was the case when he left metaphor therapy behind for 'Power of Six' methods. However, David continued to incorporate old ideas into the therapy that he conducted with people as needed. A therapist who attended some of his workshops once commented to me that David's ideas and the work he'd do in front of live audiences was phenomenal, but that he wasn't David. Point taken. David's work was absolutely awesome at times. Although it never seemed that one could be as adept as David was, he was adamant that his methods were teachable and learnable. When people would claim they were concerned they wouldn't do it right, he would tell them that as therapists they owed it to their clients to truly help them resolve their issues, and not to re-traumatize them with methods that were conventional and inadequate.

David was highly trusted and extremely intelligent. I imagine his IQ was off the charts. Our eight year old daughter Josie even recognized this when she once said without any prompting, "David has a really big mind." David also had a very witty and playful sense of humour. He loved word play and was a terrific wordsmith. He could get away with teasing that no one else could do without it being offensive. I was his "thick-headed friend Robby boy".

This came out of some early metaphor work he did with me in which there was the metaphor of a dense black fog in my head. Fortunately he eventually resolved this, however the name never resolved. Our daughter Cara loved to banter with David and tease him as well. They'd go at it.

Probably the most important thing that I learned from David was the importance of choosing words carefully so as not to contaminate the client's experience – the idea of '*Clean Language*'. This is the concept that Penny Tompkins and James Lawley of the UK have seized upon and written so well about in their book 'Metaphors in Mind'. In fact a whole industry has developed around this concept. I met Penny and James at one of the Eldon Intensives. They may have been there several times actually. Penny also attended the Lake District Intensive. The 'Clean Language' concept definitely made me a better therapist whether using David's methods or not. I find that I really enjoy using David's methods. It lifts the burden (and ineffectiveness) of being a conventional therapist slogging through painful emotions by instead learning to skilfully elicit healing responses directly from the client that fit just right. I love the idea of a therapist as the skilled facilitator of such methods. It is also interesting to listen to the metaphors take shape and to learn of their traits, characteristics, and possibilities. It can be a wild ride and quite entertaining. The healing that can be elicited can be quite complete for a person because it cuts to the core and heals at the core for a person.

Brenda and I also enjoyed a trip to New Zealand with David. We had the pleasure of meeting his lovely mother Betty, his sister Barbara, her husband Ross, his aunt Elva, friends and others who had played important roles during his formative life. David felt a very close bond with his mother. We experienced a Maori celebration which felt quite special. We took baths in holes we scratched out on the thermally heated beaches near his mother's home town. We met his best friend John in Christchurch. We absolutely loved our time there with him enjoying the fabulous bay view from John's place high up on the hill. David had a great love for exotic birds and animals. While at the Maori celebration David noticed two teenagers harassing a mother bird on a nest in an embankment. David sharply chastised these two young hooligans and took them straight to their father to give them more what for in no uncertain terms. He built a beautiful lake on his property in Eldon and would conduct therapy while navigating a pontoon boat full of people around using a quiet electric trolling motor with foot pedal controls. He had Black Neck swans that would float by, making their lovely fluting sounds. He had Coco the lama, who he would let in the house. He had Mongolian Squirrels. Cei was an avid animal lover and had Shetland Ponies, sheep, and Bazzel the goat. They had a turkey who would peck on the windows while David was working with people. It was a sublime and magical time.

    David and I shared a love of aircraft and we attended experimental aircraft shows in Oshkosh, Wisconsin; Lakeland, Florida; and in France. David bought a motorized paraglider, an engine with a propeller you strap on your back and fly with a parasail that is attached to your seat harness. He crashed it several times crunching the propeller, but getting up with only scrapes and minor bruises each time. Then he bought a two person powered parachute that's like a tricycle with a parasail that he loved to fly. I flew in it with him. It was amazing to be cruising along slowly and popping up over trees in beautiful rural Missouri fields. He didn't crash this one fortunately. David had a paraplegic friend who was an author and who he would take swimming in his pool – floating him on a raft. He also strapped him in to the paraglider with duct tape and took him flying. His friend absolutely loved it even though he was probably terrified at first. With David things were just going to happen – you might as well get used to it.

    David loved the nomadic lifestyle. He had people in numerous places around the world that welcomed him with open arms to stay. As mentioned he traveled the US in a recreational vehicle (RV) for years presenting his work around the country. He had a real love for the recreational vehicle, a transportable home that really fit his lifestyle. Once he established some roots near the very small town of Eldon, MO he began searching for and dragging home wrecked RVs to rehab. Some of these vehicles were smashed beyond recognition in the front. I remember telling him it was a losing proposition. He turned to me in all sincerity and said, "But, Robbie, this is a deluxe model that I got for a song." I wanted to tell him he had just wasted his music. It seemed like whenever I tried to disentangle part of the wreckage it just made it worse. It struck me that the wrecked RVs were a metaphor for the broken people he would take in at Eldon for healing. There was not a person so damaged that David wouldn't sally forth to salvage. No matter how battered and broken the person he would dedicate himself to provide healing for them with great acumen and always some level of success.

David also had terrible bouts of fatigue that would overtake him that he experienced for years. Sometimes he would be immobilized by it for weeks. Brenda and I would have him stay at our house to rest while we fed him and attempted to revive him. These bouts went on for years. He had been to specialists and tried numerous remedies. Sadly he was just beginning to feel better when his life ended. He'd love for people to rub his feet and give him massages. He was grateful for the kindnesses expressed to him by people all over the world during these down times. Sometimes he could barely muster the energy to work with clients during one period in his life. This was so out of character as his work usually fed him energy.

David died suddenly of heart failure. He had just been at our house in Columbia, MO working with clients out of Brenda's office which he did a number of times. He had travelled to visit another long known friend and student of his, Steve Briggs, PhD (psychologist), who lives in Kansas City. They were working together on website and video projects. Steve had also hosted a number of workshops with David. He died suddenly in Steve's home. Brenda and I hosted his family (Betty his mother, and Barbara his sister) and best friend (John from Christchurch) in Kansas City at her sister's home when they came to retrieve his body. As is customary for Maori we visited David at the funeral home daily for a number of days and had conversations with him while preparations were being made for his body to be taken to New Zealand. For the Maori death is not thought of as the end of a person's life. I like that. The word death is not even used. Brenda did a eulogy (her comments about David) on video for David that his friend John recorded. It was played at his funeral in New Zealand.

Brenda and I sorely miss David who I considered to be a best friend. I am truly blessed to have known him and learned so much from him in this life. Brenda told me the other day that sometimes she calls out to him to help her with his methods for her clients and she can feel his presence guiding her. With David you never knew when he might show up. Perhaps this is true in spirit as well. I miss him dearly and sometimes think and know that he'll show up again whether in this life or another.

Rob McGavock, MEd, LPC
Licensed Professional Counsellor

Caitlin Walker

One of the leading practitioners who worked regularly with Grove is Caitlin Walker. She has taken his techniques and adapted them for use with groups, teams and organisations in a process she calls Systemic Modelling. Caitlin decided to apprentice herself to Grove to learn his approach after attending a workshop in 1997 and worked extensively with him over the next few years. Systemic Modelling combines all forms of his work, including Clean Language, Clean Space and Emergent Knowledge. Below she describes how she came to know David and her experiences of working with Clean techniques. She has also provided two case histories on page 178.

Meeting David Grove and developing Systemic Modelling

My family background is from the US, the UK and Nigeria. Moving around a lot meant I was always keen to understand how group rules work, where they come from and how groups update them. A story I often tell when describing why Grove's work was so important to me dates back to when I moved to California at the age of nine, and found that I was not allowed to play with a new friend I'd made because he was black – the school was informally segregated. I thought, *"That's not fair. Those rules are made up. They should just change them."* This incident set me off on a path of wanting to find ways to help people identify their unconscious rules and make up new ones. As a teenager I had read Edward T Hall's 'The Dance of Life – The Other Dimension of Time' (Hall 1984), all about how different cultures had very different models for organising time and how this impacted so many other areas of their lives and led to miscommunication when they tried to work together. I became fascinated with how many levels of difference there could be between us. I wanted to find out my own models for time and make up my own rules for whom I could and could not be friends with, and for a whole host of other aspects of thinking. I studied anthropology and linguistics at university and Neuro-Linguistic Programming to help me think both deeply and practically about people's mental models and the way their language indicates how they are thinking, as well as what they are thinking. Meeting David Grove took all that study and blew it out of the water.

I first saw David at a workshop in London. He was working with a woman who was happy to share a symptom that was troubling her. He asked Clean questions to develop a metaphor for her symptom and then a landscape to allow that symptom to make sense. It was an extraordinary experience to watch a physical symptom be gently interrogated. She said she was losing her breath; and David asked her what kind of losing was that losing. She replied that it was 'a hole' and he asked whether the hole had a size or a shape. This tied in very much to the work I'd admired of Edward T Hall and seemed to be a methodology for uncovering unconscious patterns. I was very excited but needed to feel it for myself.

David put us in pairs to practice these Clean questions together and we were invited to ask: "What would you like to have happen?" and then to listen to the answer or watch the gestures of our partner. Next we took a word or phrase from that answer and asked "What kind of a … is that?" Then we asked where it was and then whether there was anything else about it. I worked with a stranger next to me. When he asked me what I would like to have happen, I said I wanted to find my path, and I gestured off to my right. When he asked what kind of path it was, I felt my attention go into my body, my heart and my hand. I answered that it was compelling and that I felt compelled to be on the path. When he asked where that compelling path was, I realised, as the words came out of his mouth, that it was located clearly off to my right, and that it was drawing me into it. It was as though the path was answering rather than my head. Finally this stranger asked if there was anything else about that path and I said that it wasn't the path I had been on. I knew in that moment that my life would change. I knew that these Clean questions were not only the methodology I had been looking for to help people uncover their unconscious patterns, models and rules for living, but that my own path had been revealed to me, one I could not help but follow.

I promptly left my PhD and my partner, came to London and turned up on the doorstep of James Lawley and Penny Tompkins, the organisers of David's workshops. At that time they were working with David so that they could learn and model his processes. I said to them, "I don't know how I am going to make a living in this field but I need to find out how to do this stuff!"

Fortunately they decided to support my transition into Clean Language and Grovean Metaphor Therapy, even giving me a position as their administrator to support me financially while I learned at their feet. I was terrible at administration and this act was a testimony to their generosity!

I attended as many events with David as I could, and this was my first real step in 'getting' psychotherapy. For me, David was my therapist and mentor and, if I'm honest, I found him a little intimidating. I was in awe of his skill and at the same time drawn to want his therapeutic attention for my own development. I learnt first hand what it meant to have long-standing issues and hidden fears reveal their sources and transform completely. It was liberating and powerful and sustainable. It was not about the therapist deciding what was right for you, it was about the therapist being present to what was there, how it came to be there and what you and your system needed to happen next. It was all about *being* rather than *doing*.

I practised with client after client to become skilled at working one-to-one with individual metaphor landscapes. I still take on an occasional one-to-one session but I could always feel the pull to use the questions to reveal the dynamics between individuals and across groups.

I created the first London Clean Practice Group with Dee Berridge in 1997 and we created group applications where, instead of exploring deeply with one client, we got the whole group to explore their models for different kinds of thinking and then shared these models to learn from one another. For example, we would explore our models for short-term memory by reading out lists of seven words, and then ask people to try to remember them. Then, instead of asking for their answers, we Cleanly modelled their process. Some people saw the words written; some were saying them to themselves over and over; some were connecting them in a story and some were simply panicking, with their minds blank. From this process we started trying out each other's processes, improving our own memories as a result of this group learning. It was a wildly exciting time.

Clean Work with Traumatised Young People

As well as developing applications within the Clean Practice Group I found a job working with ten of the 'worst' kids in the 'worst' schools in Hackney, with the aim of helping them to manage their behaviour and get back into school. This story was first published in *ReSource Magazine* and then in *Counselling Children and Young People Journal,* (Winter 2006).

I started by asking myself, "Instead of teaching these children, or trying to change their behaviour, what if I just used Clean questions to help them make models of their memories, their tempers, their time lines, and how they make decisions etc?" This would be my first experience of a live group that was made up not of well-resourced adults already interested in personal development, but of young people outside of the school system who were at risk of becoming criminals. If the questions worked here, I believed they could work anywhere.

At first it was impossible to take my eyes of the kids for a moment or they'd kick off. I got them into a circle and knew I would have to keep their attention at once: we would need to run the modelling with all of them in the moment. I also knew it would not be appropriate to use the slow, hypnotic type of facilitation that David did, because the teenagers might get bored or freaked out. I made it more up-beat and chatty and, instead of asking one kid a load of questions, I asked each kid between one to three questions and then moved on to a different kid.

We started with the very relevant topic of 'temper' and, as I rolled out the Clean questions, each child began to build up a sense of his or her own temper, while at the same time listening to one another's. One went red, one was like a switch, one like a volcano, one went quiet, etc. These are the answers of two of the children:

Caitlin:	What would you like to have happen?
Child 1:	I want to stop losing my temper!

Caitlin:	When you are losing your temper, you're like what?
Child 1:	I go red.
Caitlin:	What kind of red?
Child 1:	Blood red.
Caitlin:	And when blood red, where is blood red?
Child 1:	It's here [points to his throat/chest].
Caitlin:	And who is different to that?
Child 2:	I am, I just switch.
Caitlin:	What kind of switch?
Child 2:	I don't know it just happens so fast.
Caitlin:	And it happens so fast and you switch, and what happens just before you switch?
Child 2:	Someone gives me a look.

I kept going around the group getting them to develop metaphor models for their tempers until each of them had something. Then we did another round to help them find out about how the tempers started, using the questions David employed in order to pull back time, and how the tempers ended.

Caitlin:	And blood red is here, and what happens just before it's here?
Child 1:	[pointing to something coloured maroon] It's like that.
Caitlin:	And before it's maroon, it's like what?
Child 1:	It's purple. [Points to sternum.]
Caitlin:	And before it's purple?
Child 1:	Then it's blue. [At this his whole demeanour changed.] It's cool, like the sky. Like my mum.

At this stage I did not know what they could do with this information or how useful it would be to them; I was just experimenting. I did know enough as a youth worker to see that they were all very engaged which seemed an excellent start to the programme.

In the next session the boy who went red said to me in front of the class, "That stuff we did. When I get up in the morning and my dad's drunk: red *(indicating with his hand, red going into his body]*; I'm hungry: red; I have to put on clothes that smell sweaty and I stink: red; I've got no money for the bus to school and I'm going to be late so I'll get a detention before the day starts: red. Miss, when I get into school my red is right here *[pointing to throat]*. Is that why I hit people?"

I replied that I didn't know.

He interrupted to say, "On the way to school, when I'm going to be late anyway, I could go to the duck pond, think of my mum in Africa and look at the sky, and breathe in blue and make myself purple. Then I think I can control myself."

So that's what he did. In his metaphor he had covered enough of the landscape to find a way of managing it. Nobody in the group ever laughed at someone else during these sessions – it was as though we were creating a sacred space. And because he now had a method of controlling his temper, they all wanted one. We were modelling with a purpose – to find out enough so that we could manage our patterns instead of our patterns managing us.

And so it went on, with half the time spent simply eliciting metaphors for the current status quo – their models for time, spelling, fear etc – and the rest of the time in lively, creative debate about what they could have instead.

I realised they could not handle more than two or three questions deep, partly because they had not committed to sharing personal psychological information and partly because they got bored.

It was clear to me that this was very different from regular therapy and I needed to learn how to do it safely. Even this group work, which was a very light touch, could reveal patterns in these often damaged children that needed exquisite care and attention.

For example, once we had got past tempers and on to modelling learning and, in particular, spelling, the group noticed that one boy was spelling vertically instead of horizontally, and could not read at all even though he seemed intelligent. When I showed him a word he would learn it, but up and down rather than side to side.

He said, "Yeah, I only have a thin bit of space *[indicating a vertical line in front of him]* to see the letters in so I have to write them in single file."

I (in ignorance) walked up to him and put my hands into the space where he'd indicated that he had only had a little vertical line, and moving my hands outwards said, "You need to open up that space."

He kicked out at me, screaming and shouting, and ran from the room. I felt I had psychologically traumatised him. Later I took him aside, apologised to him and asked him if he could tell me what had been happening there because I wanted to understand it.

'How could you shame me in front of everyone?' he said.

I decided in private that I could ask him a few more Clean questions than in front of the group:

Caitlin:	Remember that space. Is there anything else about it?
Child:	*[He showed me with his hands.]* It's wavy, wavy.
Caitlin:	What kind of wavy?
Child:	Like curtains.
Caitlin:	Is there anything else about curtains?
Child:	They're curtains I hide behind.

It emerged that his father was a drug dealer who beat his mother. At the age of six (he was now fifteen.), this little boy's job had been to hide from his father behind the curtains, watch the beating and then decide whether it was necessary to run out for help or to call an ambulance.

Since that traumatic time, even though that man was now in prison, the boy could not put anything visual into his personal psyche-space because it was taken up with the trauma of hiding behind a curtain and being too young to stop his mother getting hurt. He saw things vertically because his vision was restricted to the space between the curtains he had hidden behind, watching his father beat his mother through that vertical crack.

In my naivety I had pulled open those curtains in class. Now I tried a much Cleaner approach.

Caitlin:	When you have only a vertical line to see letters in, and reading means words need to be horizontal, what could happen next?
Child:	I could make the words very small but very close up.
Caitlin:	And can you make those words small and close up?
Child:	Yes – I can see them.

And so, slowly and with the help of his friends, this clever young man re-learned how to see words horizontally and was able to teach himself to read. I did not attempt full healing sessions with him, even though I knew how to, as I had neither a psychotherapeutic contract with my employers nor qualifications to work as a child therapist. I needed to coach these children to manage what they had, rather than help them heal their systems.

This case history was part of a mentoring and education project which my team were undertaking, and our Systemic Modelling was the education side of it. We won the European Crime Safety award for this project because 60% of the kids were back in mainstream school within nine months.

Metaphors at Work

As well as working with young people, I was invited to use this process with a business team, which took me way out of my comfort zone at the time. Remarkably, it was very similar to working with the kids. I was asked by the leaders in a software company to help them develop a shared company vision. Their programmers were having trouble communicating with the marketers in the organisation.

I simply used the same principles as I had with the kids' project and started them off in small groups, asking them Clean Questions and helping them first of all to develop individual metaphors and then, as they listened to one another, to develop group metaphors. This was another big shift away from Clean one-to-ones and helped me to think about how the techniques could be used as a group development process. Using this Clean approach, the company was able to create one shared metaphor for the organisation, not imposed from the top down but built up through the self-awareness of each individual and each small group.

I called this process *Metaphors at Work*, because it is about helping groups of adults to understand their personal embodied metaphors, how they affect the way they work and how they can cause issues between individuals that may not even be conscious of. Once this is out in the open then they can devise ways to work with each other's metaphors, finding common ground and rules for engaging collaboratively.

In business, people are not familiar with Clean language training, so I introduce the questions more as a tool to improve their listening and observation skills, and treat the metaphors as 'sticky' or memorable ways for them to understand how different they are from one another. The Clean questions are a common language for creating shared meaning. I do not stop people asking 'dirty' questions or sharing their assumptions, but I encourage the group to notice the difference and to call one another out when they are making too many assumptions without checking what someone actually means.

During this early piece of work, a forward thinker at the Open University asked if he could film the sessions for use in their MBA programme, as a module on creative management. This made it more acceptable to other groups and businesses, giving it legitimacy. I was living my dream and being asked to bring the process into team building, police interviewing, mergers and acquisitions and helping the long term unemployed to find sustainable employment. The possibilities seemed endless.

I ran my Clean projects according to what I had learned from David. I would start by asking the project sponsor what they would like to have happen. I would spend the first session just modelling their answers, helping them to become really clear about what they wanted. These modelling sessions often resulted in big shifts in their thinking and the projects were very innovative.

After a few successful pilots in helping the long term unemployed become a peer coaching group, able to support each other to find the work they needed and wanted, I was invited to help set up a whole *Welfare to Work* company based on Clean modelling principles. This was exciting, recruiting a workforce based on their ability to ask Clean questions, be curious about people's answers and trust people to make the right changes for themselves, instead of shoe-horning them into jobs they didn't want. Eventually I built a small troop of people trained to do Clean modelling in groups, and I was just starting to be able to articulate the rules and principles.

Co-working with David Grove

In around 2001 I got together with David in the Lake District where he was working with Georgina Evers. He was developing Clean Space and working out the principles governing that process. I was desperate to share the ideas I had about getting groups to self-model. We found lots of commonality between the meta-rules of my process of Systemic Modelling and David's rules with Clean Space, some of which were: no more than two or three questions per person; no need to challenge or get involved in people's answers but by moving around (the group in my model and spaces in David's model) the system began to learn about itself. This led to Emergent Knowledge, sudden insights and exhilarating learning. I was delighted at the correlations and felt even more certain that my Systemic Modelling was worth pursuing.

At the same time I was becoming clear about how the interchanges between facilitator and learners were crucial to group learning, and I started 'throwing my weight around' with David. I remember a workshop at Penny and James's, where he was teaching a Clean master class, when he asked one learner, "What is the next question to ask?' They would say what they thought and he would say 'No' to their reply and carry on around the group until someone said something he agreed with. I confronted him, saying "David, are you asking me what is my next question, or to guess what is in your head? If it's to guess what's in your head I'd rather wait and you can just tell me what you think as this isn't suiting my learning style." From my work with the children, I had a language to challenge teachers with, in the same way that the children had challenged me, and felt I had a right to be in a good learning state, even if I was with my mentor. Luckily, David liked being challenged in that way and we moved from mentor/mentee to more of a collegiate relationship.

Clean Healing

While running the practice group, I had become interested in asking Clean questions on physical as well as emotional issues, and around 1998, Dee and I had run a small workshop we called 'Working with Dis-Ease'. This shifted to a new level when I met a muscular skeletal physiotherapist called Catherine Saeed in 2002. I had been teaching her Clean questions and modelling embodied metaphors, and she became interested in how people's muscles, postures and breathing changed as they went through big changes in their metaphors. She brought along a colleague of hers who was a physiotherapist and also a competitive runner. The colleague had an injury that was not healing and Catherine wanted me to use Clean questions to help her to model the symptom. After around twenty minutes of questions she started to describe it as "a spring that had a kink in it". She said that the more it was stretched the more the kink was weakening. She drew her metaphor and then she and Catherine looked at it from their professional point of view and realised that it helped them to re-diagnose the injury. Contrary to the previous diagnosis, it was not a tight Achilles that needed stretching off, but a small tear in the tendon that needed complete rest to heal. They changed their course of treatment and within six weeks Catherine's colleague was running competitively again.

Catherine was so impressed that she devised two-day retreats with me and brought along patients with intractable issues so that we could work on them together with metaphor development and physical interventions. They were very successful, often with miraculous results, especially where people linked current symptoms as expressions of past trauma. At times it felt almost like faith healing except that the healing was all being done by the clients themselves. Our contribution was simply to train their attention on their issues, allow them to understand what was happening and work out what needed to happen next.

Penny Tompkins came on one of those early retreats and had a wonderful personal experience healing her ongoing back problem. Catherine and I worked directly with David who was suffering from postural problems. We combined our approach with Clean Space and he regained the posture he felt he should always have had and raved about the approach.

We would have loved to continue this work but found it difficult to raise the funding and to prove the cost effectiveness of it. I wanted to bring it into mainstream offerings for clients. I was not prepared to offer it only to private paying clients as this did not fit with my path of making Clean processes available to all.

Developing Emergent Knowledge and the Six Degrees of Freedom

The next shift in my association with David was when I moved to Hull and David met my husband Shaun. We had bought a huge old house for a big Clean project I was running (on the basis that it was cheaper than putting all the Clean facilitators up in hotels). There were fifteen of us staying there at different times including Penny Tompkins, James Lawley, Michael Mallows, Phil Swallow, Judy Baker, Chris Grimsley, Nancy Doyle and of course David himself. It gave us the chance to bring together different developments and models and bounce them off one another. David was developing Clean Worlds and Emergent Knowledge and he and my husband got very involved in the design and thinking around Clean Directions and David's idea about helping people obtain Six Degrees of Freedom. He wanted to find out whether if you gave people the chance to shift their body position, say with a chair that spun or even better a gyroscope that could move in any direction, what might their bodies know from those different positions? Shaun joined in David's design and building of what came to be known as the 'Whirly Gig'.

One couple who worked extensively with David and with us during this period of devising the rules and principles of Emergent Knowledge and Clean Space was Chris Grimsley and Glenda Sutcliffe. They work in the Northwest of the UK and run an NLP training centre; NLP in the Northwest. They are particularly skilled at bringing Clean approaches to local people who put them into use in schools, communities and businesses. They excel at making new ideas seem straightforward. They had first encountered Clean through my *Metaphors at Work* process and quickly built their own relationship with David, eventually becoming very close with him.

Like David, Glenda had been raised within the teachings of

the Salvation Army and they talked about their need to serve and to help others, and how this had developed from their respective childhoods. Chris and Glenda still train Clean Language and Clean Space and host Shaun to bring along the Whirly Gig and give people the experience of Six Degrees of Freedom. Glenda was a great mentor in helping me see David not just as a genius thinker, healer and teacher but also simply as a man who needed friends, love – and firm boundaries when he was out of order.

We ran a number of different Clean experimental trainings at the house, bringing together engineers, medicinal herbalists, art therapists, teachers, managers and body workers. One student of David's was Jeni Edge who developed a bodywork approach combining Emergent Knowledge and massage. She started asking the clients "Currently your symptom is like what? Then, "Whereabouts would you like attention?" "What kind of touch?" and then she started making six movements and re-asking the clients what they wanted to have happen next. It was a great time of personal insight and professional creativity.

We called the house 'The Practice' and this began Shaun's endeavour of creating a centre where Clean practitioners from all fields could get together and share their ideas and look for crossovers between approaches. Shaun now leads an annual event he calls 'The Northern Taste of Clean' which aims to develop new, leading edge applications of David's work.

Later experiences with David Grove

After this we moved from Hull to Liverpool, where we live now, and David decided to make our home one of his regular UK bases. At times it was as though David's capacity to create new ideas was out of control. In the autumn of 2005, he and Shaun bought a lot of computer hardware because he wanted to wire up his patients to biofeedback programmes and track the internal physical changes that occurred while he was working with them, particularly when big change and resolution took place. One day in December, I went into labour with my second baby and David was a reluctant houseguest during the planned home birth as the weather was too poor for travel. The house had three floors and between contractions I wandered around wondering where my mother was. I found her in the office with David, wired up to his machines while he asked her Clean questions and I shouted, "No! Not today! My mother's attention needs to be on me!"

David was a wonderful support, emotionally as well as professionally and after the birth we made him, along with the other attendees, one of my son Guy's guide parents. When I was pregnant with my third child, David insisted that Shaun and I come out with the family to New Zealand to meet his own family. He had a new idea about working in doctors' surgeries and wanted Shaun to support him. While David had been in and out of doctors' surgeries himself he had taken to asking the doctors what they thought of his own symptoms, and he would use six questions to help the doctors develop their thinking. I'm sure that this was a new experience for most health professionals, having their patient use a process to hone their diagnostic skills. David became convinced that this would be a useful tool for doctors in general! We flew out and Shaun and David worked with a doctor for a few weeks. For example, if a client came in, and the issue was an obvious pattern, this doctor would prescribe sessions with David, to explore the metaphors and the issues underlying the symptom, as well as mainstream pharmaceuticals. Like lots of the applications towards the end of David's life I think this has great potential and hope that someone picks it up and develops it further with some supporting research.

Clean Health & Safety in Factories

While I was in New Zealand, David introduced me to a colleague of his who worked in the poultry processing industry. She, like me, had learnt Clean questions from watching David do therapy. She had taken the concept and applied the questions as an investigative tool after factory incidents. She had the highest safety record of any of the plants across New Zealand within this company. She said that the South Sea Islanders, who made up the majority of the workforce, had a reputation as being uncommunicative after accidents. However, she never found the workforce secretive or closed and believed that it was simply that they were being asked conceptual questions like "How did the accident start?" and "What time did it happen?" These were questions which they found difficult to respond to while they are still in the trauma.

Instead, this woman's approach to investigative interviews was to spend the first thirty minutes asking Clean questions like 'This accident, it's been like what?" The answer might be, "It was a mess' to which she would ask, "What kind of mess?" and "What happened just before that mess?' This type of questioning allowed them to build a model of their experience and to be able to articulate it clearly. The problem with the existing investigative interviewing was that the people being interviewed might just have witnessed someone's arm being severed by a machine, or fingers cut off. The interviewee would then be in trauma and unable to process his or her experience. Once she had helped people to settle the incident through her gentle Clean questioning, and to process it, then it would be possible for them to answer the detailed investigative questions that helped her to work out what needed to change in the factory process to make things safer in the future. It was her Clean approach that allowed her such a high safety record in her factories. I spent some time with her helping to model out what it was that she was doing differently so that she could teach it to others in the company. This is another example of how diverse the impact of David's teachings could be.

The Death of David Grove

When we returned from New Zealand, David was very keen to work with different people to record his tacit knowledge and to help him articulate his current knowledge. While he was staying with us, our relationship alternated between learning whichever brilliant new idea he was having, to helping to take care of his failing health. Shaun would drive him to wherever he was going to work, make sure that he ate good food and would fill in taking over clients or groups when David wasn't able to work. I spent time encouraging him to spend a little of the attention he gave to others on his own health and wellbeing.

David was in the US and France when my third baby, Grover, was born. Although we talked by phone I did not see David again after the summer of 2007.

In January 2008 I was just celebrating the conclusion of a piece of work when the phone rang and David's dear friend and colleague Dafanie Goldsmith told me that David had died of a heart attack.

I cannot describe how that evening and the next few days went. I was so lost. I flew out to New Zealand for David's funeral, taking just the baby and leaving a heart-broken husband to watch our other two children. At the funeral, Grover was a welcome distraction for everyone's grief and I have to admit that it was not until I overheard someone say that he was named for David that I made the link between the name Grover and David Grove. He was named after Grover Washington Junior, the saxophonist, but perhaps I had, unconsciously, named him for my friend and mentor.

After the funeral there was a little unrest in the Clean community and worries about who really knew which processes the best or who had a right to write down his work. I liken it to the children's story 'Seven Dinners Sid' about a cat with seven homes. David was very precious to many people, as a therapist, a mentor, a teacher and most importantly as a friend. He inspired us, had adventures with us, developed new ideas with us and downloaded his thinking to whomever he was with at the time. Each of us held fragments of what he was thinking at any given time. After he died it took us a while to get to know one another and find the space we needed to share our experiences of David now he was gone.

I am just writing the book he told me I needed to write and I know he would be proud of me having found the courage to do it. The work is coming on apace and I hope that within my lifetime there will be significant improvement in international relations as a direct result of there being global access to David Grove's work.

Caitlin Walker
www.trainingattention.co.uk

Jennifer de Gandt

Jennifer de Gandt is regarded as the Elder of the French community of Grovian practitioners. She started the exchanges between the French group and Grove, Tompkins and Lawley.

I first met David on the recommendation of my friend Graham Dawes, who was told by Joanne Hogg that there was a very interesting person called David Grove giving Healing Retreats in the Lake District. So I went.

I have been in personal development work for a very long time starting with Jungian Analysis in London in the late fifties then blossoming into the whole Humanistic Movement that arrived in France, where I was then working, in the late sixties and early seventies. My work has always been with teaching and with learning in groups, first in Universities around the world sponsored by the British Council and then in the seventies in IBM France, where we ran a very experimental language programme for IBM managers from all over Europe. As I was in charge of "methods" I was always chasing new ideas and trying them out in various contexts. In 1983 I discovered NLP through Gene Early who gave the first course in France. Then I was on assignment to the US with my husband and the NLP world exploded upon me and I became a trainer.

Back in France in 1986, I set up on my own and brought NLP to Hewlett Packard in Grenoble. The mixture of business groups and therapy groups was very stimulating and the nineties were full of discoveries. So it was quite natural that I would have been drawn to David's Clean Language work and off I went to Georgina's farm in November 1997 to meet David.

The impact was sudden, I arrived late and as soon as I walked in, he started asking me questions and sending me off into strange inner spaces. I noticed that he had no feeling for the group as such but was laser sharp in his attention to each participant. In a few minutes I was seeing the spaces where I held my feelings about England and France and found myself on the boat between the two. David wanted to know why I was watching each coast from the back of the boat! Good question!

What I was attracted to in his work was the ease with which he could direct my attention to my inner space. I was used to going to this space but had never had such a present and perceptive companion.

The times alone with the drawings and musings also suited me. And I was very interested in the spaces that emerged for other people. He was at that time in Metaphor Therapy, age regression, soul retrieval and generational healing, all flowing in unstoppable rivers of meaning. I noticed that there were people there with traumatic history, who appeared to turn up whenever David came to the UK. He took his time with them, no promises of this or that, just the next part of the exploration. He also used his space freely, going off to climb hills or buy wellington boots for clients whose symbols demanded to be manifested in the here and now.

I loved the freedom of it all and took up other chances to work with him. Sometimes this was another Healing Retreat and sometimes a Therapists Training group. Then I linked up with Penny and James in London to see a much more systematic approach to his work. In 2000 I organised their first appearance in France at our NLPNL Congrès and we set up Trainings together. In 2003 David came to my house in Normandy for the first time and we began a very intense exchange of ideas and experiences.

Many strange things occurred: the garden became a birth place for Clean Space and I have fond memories of Phil Swallow desperately trying to film John Joint as he strode across my land to my neighbour's field, an unheard of crime in Normandy. David was meanwhile warming himself with trips to the sauna and wrap ups in warm blankets. It was summer in New Zealand, he remarked ruefully. I remember one year when he came with Sandy, a fellow New Zealander, who said as her introduction of herself "I am here to make sure David gets here!" Thank you, Sandy!

Then the next year David appeared with the Gyroscope and we had participants out on a frosty night moving under the stars to find their lost parts! The way David made machines work for us was quite new to my experience of therapy and people loved it. We swung in hanging chairs and turned our perceptual positions on their heads and we certainly saw differently. Or rather, in my case, I saw through old images long installed in memory. In the twist of the gyroscope, I felt an ancient fear of falling that translated into images of high cliffs and a false step, then the angle turned these images into pure sensation and created a feeling of pulsing energy that removed all fear.

In 2006 and 2007 the French network of Clean Language practitioners were privileged to have very close contact with David's new ideas for Emergent Knowledge. We tried out variations on his ABC distinctions and of course the power of six through downloads. Just before his death, he was exploding with projects: Table Work in Business with Lynne Burney, Vision with Lynn Bullock, Epiphanies with me, Fibonacci numbers with Silvie de Clerck, New Stories with Sophie de Bryas, Emergence with Maurice, and Anthropological Journeys with Tania Korsak, to name but a few. He had an enormous capacity to tune in to the ideas and passions of other people and an equally strong desire to turn ideas into things people could do to grow into fuller human beings.

I am continuing his work in France by running three communal events: 'Le Salon de Printemps' in March each year takes place in Paris, Montmartre, where the French network present their current work with Clean language, Symbolic Modelling, Clean Space and Emergent Knowledge to each other and the public. The second event is the Université d'Eté, held the last week in June, which includes two days of Supervision for Facilitators with their Clients, then three days for further presentations of work in progress in the French Community. The last event is in November and is an Emergent Knowledge event when we carry on the work we started with David and which we are now developing in France.

Jennifer de Gandt
jennifer@innovativepathways.net

Tania Korsak

Tania Korsak worked with David Grove in France in 2004. She now runs a private practice in Brussels helping pregnant women and is involved in clinical research in Paris helping parents to manage severe epilepsy in their child. She incorporates Grove's Clean practices into both of these activities.

When I met David Grove, in 2004 through Jennifer de Gandt, three things struck me about his work: it was rooted in Polynesian culture, it had some magical component (from an anthropological perspective) and it was a refined tool to "learn how to learn".

In 2004, in Jennie's sitting room, David was presenting to a small group of people his model of facilitating a client from A to B. I was then struck by how this form of journeying resembled Polynesian navigation, which I had come across in my studies in anthropology. The next day over breakfast, some confusion had emerged among participants about David's presentation. Questions were being asked about how to facilitate a client's shifting perceptions and whether a facilitator should remain focused or not on the client's initial request.

It struck me at the time that I had a different paradigmatic understanding, and a comparison between different navigation techniques the day before had helped me understand David's model in a different light to what was being questioned. As Western navigators the origin and the destination of journey are predetermined. The journey is about trying to keep to a straight line from A to B. Whatever storms or currents; the challenge consists in the ability to remain as close to the map route as possible. Facilitation in those terms would be objective-driven. On the other hand, Polynesian navigators do not predetermine their destination; it is the ability to grasp information in the moment and navigate with it that will determine the destination. In this case the journey begins in A and the process reveals the position of B; what is found in A and on the way to B determines the nature and the place of B. It struck me then that in order to grasp David's model we needed to give up on our western navigation technique and seek to become a little more Polynesian, by thinking of facilitation as process driven.

David replied, 'Where do you think I come from? I'm Polynesian!' I had no idea, I thought then he was American. I had created this metaphor without knowing his background. It turned out that his mother was part Polynesian, descended from a long line of Polynesian navigators. He then felt I had some understanding of the structures that pre-empted his way of facilitating. It was the beginning of many conversations, mainly over the phone, riddled with challenges, surprises and giggles.

I presented the metaphor of the Polynesian navigators at the Clean Conference in London in 2009. I called it "A Polynesian Journey through Childhood: Understanding the Sensorium". My paper suggested a journey through the development structure of lying and the hidden developmental functions of being economical with the truth and how Clean and Polynesian skills could help us reorganise and understand in its complex form, this very human behaviour.

This talk was infused with another recurrent topic in our conversations, the ability to metamorphose as if under a magical spell. Indeed, during a Clean session, clients journey in the land of the psyche and experience sensations, emotions and thoughts. It gives the explorer an opportunity "to learn to learn", as it stimulates one's ability to experience and organize old and new information emerging through the Clean symbolic process. It gives the explorer a chance to re-interpret and often find wisdom in his new understanding.

As I began watching David facilitate I became particularly interested with the strange ability clients had of metamorphosing as if the experience they were going through necessitated physical malleability. I also experienced it as a client. Clean questions and re-iterations seem to prompt clients' ability to transform. Today, I have become very focused on how clients in a Clean session are always morphing. Clients impersonate different ages, different roles and sometimes – different animals, objects or energies as if some magical spell transforms them into something else to help them on their way.

David used to tease me on what I was perceiving: *"Which age, which learning structure?"* And test me out with the question: *"And how old [my words] could that be?"* (I usually got it right.)

However, this was no magical trick, I was running at the time a little Montessori home school structure in the south of France helping children and parents. Over the years, I had spent countless hours observing children and adults learn and transform. I learned through this experience that we do not learn as individuals but that we in fact learn through the relationship we create with others, the environment and ourselves. At different ages these relationships change in structure and in focus and seem to determine the nature of some identifiable developmental pattern. Clean facilitation is to my mind a means to facilitate the client's ability to both regress and explore these learning patterns embedded in our ability to self-organise.

This was another way of approaching the way David had worked with trauma that also became the centre of some of our conversations and his supervision. For David, Clean facilitation was a way of retrieving some lost part of oneself, something that was stuck, frozen in time or space and that was related to some traumatic experience. In my words, it was as if the client had a certain density in some developmental pattern, *something* undergrown that was pulling him back that could be through a Clean process, differentiated and learned. This *something* requires the explorer to work deeply with his perception and embody the nature of the symbols at play, often palpable for the observing facilitator. As the process unfolds the client drops this momentary transformation and appears somewhat more himself, more mature, more whole. From an anthropological perspective, one could say that the client is the shaman of his own process of transformation capable of embodying the nature and the patterns of his learning experience. Clean is in this sense a magically transformative and a self-empowering tool.

These exchanges enriched my experience and my practice. They led me to create, with the support of the head of the Neuro-paediatric ward of the Necker Hospital in Paris, a clinical trial using Clean facilitation as an analytical tool. The research aims to understand how parents deal with the impossible burden of having to raise a child suffering from a rare form of epilepsy. In my preliminary study, I discovered that parents are experiencing some form of traumatic struggle similar to the clients I would talk about with David. In order to help parents learn about and exchange their reactions I created a developmental kit. It consists of seven games, or tools that give parents the possibility to relate in a different way to their reactions and help them identify recurrent patterns. The games have a learning constraint that corresponds to a given developmental pattern. The material both supports and limits the exploration. So it is not saying, 'What would you like to have happen?' The material aims to guide parents at a very specific level of their understanding. Regarding the experience of having a sick child, it is more about 'OK, we can organise information like *this*, let's see what happens if we begin to organise it like *that*. The material acts as a catalyst for specific processes.

In May, last year this toolkit was presented in a contemporary art gallery, Roots, as an installation. *"Clean-games insights"* aimed to suggest a journey through the multi layer patterns of our perception. As in a dig, I displayed my games as the tools of a new school, *the archaeology of perception*. Once the clinical research is completed, I hope to organise a second installation showing this time my findings into the dig of our ability to self-organise.

Otherwise, I have also been interested in training facilitators and explorers in Clean. In my experience, I found that facilitators need to acquire symbolic maturity, the ability to become malleable in all the multi-layer patterns of perception. One of the difficulties new facilitators seem to have is a lack of understanding and experience of how Clean questions affect the process, and therefore do not know which question to ask and when. To this end, in March 2011 at the French Salon organised by Jennifer de Gandt, I presented a Clean formula, a mnemonic trick to help facilitators learning about Clean to use given question in a given order. It has helped new comers to slow down and support facilitators in their ability to become sensitive to the emerging process.

In my practice in Brussels, I mainly work with pregnant women. Pregnancy is a rite of passage in a woman's life. Women come with question about their bodies, their sexuality, and their relationships. As a Feldenkrais (Feldenkrais 1991) practitioner, I often begin my sessions with Functional Integration and incorporate Clean as the session evolves towards other concerns. For example, I might begin with Feldenkrais to help pregnant mother overcome a general sense of anxiety by supporting the patterns they are using to carry the baby. I then suggest Clean as a way of unfolding at the symbolic level what is happening in their experience. I rely on my developmental model to check out for some of the learning that could be usual for the new mother. I often have the privilege of watching these women transform into beautiful Madonnas, icons of renaissance graces, as the beauty of their newfound wisdom embodies pregnancy. I would love to work with a photographer that could capture these moments of deep transformation. It is a humbling privilege.

I am deeply grateful to David and all the Clean community for their sharing and support.

Tanya Korsak
www.Cleaninsights.com

Philip Harland

Philip Harland is a playwright, scriptwriter, author, and a Clean Language and Emergent Knowledge psychotherapist. He was born in Yorkshire, won a scholarship to Bradford Grammar School, studied architecture at Durham University, and was commissioned in the Royal Artillery, where he spent national service prosecuting and defending courts-martial. After training in analytic, humanistic, and neurolinguistic psychotherapies, he worked closely with the David Grove until Grove's death in 2008. He published many articles on the Clean treatment of addictions, compulsions, and emotional and cognitive problems, and two books: 'The Power of Six' and 'Trust me I'm the Patient: Clean Language, Metaphor, and the New Psychology of Change'. (Harland 2012) Below is his account of his relationship and work with David Grove.

I first met David Grove in June 1996 in London at a Clean Language introductory workshop called 'Grovian Metaphor', and went on to his first London training with Tompkins and Lawley (in 'Grovian Metaphor Therapy') in September 1996. I was invited to join a new Clean Language research & development group hosted by Tompkins and Lawley (along with Caitlin Walker, Dee Berridge, Clive Bach in Highgate. Then I met and worked regularly with David over the next ten years or so in London, France and New Zealand.

I worked with David on most aspects of Clean Language and metaphor – trying out and helping to develop ideas for new questions, such as: "Where did you come from? Where did you come from before you were born?"; the nature of alternative universes; the development of Clean Space and Emergent Knowledge/Power of Six from near the start.

I had trained in analytic, humanistic, cognitive behavioural and neurolinguistic psychotherapeutic methodologies but found them all too directive/suggestive for my non-authoritarian, pro-self-realization tastes,

David had a readiness to go wherever the work took him, an ability to focus exclusive attention on the client and an utter conviction that the client knows best. He was a genius, annoying, touching, generous, thoughtful, enquiring, stimulating and witty. We shared a delight in the ambiguities, puns, carriwitchets and etymological echoes of language. Pretty much the only thing he would defer to me over was a knowledge of wine. I remember his giggling, his long, long hugs after absence, our long walks after working in France and New Zealand, when he would go over and over what had happened during the day, looking for what could be learnt from it, and envisaging what we would do tomorrow.

I experienced huge sadness over his illnesses and my loss of an inconsistent, unpredictable and loving co-facilitator, colleague, mentor and friend.

Philip Harland
philipharland@gmail.com
www.wayfinderpress.co.uk

Lynne Burney

Lynne Burney worked with David Grove in France from 2004 onwards. She is an MCC with the International Coach Federation and founder of the LKB School of Coaching in Paris.

I met David Grove at the Normandy Retreats (Les Salons) in a doorway at Jennifer de Gandt's house in November 2004, and I went on meeting him in the same doorway at the same time of the year for the following four years. When I count up the number of days spent in his company it only comes to something like fifteen, but those fifteen days radically changed my inner self and the way I coach and work with other people. It seemed extraordinary to me to meet a fellow Kiwi in a garden in France; one who had been to the same university but who had followed such a radically different road from mine. In the kitchen it was like we were old mates but in the "salon" (learning space) he was the master and I, the willing "voyageur".

These three to four day retreats at Jennifer's house were essentially an opportunity for David to test run his latest ideas so when I met him he was well into Clean Space, Small World Networks, edges and infinity. He worked in close association with Jennifer and enjoyed the loose structure of these days and the French flavour provided by the small group of "femmes fatales" who attended the "salons". In 2004 his work was a very new phenomenon in France and was unheard of in coaching circles.

From a personal point of view, these retreats or "salons" were an opportunity to do some deep personal journeying in a very safe environment with a profoundly humane person. Whatever "technique" or experience that I experimented with on myself during those retreats, I made available to the coaches that I supervised afterwards. In this way I helped develop the "Clean field" in the coaching community in France. My enthusiasm for his work cost me one or two clients in the early days of my work with David but by the end of 2007, with his support and creativity, I was ready to take Clean Space and the Power of Six back into companies where they could work their "magic" with teams and groups.

What drew me to this work was David's voice. It invited me to go down the rabbit hole and to stay there long enough to meet the white queen. I was also attracted to the rigour inherent in his work. Many years of yoga practice had given me a fine appreciation for mind-body detail, and working with Clean techniques required the same patience and attention to detail as any yoga asana or meditation practice. And in that patience and attention to detail lies love and a gentle harbour. From a personal perspective it was about the power of the inner journey that took me through the dark night of desolation and pain to a meeting with a midnight star, a garden table and a deep and easily accessible inner peace.

In terms of my clients, today I work almost exclusively with Clean Language, Space and Iteration in my one on one coaching sessions and I use Clean questions with practically any other technique, tool or exercise that I use with company teams. There were some challenges along the way. The very first time I decided to try out iterating the question, "And what do you know about…?" with four senior managers in France's biggest aeronautical company, one of them walked out! He had warned me at question four that if I asked the same damn question again he would leave. I did. He did. Two of the others stuck it out and had a fair to middling experience but the one manager who "went for it" had an epiphany.

What I learnt from it was, yes, this is powerful work! And it would also be a good idea to take care of the learning frame before assuming that everyone is on board; and there may be a few preliminaries necessary to prime the field beforehand; and above all, make sure the participants are present at this workshop voluntarily; and, oh by the way, God will not strike me down if I don't ask six of the same, but nothing much will happen if I don't either! In a multicultural context, the amount of "prepping" is likely to be influenced by the culture of the organisation, power relationships and of course the purpose of the workshop.

I started teaching coaches to work with David's techniques in April of 2008 in Marseille. The workshops run six (what a surprise!) times, for two days every two months. They have run in Paris since 2009 and also ran in Nantes in 2011. The last module is a validation process run by Jennifer de Gandt and myself. The language of tuition is French.

I started a Clean research group in Marseille in 2011 and it will continue both there and in Paris in 2012. This year, 2012, my work with coaches in these two research groups will focus on where Clean techniques can meet and marry with other well known techniques such as Constellations, Process Work, Narrative Therapy etc.

I have also developed David's techniques very clearly in companies, mostly using space and iteration. The last discussion I had with David at the end of November 2007 was about how to bring the table successfully back into the meeting room. I had always argued that the table was an antidote to creativity and communication but, following my personal work with David, I began to explore the idea of people rotating around a table with a coloured pen, jotting down their responses to the same question on the piece of paper they found in front of them. The paper was stationary, the people mobile and the result was a simple way to create a little chaos while informing the system of what its individual members were thinking.

Today the number six informs much of the work I do in companies; not necessarily in an overt way but if I am running a world café I am going to be looking for multiples of six (six tables, six people per table, six conversations etc). I am going to be asking each group six questions about whatever their topic is. This does not imply the over use of the iterative question but rather a knowledge that six of anything is more interesting to a system than three of it.

When I am supervising coaches and they are describing

something that is troubling them about a client relationship, I am sure to ask them what session they are in. When I am working with a client's systemic representation of his issue, I work on the basis that six representational elements are probably enough for some sort of change to occur. Six guides my patience and gives structure to the work and the seventh question dénouement is invariably present at the end of any team or individual coaching session. Moving a team in space moves its thinking and its body-sense of itself. From this, change can come of its own accord.

David Grove's work is an ongoing experiment and exploration into the working of the mind-body – the techniques in themselves are nothing without the humanity of its user and the use of these techniques requires that we be our first clients. Not all clients are ready to let go of the outer relationship with the coach to journey inwards. That is OK. You don't have to do a lot as a Clean Coach but you sure as hell have to be present and "engaged" with the world of your client.

As an assessor of coaches for ICF, I would like a lot more coaches to "Clean" up their act!

Lynne Burney
Courbevoie, France
14/1/12
www.lkb-coaching.com (website)
www.lkbheartlines.com (blog)

Penny Tompkins and James Lawley

Learning from a Master

We first saw David Grove working in 1993 and were bamboozled by what we saw. Fortunately Penny had a "pull" to find out more so we attended two retreats thinking we could figure out what he was doing. Watching David work with others close up and experiencing the amazing effects his questions had on us was fascinating and transformative, but did not get us much further with our figuring out. So we made a decision to model him as an 'exemplar of excellence'. That was in 1995.

Modelling is a process for accelerating learning and acquiring new ways of doing and being. We soon realised that if David's work could be generalised it could be applied outside of psychotherapy and even more people could benefit from it. We called our description of his work Symbolic Modelling to make clear that we were not aiming to replicate exactly what David did, but rather to create a model whereby others could use the principles and practices of a clean approach in a wide range of contexts.

To say David proved a more complex exemplar than we envisaged would be a gross understatement. It took us five years before we were ready to publish 'Metaphors in Mind: Transformation through Symbolic Modelling'. Our book took into account many of David's developments in the fifteen years up to 1999. But David never stopped innovating. No sooner was our book out than he started working on his latest idea, Clean Space. And that meant we could never stop learning from him.

We last spoke to David when we telephoned him from Texas over Christmas 2007. As always he did his best to persuade us to drop everything and come to a workshop in California where he was experimenting with his latest ideas. As tempted as we were, we had family obligations and told him we would catch up with him on his next trip to the UK. Two weeks later as our plane touched down in London, our mobile phone rang with the shocking news of his death.

We could say much about our relationship with David but we would prefer to honour his legacy by describing what we have learned about how to master the master's work, and we have chosen six pointers for this:

See the work in context

Get to know the nature of metaphor
Think space, space, space
Separate behaviour from commentary
Examine the relationship between questions and answers
Adopt a clean stance

See the work in context

People who gathered at David's funeral were invited to bring photographs of him, and to lay them out on a communal table for everyone to look at and tell stories about. We soon discovered that his supporters were loyal to the aspect of David's work that he was developing when they met him. Those who knew him in his Healing the Wounded Child Within days brought photos of a younger David, and they described how metaphors took shape inside the body and transformed in unexpected ways. Others described strange forays into perceptual space outside the body and journeys back through time, through the generations to sacred redemptive metaphors. Yet others said the simplicity of Emergent Knowledge and Power of Six superseded his previous work. You would have thought they were talking about different therapists.

We don't see the span of David's work as a strict developmental sequence. Of course his later ideas evolved out of his earlier work, yet the later work is not necessarily 'better than' nor 'more advanced' – it is simply 'different to' and was developed for a different purpose. David's thinking seemed to take a huge leap every few years while continuing in the same general direction. His pursuit of a new idea often meant that he would temporarily dismiss his previous ideas – to the dismay of those who had spent years trying to master his techniques.

David had several attempts (helped by a number of devoted supporters) at integrating all of his work but his speed of innovation meant than none of the proposed frameworks lasted. In the mid-1990s for example, soon after developing his Quadrant Model[1]

David came up with a "fifth quadrant" which sealed the fate of that framework.

Within the three major epochs of David's developments – early (Inner Child), middle (exploration of perceptual space and time) and end (Clean Space and Emergent Knowledge) – he devised dozens of practices, and came up with many principles and explanations for each. He continually refined these, each time getting cleaner and simpler. So, when you go to source and study David's work, it is worth considering the context in which the session took place. When did it happen? Where did it come from? And where was he going with it?

Get to know the nature of metaphor

For ten years David and his wife, Cei, set up camp every six months or so at Georgina Evers' retreat centre in the Lake District of England. After we had been studying his work for a year we asked him "If there was one thing we should concentrate on until you come back, what would that be?" David's surprising reply was "Get to know the nature of metaphor." At the time this seemed like a Zen koan, and perhaps it was because our contemplation revealed layer upon layer of meaning.

David said he "chased ideas and wrestled with them". He sought to understand the nature of things, and did that by completely absorbing himself in a topic. A classic example elsewhere in this book is Rob McGavock's story about David's experiments with flying machines. He used these contraptions to understand the nature of "thin air". And his desire to cross the Pacific Ocean on a self-made pontoon (which thank goodness didn't happen) was driven by his desire to understand the nature of space.

Understanding the nature of something is more than having a cognitive appreciation of the subject. It is about having an intimate relationship with it's essence. This comes from spending time in its company, recognising it's multi-faceted nature and being changed by the relationship. We think the subjects at the heart of David Grove's work over 25 years are: metaphor, perceptual space and time, emergence, and of course, a clean approach. We would add 'modelling', whether that is as a learner, a facilitator, or a client who is self-modelling. Although David baulked at the word, he was a master modeller – one of the best we've ever seen.

Think space, space, space

David experienced the world very spatially. He shuttled between retreats in New Zealand, UK and USA. Lord knows how many times he circumnavigated the globe. His Maori ancestry imbued him with a remarkable sense of space and a physicality of time.

David's funeral in New Zealand included four days of traditional Maori rituals which were followed by a Christian burial. The rituals included laying his body in his tribal marae and his family and friends sleeping there with him the night before his burial. A marae is an indigenous building constructed by previous generations that holds the visible and invisible tribal history. Tribal elders lined up at the door to receive all of us. We removed our shoes and received hongi – the pressing of nose and forehead to each elder for the "exchanging of breath" – and a welcoming greeting in the ancient language. Inside the marae where everyone stood or sat had significance. As the Maori leader pointed up toward different spaces near the ceiling, it was explained to us that these were where the history of previous generations resided. He described the history in such vivid detail it was as if the ancestors appeared before us. This felt strangely familiar to working with symbols in a metaphor landscape. No wonder David's locating of invisible symbols in an individual's mind-body space took on such realness and believability.

David said "change takes place in a context" and therefore he "made words physical". The effect was to turn metaphor on its head. By definition a metaphor is not a literal description, but

David worked with metaphors as if they were literal. This was an astounding leap in the 1980s when the significance of metaphor – and in particular, the pervasiveness of spatial metaphors – were just beginning to be understood by academics.

Location and spatial relationships were at the heart of all of David did. Whether you are studying his work or applying it in practice you will get better results if you think space, space, and space.

Separate behaviour from commentary

David loved ideas and we often discussed his latest theories long into the night. He would send James off on quests to research topics between visits. During the creation of Clean Space, David was particularly interested in James' knowledge of network theory (since James had once managed one of the largest pre-Internet computer networks in Europe).

David often commented on what was happening during demonstrations. It took us a year of modelling him before we figured out we needed to keep what he did and his commentary separate. They were both valuable but whenever they appeared to be incompatible we learned to favour the behaviour. For example, David created lots of theories about trauma, the role of metaphor, the numbers 1 to 6, and these changed over time. Whereas, although he added to his Clean Language question set the basic questions hardly ever changed.

The transcripts Carol Wilson has provided in this book are a wonderful resource. We maintain that if anyone is going to master David's clean approach, and facilitate similar results, first and foremost they need the knowledge of what he did and how he did what he did deeply embedded in their neurology. Then taking on his fascinating and seductive explanations is more a matter of choice.

Examine the relationship between questions and answers

David did not get his wonderful results because of any particular question asked at a crucial moment (although on occasion this could help). While a question might seem to have magical qualities to transform, it only had such impressive qualities because of the groundwork laid by all the previous Clean questions (and instructions in Clean Space). In a Power of Six process for instance, the sixth question rides on the back of the previous five.

Over and over we saw David's questions establish the physical configuration of the immediate environment, then bring to life the client's inner landscape, out of which the psychoactive relationship between client, their metaphors and their surroundings could emerge.

David demonstrated that a key part of the facilitator's role was to preserve the integrity of the client's process; to keep the client's metaphors in his or her attention; to "bless" the arrival of each new symbol by supporting it to find its place within the network of relationships; and to respond to the client's idiosyncrasies. Without this level of care and attention, iteration cannot do its job and painstaking groundwork can be lost in an instant. David was only half joking when he said: "You're only as good as your next question!"

To appreciate the relationship between client and clean facilitator we studied many transcripts of David's sessions, modelling each question in the context of both the client's previous response and their next answer. Moving our three-pane window (response-question-response)[2] down the transcript one question at a time revealed the background patterns and logic of David's process. Once you've mastered three panes, you can try five, then seven, etc. It takes time to do, but the richness of understanding and learning gained makes it worthwhile.

Adopt a clean stance

David approached a client's inner world like nobody we had ever seen before or since. Getting good at using Clean Language, Clean Space and Emergent Knowledge will take you a long way. Becoming proficient at modelling will take you further. But the glue that holds it all together is how you 'position' your perspective in relation to a person's inner life. We call this the 'clean stance'. Of all the learnings this might be the toughest to grok, to get, to understand its nature. We acquired it through direct modelling but it took many more years to find a way to adequately describe it.

It was a comfort to find that someone else, the Chilean neuroscientists, Humberto Maturana and Francisco Varela, were using a similar perspective which they called "biological phenomenology". Ken Wilber described this as "a third-person conceptualization of a first-person view from within the third person or 'objective' organism". Unless you are academically minded this kind of language is not easily accessible.

In short, a clean stance is being able to appreciate the inside perspective of a person or group as they perceive it while simultaneously retaining an outside view of the larger system. We discovered that David could work with people who had suffered the most terrible trauma, in part because he did not take on their feelings in his body, but left them where they resided in the client's perceptual space. At the same time clients knew he was intimately connected with their personal experience. Eventually, thanks to Raymond Tallis, we discovered that a simple metaphor for describing this unusual perspective existed right under our noses – pointing.[3]

When you watch, read or hear David working, the session will make a lot more sense if you keep in mind at every moment: 'What is the client pointing to?', 'What is David pointing to?' and 'What is the relationship between the two pointings?'.

And finally…

While most people would be happy to make one significant contribution to their field in a lifetime – David made so many that it is hard to count them all. There was only one David Grove and no one else can ever quite do what he did, but with "due diligence" we can all use his work to enrich our own lives and the lives of others. We sorely miss our teacher, mentor and dear friend.

We hope our brief description of these six pointers will support you to learn from and apply David Grove's marvelous legacy in your area of expertise, be that therapy, coaching, health, education, business, organisations, research...

James Lawley and Penny Tompkins
12 September 2014
www.cleanlanguage.co.uk

Endnotes

1. cleanlanguage.co.uk/articles/articles/4/1/Problem-Domains-And-Non-Traumatic-Resolution-Through-Metaphor-Therapy/
2. cleanlanguage.co.uk/articles/blogs/54/Analysing-transcripts---the-3-paned-window-method.html
3. cleanlanguage.co.uk/articles/articles/326/1/Pointing-to-a-New-Modelling-Perspective/

PART FOUR

CASE HISTORIES BY DAVID GROVE'S PRACTITIONERS

KEIKO IZUMI
Workshop with David Grove at the World Bank

CAITLIN WALKER
1. Clean Sports Development in a University
2. Clean Team Building in a London Business School

IAN HALDANE AND DIANNE EMMERSON.
Clean Language and Clean Space Workshop for the Te Ihi Tu Programme

CAROL WILSON
1. Transformational Change through Metaphor delivered by Carol Wilson, Angela Dunbar and Wendy Oliver 2007 at the BBC
2. Project for Doctorate in Professional Studies: an Exploration of the Use of Clean Language and Emergent Knowledge Techniques by Corporate Coaches delivered by Carol Wilson 2011 at the BBC
3. Clean Language Session with a Business Executive

The Work and Life of David Grove

ANGELA DUNBAR
1. Clean Worlds Session delivered by David Grove

2. Clean Language Session Transcript

ADRIAN GOODALL
Clean Space Corporate Workshop

KEIKO IZUMI
Workshop with David Grove at the World Bank: an Experiential Journey through Emergent Knowledge in a Time of Uncertainty

Keiko Izumi currently coaches staff and managers at the World Bank. She co-facilitated a series of cultural learning orientations for new staff to help them to work comfortably in their new, highly cross-cultural work environment. She learned David Grove's Emergent Knowledge (EK) from David Grove and closely worked with him in 2006 and 2007. She incorporates EK in her coaching with excellent results.

Background

This case history describes a workshop David Grove and I designed together and which he conducted at a large organization in 2007.

Our client group wanted the workshop to deal with their work situation which was affected by a major restructuring process in their organizational division. Accordingly, the purpose of the workshop was designed to provide the participants with sufficient time and space to reflect on where they stood in their career paths and think through how they would move forward professionally in a time of uncertainty. By the end of the workshop, we wanted the participants to gain clearer understanding and insight on:

1. What shaped their current goals and mission statements by walking back through their past goals and mission statements.
2. How they encoded time and how it affected them in the process when they wanted to move forward.
3. What forces motivated them to move forward with their career.

The workshop consisted of three main exercises conducted for a one day retreat. The group consisted of 35 people and was designed to facilitate 100 people in the future.

Workshop

This is the structure of the workshop at a glance:

1. David's brief description of ABC Small World

2. Ice Breaker: Power of Six

3. Main Parts
   a. History of Your Goal: What are Your Goals ?
   b. Time-Scape: How Do You Encode Time ?
   c. A Short Play: Communication Exercise
   d. Force Majeure: Strange Attractions and Drivers

4. Restatement of Your Goals and Reflection

David's ABC Small World has been discussed many times and we will not review it again in this case history.

Our Icebreaker was a brief demonstration of his "Power of Six" exercise. We adapted this exercise to be able to let participants physically move around. When a workshop is conducted inside an organization during normal business hours, they tend to continue to think about their daily business matters when they enter the workshop room. It is useful to have participants physically move around during the Ice Breaker rather than letting them sit and talk. This is to allow their emotional and mental state to shift so they can be fully ready for the workshop.

For this brief exercise, we asked the participants to select a 'not-so-serious' problem and write it on a card. They were then asked to move to another space, rewrite the same problem on a different card and repeat this process four more times. Altogether they experienced six different spaces with six different statements of the problem on six different cards. At the end of this session, the participants were surprised that their statements had quite dramatically changed. Their feelings on their respective problems had changed too. Some said that they had gained insight about the problems.

Main Parts consist of three main exercises. The participants were asked to draw and/or write in response to the questions asked by a moderator. We first examined the history of the participants' professional and personal goals and missions. We

History of Your Goals

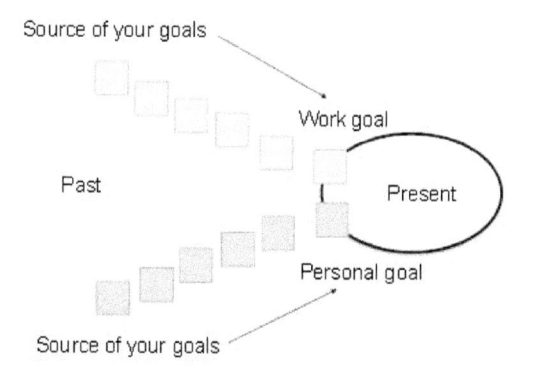

went through professional goals and personal goals separately. The participants were asked to pull back their current goals at least six times into their past, draw and/or write goals at each stage on a piece of large flip chart paper, and then put it up anywhere on a wall:

Secondly, the participants were asked to identify how time was encoded inside and outside them, and relate their ways of encoding time to their work. The questions asked were:

> "Is your past, present, future located spatially?"
> "If so, where?"
> "And how?"
> "How much of your past is in your present, and future?"

For example, if you are inclined to dwell in the past while attempting to create future goals and a significant amount of your past is in your future already, what is likely to happen when you are attempting to create your future goals? With the help of other questions, the participants drew the way they encoded time inside and/or outside themselves. We also explored the relationship of their time encodement with their work and goals. For example, we asked whether their way of encoding time helped or hindered their job, and if so, in what way?

Time-Scape: How time is encoded

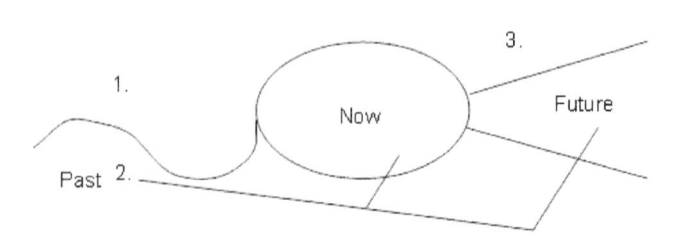

As an intermission, we decided to do a short game to generate a relaxed, fun environment. David called this exercise 'Sound-Scape in Communication'. This exercise enhances awareness of how our own communication is received by others. The game proceeded as follows:

Two volunteers drew their bodies on a flip chart and put them up on a wall. David asked one volunteer to stand at three feet away and had them greet each other. The first person was asked to draw in which shape she intended her voice to travel toward the second person and to indicate where in the body she intended her voice to land, and thought that actually it landed. Then, the second person was asked to draw in what shape the first person's voice travelled towards her and where in her body it landed. Because the two volunteers were not English native speakers and shared the same mother tongue, they tried the above process in English and in their mother tongue:

Sound-Scape in Communication

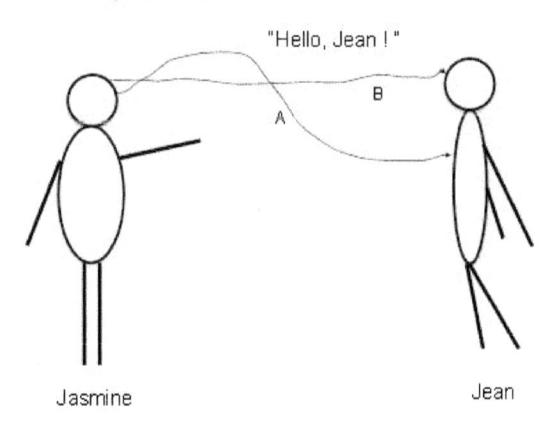

"Hello, Jean!"

Jasmine   Jean

A: How Jasmine intended her "Hello" to travel and where she intended it to land in Jean.
B: How Jean felt it to travel and where she felt it landed in her.

Next, we moved on to identify the source of our motivation. Sometimes, we do not clearly understand what drives us into action towards the future. It may be that we want to escape from something or it may be that we have created such a strong vision in the future that we are compelled to move forward. The participants were asked the questions like, *"What is the source of your motivation? Is your motivation to escape from your past or to be drawn to a vision in the future?"*

The participants drew their bodies and identified four major directions that pushed or pulled each towards his or her vision. We then further explored the relationships of their four directions:

After all the above exercises were done, the participants were asked to go back to their initial goals and missions, and rewrite/redraw them.

Force Majeure: Strange Attractors and Drivers

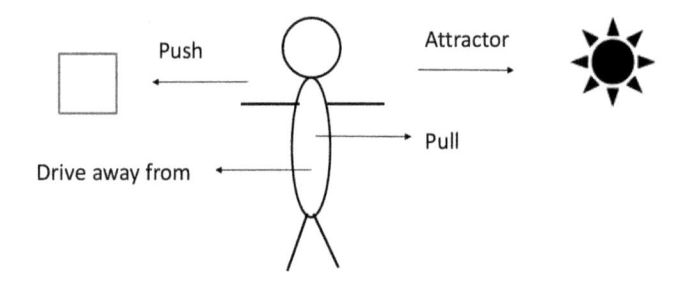

Postscript

I think that it was rather ambitious to incorporate all the above exercises into a one day time frame. Two days for the exercises would be more appropriate, given the time the participants need for drawing, self reflection and integration of all the materials. Because of this time constraint, the three main exercises may not have been tied together as well as we had intended. Further, the second and third exercises may not have been perceived to be adequately connected with the initial goals and mission.

With more time, the second and third main exercises should be clearly connected to the initial statement and/or drawing of goals and mission. At the end of each exercise, we would have asked the participants to reflect on the insight gained through the exercise, and then go back to their initial goals and mission statements and consciously incorporate their new reflections and insights into them. For example, during the second exercise, if they found that time was encoded inside them and that a significant amount of their past was in their present, then we would have encouraged them to think about the way they encoded time, and how that influenced the goals and missions they initially stated and/or drew. When all of the exercises were finished, the participants would have been given time to integrate all the insight they gained at the end of each exercise, and to rewrite/redraw their individual goals and mission statements.

Secondly, the way David facilitated this workshop was quite different from the way professional trainers often do in corporate training sessions. He phrased an instruction into a question, and rephrased the same instruction in a slightly different question and continued with the exercises. We were aware that throughout the whole workshop the participants asked him to repeat the instructions only a few times.

When we think about how we can use the exercises for our own coaching sessions and workshops, each exercise could be expanded as a stand-alone module. If you are a coach, and have a command of David Grove's Emergent Knowledge, you would be aware, for example, that during the first exercise you could further explore each past goal and their relationships and then, at the end of the session, ask, "*If you write or draw your goal again, would you write or draw exactly the same?*" You can then ask your coachees to redraw all of the drawings. Given that the coachees are absorbed into the process, their drawings and statements of goals are likely to change in significant ways.

Keiko Izumi
Contact Address: Izumikyoto@yahoo.com
Website: www.cleancoachingUSA.com

CAITLIN WALKER

One of the leading practitioners who worked regularly with Grove is Caitlin Walker. She has taken his techniques and adapted them for use with groups, teams and organisations in a process she calls Systemic Modelling. Caitlin decided to apprentice herself to Grove to learn his approach after attending a workshop in 1997 and worked extensively with him over the next few years. Systemic Modelling combines all forms of his work, including Clean Language, Clean Space and Emergent Knowledge. On page 128 she describes how she came to know David and her experiences of working with Clean techniques. She has also provided the two case histories below.

Clean Sports Development in a University

One inspiring project, which has been completed and is now running independently from me, is with a Faculty of Education Sport and Leisure, where I was commissioned to develop a culture of peer coaching across the department.

I am sometimes asked how it is possible to sell Clean Language and Systemic Modelling into an organisation. In the case of this university, I was originally invited to run a creative thinking session. When I ask Clean questions conversationally it makes people think carefully about their outcomes and to challenge the assumptions they are making about change processes. By staying Clean, and unattached to winning the work, I often find that I am given a much wider remit than my clients originally planned.

For this project, I was asked to work across the whole department, whose main goal was to help their students to make the most from their time at university. One of the plans was to make a DVD featuring sports personalities as role models, to inspire the students. I suggested that I could start by interviewing a number of students and adults who had exceeded their potential at university, to find out what had made the difference that enabled their success. In a series of focus groups I asked people:

"You are senior lecturers. Assuming that you liked university enough to stay, what motivated you to make the most of your time at university?"

They gave answers like "My granddad. He believed everyone had a right to education and that I shouldn't waste any of it"; "Money. I had taken time out of my career, I had to make it count"; or "The need to please my lecturers".

There turned out to be a series of themes that were common across interviews:

- Knowing one's learning style
- Understanding and being able to use time effectively
- Being able to make good decisions
- Knowing what inspired and motivated the person (which could be religion, family anything at all) and being able to draw on that when times were tough
- Having a strategy for learning from failure
- Being able to take and learn from feedback

These became the main themes for the whole project. I figured that if these themes were so important to naturally high achieving students, it would be useful for all staff and students to know more about these themes for themselves.

Even though this was a sports department, not one of these lecturers had been motivated by a sports person, which had been the original thinking behind the DVD. Since the sports personalities were already booked, I decided to start by interviewing them. Some were athletes such as Kate Walsh, Captain of the British Hockey Team, and Beth Tweddle, the medal-winning gymnast. Others were involved in teaching sport or in sports development overseas. The interviews went smoothly, starting out conversationally and then developing into Clean modelling sessions around each of the themes.

This DVD meant that as students developed their own models, they could also compare and contrast them with, for example, Beth Tweddle's, and draw some learning from her inspirational story. This DVD is still in use at the university and can be bought as a separate product for people wanting to see Clean modelling in practice.

After making the DVD, it was time to bring Clean into the staff team. My Systemic Modelling always encourages teams to lead change processes by example, so I brought these themes to the ten staff via their monthly meetings. I would start by giving them questions like:

"When you're teaching at your best, you're like what?"

I would ask a few questions of each member of the team and then get them to develop their metaphors with one another, map them out and then share how their different metaphors showed up in their teaching preferences. I encouraged them to use these differences to coach one another in areas that they found challenging.

Next I asked about time "Time is like what?" and so on.

Once the staff team had done this they start to behave more like a self-organising system. They used the knowledge they had about themselves and about one another to co-develop a student handbook for use in their student tutorial groups, incorporating my questions. So the students now start their University journey by being asked, "When you're learning at your best, you're like what?" Then the questions move through the topics of time, making decisions, and so on.

The staff, independently of me, have changed the way that their students begin life at university: for the first five weeks students simply spend time getting to know their learning styles and unconscious models, and building relationships in small groups so that they have a network of support to see them through the three years.

During the second year of the project, one leading member of staff started embedding the Clean modelling themes into the curriculum. This meant that while the students were learning about their own and one another's models for time in their tutorials, they would then cover the same theme in a number of their lectures. For example as students learn about their internal time, they also learn about how time impacts on elite athleticism, or which people take up community sport et al.

So if the next iteration is about decision-making ("Making decisions is like what?"), then in the first week they create their own metaphors, and in the next week put their learning from eliciting their own and hearing other people's metaphors into discrete action, setting a goal and giving themselves feedback on how well they put their learning into practise.

The impact of Systemic Modelling in these circumstances is that instead of saying "My time management is rubbish", thereby labelling oneself as either good with time or poor with time, a participant might say:

"This is my model for time; here are some of the other models for time; given that this is my goal for being at university and these are the demands that will be made of me and my time, what I am going to do about this?"

After a week of self-reflection the students are expected to put that learning into action. The following month there is a new topic until, over the course of a year, they have six iterations.

It is a beautiful model and clearly has impact. At the time of writing, it has been put into action over five years, during which their results rose from an average of 49% achieving 2:1 degrees and above to between 73% and 75% year on year. At the entrance to the department there is an enormous mural of students' learning metaphors and up the stairways there is writing that asks: "When you're learning at your best, you're like what?"

Clean Team Building in a London Business School

I have taken Clean language and Systemic Modelling into many sectors, including Welfare to Work, fast moving consumer goods, schools, mediation, conflict resolutions and mergers and acquisitions, in order to find out how the techniques need to be packaged differently for different audiences. They seem to work in all sectors, including business, education and community. While I was beginning to articulate the model of Systemic Modelling, and its principles and rules, I was invited to try it out in a context that was quite intimidating for me. I was invited to work with an institution rated as "the UK's top business school for providing executive education" by the Financial Times. My first reaction was to wonder how it would be possible to facilitate the country's top facilitators and help them find something new.

I was invited, alongside artist colleagues, to support the programme development team to become more of a learning community. The leader wanted them to share their expertise so that they could not only be the best in the country but could move up to being one of the top five in the world. I started by Cleanly eliciting metaphors for how they design their programmes. I asked Clean questions conversationally at first and then brought in the fuller syntax, helping them to access their unconscious triggers for choosing, say, this course format or that one. Once the sessions were underway, the clients stop paying attention to me or to the artist, who was sketching away in the room. They became deeply involved in learning about their own unconscious choice points and intuitions, building rapport with the unconscious wisdom in their systems.

Once three members of the faculty had completed an individual metaphor session, a colleague would paint their metaphor into a beautiful two-dimensional visual landscape, working closely with the client to ensure the symbolism was accurate.

Next, I would facilitate three of them to share their metaphors and to ask one another Clean-ish questions to interrogate the differences between them. From this position, having developed a metaphor for their unconscious processes, these skilled professionals were able to access the deeper structure of their thinking and have rewarding discussions about their knowledge and expertise and about the differences that made their programmes so successful.

The process seemed to develop a sense of collective trust that allowed them to express their vulnerabilities and engage in learning conversations to share their expertise. This was a relationship that they had struggled to have previously.

Once the first three were happy with sharing their metaphors, they presented the metaphors to the wider professional forum to stimulate discussion and learning. I went on to elicit metaphors from six more programme leaders so that as a programme design team they now had nine diverse examples of excellence to learn from.

Caitlin Walker
www.trainingattention.co.uk

IAN HALDANE AND DIANNE EMMERSON

Clean Language and Clean Space Workshop for the Te Ihi Tu Programme

Te Ihi Tu was a successful tikanga-based Maori Community Residential Correction programme for all high risk recidivist prisoners from prisons throughout New Zealand. Incorporated in 1995 as a trust, Te Ihi Tu ran a thirteen week intensive on site from its premises in New Plymouth.

The programme gave inmates a Maori world view, an understanding of the Treaty of Waitangi, decolonization workshops, te reo Maori classes and group facilitation. There was zero tolerance for violence and drugs. There was also a demanding health, fitness and dietary programme that had waka ama (traditional Maori Polynesian Outrigging canoe) and outdoor mountain climbing sessions. Computer literacy was also a component.

The problem – before

The problem was to cut to the chase quickly to use limited time and resources to get an effective rehabilitation outcome with these prisoners.

The trust had just a thirteen week window of opportunity with inmates to get a result. They wanted to work more intensively with those inmates genuinely committed to making changes. And to cull those who were just going along for the ride.

Behaviour patterns of prisoners who have been in prison as repeat offenders is often entrenched. Breaking these patterns and getting inmates to adopt new patterns that avoid risky behaviours and reoffending was the trusts' major challenge.

The trust tried a number of innovative ways to overcome resistance of prisoners to face up to the consequences of their behaviour patterns. These included week long Vipasana meditation sessions.

Clean Training

In order to improve outcomes and to direct resources effectively Te Ihi Tu asked Dianne Emmerson and Ian Haldane to conduct a three day Clean Language and Space workshop for Trust coaches, manager and admin support person.

The three day workshop included:

Basic Clean Language concepts:

- How to run a meeting using Clean language
- Asking the questions in a facilitation sense
- The importance of understanding same word different perceptions – interpretations

Moving back three levels in questioning:

- Unpeeling the top layers of the sub conscious
- Avoiding deep level counselling
- Unpacking words and metaphors at the same level

Basic Clean Space concepts:

- Six moves to move from problem statement to resolution
- Use of space to overcome cultural and linguistic barriers

- Observation and interpretation of moves that people make around the space they choose to occupy
- Use of space to work cooperatively with language metaphors and further unpeel / unpack what has been expressed by the participant
- Identifying where people have progressed to in a typical six stage sequence of problem statement, affirmation, wobble, deconstruct and reconstruct

The training provided opportunity for staff to rehearse and practice concepts with their whanau (family) in a home-based context. Significant shifts occurred in some instances.

Staff commented particularly on:
- Outward simplicity of the concepts – but underlying complexity in terms of interpreting data elicited
- Neutral non threatening manner of the methods
- Speed with which results were achieved

After

Te Ihi Tu coaches completed the second intake of inmates where the Clean process was been used. Four inmates completed the thirteen week programme from an original intake of nine from the first. One completed the second programme from an intake of three.

Because Clean provides a tool for facilitators to quickly unpack what is being represented to them then "It sorted out early on who was going to go the distance and who wasn't" – "*Moreover we had three hold their hands up and drop out of their own accord – that never happened before*" (Coach One).

Before and After Interviews with Coaches using Clean

Individual interviews with trust coaches elicited the responses in the table below. We used the first Clean question "And before the introduction of Clean at the trust, the situation was like what?"

From an original statement each coach was guided through six download positions from that statement, as illustrated below. Coaches then made observations in response to the second Clean question "And after the introduction of Clean, the situation at the Trust has been like what?"

Coach One – Before

Opening statement – "Frustrating – it was like pulling teeth"

	First download	Second download
1	"There was strategizing by coaches"	" hmm.... creative"
2	"There was resistance by the clients" – (resistance to what?)	"to the truth"
3	"Clients create myths to shield themselves from the truth"	
4	"Look to ways to avert and avoid"	
5	"They avoid truths in order to protect the myths"	
6	"A lot of this is running away from the original pain"	

Coach Two – Before

Opening statement – "A bit of confusion"

	First download	Second download
1	"No connection with the men"	"Bullying by some coaches"
2	"Pressure" (what pressure was that pressure?)	"To perform – for the men to meet the objectives of the programme – and for the coaches to chase them down."
3	"Me, probably in with the confusion… dunno how to say it…"	"Expectations too high" (whose?) – "The coaches – some bullying by the coaches."
4	"Intrusive"	"For the men to go where they don't know … and maybe don't want to"
5	"Misunderstandings" (whose?)	"Between the men and the coaches"
6	"Disrespect"	"In that way pushing too far – even to the point of breaking them – maybe some of that is needed."

The question "what do you know now?" elicited this response: "We needed to look at ourselves… is the work we do about us or is it about the men?

Coach Three – Before

Opening statement – "Amazing"

Te Ihi Tu Case Study

	First download	Second download
1	"Unique"	"People" – differences"
2	"One of a kind"	"Special"
3	"Wairua"	"For me it part of what's been going on"
4	"Special"	It's the uniqueness of what a person brings from their own lives' – experiences"
5	"Nah .. that's about it"	"There's heaps"

Coach One – After

Opening statement – "Practical"

	First download	Second download
1	"Realistic thoughtful"	
2	"Humanity, complexity" (whose?)	"Everyone's"
3	"It's just about living"	
4	"Being at ease"	
5	"Common sense"	
6	"Planting the seeds is enough (for what?)	"In helping someone come to their own understanding"

Coach One commented that Clean had reoriented the Trust back to core Maori values of tika (accuracy), puna (truth) and maramatanga (awareness).

Coach Two – After

Opening statement – "More respect for the men"

	First download	Second download
1	"More respect for ourselves"	"Things don't bite"

2	"Easier to work to a point"	"The men are more open"
3	"More… understanding from the men and from ourselves on what was needed"	"Because of the Clean mahi (work) we knew where the men were and they did too"
4	"A lot quicker results"	"We didn't have to work in the mud as much"
5	"It made all of the rest of the work we do a lot easier… not all the time… but on a percentage scale"	"…because we were working at their (the men's level) they reached their objectives a lot quicker… and the objectives were their own… not ours (objectives)."
6	"We started working more on the men's level separately"	"Each different and has different expectations" "So to get the best out of them… that's what it took" (Clean?)

Coach Two observed independently that "Clean had allowed the programme to refocus more on core Maori values in particular aroha." And that it had "modified us being too pushy in our own expectations of the work that we could do with the men."

Coach Three – After

Opening statement – "Quick"

	First download	Second download
1	"Fast"	"In identifying the issues – identifying the strengths weaknesses opportunities and threats – it's like the whole package"

2	"Amazing"	"It's getting to that SWOT, then watching the men come to their own place – it sits with the person then it's up to them to make a choice based on their own insights. it's about me working as a coach"
3	"Special – unique"	"Every person has their own specialness uniqueness" I'm part of that and they (the men) allow me to become part of that"
4	"One of its kind"	"That's the korero I've been sharing with you – that's what the person brings – each person is different even though the issues may be similar"
5	"'Universal"	We've done work here with Maori and Pakeha – we're now working in the community itself with this (then referenced his whanau, marae, hapu and iwi as places where he now practices Clean)
6	"Exciting"	"That's it see!" – "It's fast – we clean up, mop up instead of being stuck!"

Coach Three then observed that *"Clean works – it's simple – I'm going places I might not have gone before – it's becoming unconscious – it's becoming part of my life"*

Conclusion

Clean has allowed the trust to:

- Obtain results quickly from people deemed by Corrections to be high risk recidivist
- Realign their own work with core Maori values and world view
- Work at the pace of the men through this bottom-up process
- Operate in a facilitative mode compared to directive

Some of this is contained on these observations:

Observation	Comment
"The poems on the wall tell the story – the ones before Clean language training tell about what happened to the person – in a sense the inmate is making a rationalization for their past behaviours without any sense of resolution" "At the poroporoaki (farewell graduation) after the Clean input the poems were in the now and expressed a desire to go forward"	Clean allows people to acknowledge what they have done and take responsibility for it. They may not like what they see or experience, but they can't avoid it. They own whatever ugliness, chaos, grief etc has been unpacked through the Clean process. The critical thing is that it allows people to take a perspective on this, move forward and resolve past issues.

CAROL WILSON

1. Transformational Change through Metaphor: Delivered by Carol Wilson, Angela Dunbar and Wendy Oliver 2007 at the BBC.
2. Project for Doctorate in Professional Studies: an Exploration of the use of Clean Language and Emergent Knowledge Techniques by Corporate Coaches Delivered by Carol Wilson 2011.
3. Clean Language Session with a Business Executive.

Transformational Change through Metaphor: delivered by Carol Wilson, Angela Dunbar and Wendy Oliver 2007 at the BBC

The BBC has trained and accredited a group of internal executive coaches to a high level. These coaches receive regular training in advanced coaching skills. We were asked to deliver training that would further enhance and deepen their executive coaching skills. With Angela Dunbar, I designed and delivered 'Transformational Change through Metaphor', a course based on the programmes I created with David and on Angela's work in Clean techniques.

24 internal executive coaches were trained in a two day course, spread over one month with paired practice in between. The terms and principles were aligned with the training which the coaches had already received.

After some initial scepticism, the coaches became ardently enthusiastic about the new skills, once they had experienced them in practice. All reported that they are using the skills and that both their coaching practice and leadership styles were markedly improved by the new training. Head of Coaching Liz Macann, who created the coaching force at the BBC and designed their training, said,

> "It gave me a way to explore emotions and feelings safely, staying within the boundary that separates coaching from therapy. It was also a revelation to see where the clients mind went to when it was freed from its usual verbal restrictions when exploring an issue. An unexpectedly great way of working."

Reactions from other course participants included the benefit of Clean Language as a new tool in the coaching toolbox, the benefit to participants' leadership skills and the ease with which Clean Language can overcome any blocks that clients might be experiencing.

Project for Doctorate in Professional Studies: an Exploration of the use of Clean Language and Emergent Knowledge Techniques by Corporate Coaches Delivered by Carol Wilson 2011 at the BBC.

In 2011 I embarked on a doctorate at Middlesex University Work Based Learning Unit to explore Clean techniques. I trained 16 of the BBC's highly qualified internal coaches in Clean Language and Emergent Knowledge, and am exploring what happens as they use the techniques with their clients and each other. My reasons for undertaking the doctorate are partly to continue my research into David Grove's work and to draw attention to it, and partly to bring some academic rigour to bear on the processes.

The field is relatively unexplored academically so I did not set out with any hypotheses to prove, simply to find out and record what happens and identify any trends that emerge.

I do not believe that the number of participants I am working with, up to sixteen, is large enough to provide any reliable statistical survey information. This would require working with many groups at the same time and I do not believe I would be able to devote sufficient time to make this approach effective, or that it would best suit my learning style. For this reason I am not working with large surveys or attempt to draw the statistical conclusions demanded of hypotheses testing experimental research.

The information I record from working with my sample group is intended to be useful to the Clean community. I am recording what the coaches experienced, what conditions and processes brought results and what was most meaningful to the participants. The emphasis is on what actually happened, rather than their expectations of what might happen, and they will be encouraged to explore the parts of their sessions which did not seem to be effective, as well as what gave rise to the more successful parts of the sessions, and what unexpected events took place.

I chose the BBC because I believe that the coaches are of a high level of intelligence, adhere to demanding standards, are ethical and, mainly, because people who work in media tend to show a healthy level of cynicism.

The case history which follows is an account of the sessions between two of the coaches, Claire Taylor, acting as coach, and Anna (not her real name) as the client. The session combines Clean Language and its metaphors with an Emergent Knowledge technique called Clean Boundaries. The framework for the questions is:

- Clean Start (enabling the client to find the right space from which to start the session)
- And what kind of space is the space around [xxx]?
- And is there anything else about that space?

- And does that space have a shape or a size?
- And how far does that space go?
- *And what kind of boundary or edge does [xxx] have?*
- And is there anything else about that boundary?
- And what does that boundary know?
- And what does the space between those two boundaries know?
- Clean Finish (enabling the client to finish the session comfortably and consolidate what has been learned).

Anna described her situation as follows:

"I was faced with a relocation decision that felt like a zero-sum situation, rationally positive but emotionally negative. Logically thinking it was clear to me that the relocation presented a great opportunity, but there was an emotional aspect that made it feel very negative too."

Claire asked questions using the Clean Boundaries framework above and this is how Anna described her journey during the session:

"I initially found it difficult to look outside the ugly rock that this 'zero-sums' felt like. The coach continued with the questions and I was able to move away from the rock and look at the space outside it that felt vast and beautiful like the universe and the milkyway. At some point the word "edge" sounded louder in my head. I think that was a shift moment that just the sound of the word somehow unlocked something, and I was holding a baseball-bat, swinging it to hit the rock (that had already turned into a somewhat more flexible, semi-milky transparent object that I was pushing to expand from within) to effortlessly see it move in space and become one with the milkyway. It felt that it always belonged there and I didn't need to hit it, I only had to grasp the bat and swing in a dance kind of movement for it to get in its place, and this will make ripples in my world to move what felt like an ugly, solid, difficult to change semi-milky inflexible blob/rock into an amazingly beautiful milkyway. Writing the previous paragraph, I am smiling and my whole mood is lifted. I don't play base-ball, although this symbol was present in this journey and is linked to my kinaesthetic-self."

The changes brought about by Clean sessions take place at the deepest level, below consciousness, and can continue to effect changes for days, months or years after the session. Five days after the session Anna reported:

"What happened in the following days was like a flood that started and was impossible to stop and I had to experience it fully and hold on and see what would come on the other end, when the flood waters subside. I spend two days mourning deeply for what had happened, crying and sobbing at times that I least expected, being unable to move forward, frozen by the irrational fear of what would happen if I relocate and I feel utterly miserable. But at the same time, something was healing, something deeply traumatic had come back but it was healing itself. I am not yet at peace with it, but at least through this process I was able to understand that my research and professor past was screaming to be part of me again. My technology expert self, so eagerly abandoned to escape an "ugly blob" of the past, has lifted its head thinking that there is an opportunity to find ways to become whole again and all this thanks to the impossible challenge of relocating and the journey through feelings and emotions and the help of Clean Boundaries and metaphors."

The 'becoming whole' comment that Anna made crops up frequently in Grove's work. Traumas are often embedded at a young age and then forgotten by the conscious mind. Meanwhile, defensive mechanisms are set up deep within the psyche, growing more convoluted and irrelevant over the years, and grinding into action when triggered by events reminiscent of the original trauma. These mechanisms use energy and resources which could be put to a positive use and when resolved often result in clients uncovering a talent or ability previously unknown to them.

Claire, the coach, commented, "One of the areas I want to improve as coach is to allow and help the client explore more their space, issue and thinking and avoid a tendency to get to action space too quickly. I found the boundary approach gave me this "permission" to explore almost for the sake of exploration. The client presented an amazing richness of metaphors and visual spaces. I was almost lost for choices and the boundaries gave me the tool to explore this richness rather than feeling lost in the wealth presented to me by the client. It also felt more natural to mix questions from Clean Language with the Clean Boundaries, and the client commented that this helped her and felt like a richer coaching experience too."

This type of exploration exploring 'for the sake of exploration' is required more frequently from coaches now that clients often find themselves in uncomfortable situations that they have no control over: all that can be altered is how the clients feel about and react to the pressure they are under. Clean Language and Emergent Knowledge techniques help people develop greater resilience in such times of stress and uncertainty.

CLEAN LANGUAGE SESSION WITH A BUSINESS EXECUTIVE

In this transcript of a Clean Language session I delivered to a business executive, the client had a fear of public speaking. He regularly had to speak at events in the course of his business and although he usually performed reasonably well at the event, his anxiety would affect his work and relationships for a week beforehand. Using only Clean Language questions, and repeating his own words back to him, the coach helped him to develop and explore a metaphor. Below are some highlights of the session:

Coachee:	I get nervous for a week beforehand.
Coach:	And when you get nervous for a week beforehand, that's like what?
Coachee:	It's like the nauseous feeling before going on a rollercoaster at a fair.
Coach:	And when it's the nauseous feeling before going on a rollercoaster at a fair, what kind of nauseous is that?
Coachee:	It's being in one's shell, with the volume turned down.

The coach continued to explore the metaphor, using Clean Language questions, then asked:

Coach:	And what happens next?

Coachee:	I am seeing light at the surface, and sunshine. Gravitational pull from above, like when you've been scuba diving. There is pressure on your chest from the water. I can hear people talking – a dull quiet sound through the water. I need the gravitational pull.
Coach:	And what needs to happen for the gravitational pull?
Coachee:	The pressure needs to turn.
Coach:	And can the pressure turn?
Coachee:	There is a pressure wave, I can move it. It can take me to the surface.
Coach:	And what happens next?
Coachee:	The sun's coming out. Serene, relaxing and enjoyable. It feels great. I am on the surface and the sun is reflecting on water. All is quiet. The dull, quiet sound through the water has gone.

The result for the client was that his customary week-long anxiety never occurred again. In addition, as is often the case with Clean Language, he noticed some additional benefits in that he became less stressed in his life overall and found it easier to focus on taking his business forward.

ANGELA DUNBAR

1. Clean Worlds Session delivered by David Grove.
2. Clean Language Session Transcript.

Clean Worlds Session delivered by David Grove: "My Personal Journey"

Angela Dunbar is an accredited coach and trainer, a Master NLP Practitioner and a Certified Clean Language facilitator. Angela worked with David Grove and Carol Wilson to develop their Clean Coaching training and now delivers and develops the training to individuals, corporate clients including the BBC and Oxford Brookes University, as well as delivering Clean Language and Emergent Knowledge sessions to individuals. Below she describes a workshop with David Grove.

This session took place during the first of two events facilitated by David Grove in London in November 2004. It was described as self discovery by way of a 'Personal Journey' within the setting of a small, supportive group. Philip Harland hosted the event at his house, within which we would be working — his space would be ours for the next two days.
When all had arrived, David gave us a detailed presentation on the process we were to take in order to physically chart and explore our metaphorical 'psychescape'. We then simply got on with it, working mainly on our own initially to map everything out. These were his instructions, in six steps:

"Step 1 – Describe your Mission Statement. Where do you want to get to? Write it down as verbosely as you like. Once written, investigate the words and the letters you have chosen – words have had a personal journey through history as well – it may be no co-incidence that you chose this one. Pay particular attention to any mistakes you have made – what are you subconsciously trying to tell yourself? Finally, find the space that represents where you want to be."

Having done some 'Clean Space' work on my Symbolic Modelling course, I knew what David meant: for each of us to intuitively locate a place in the space around us that felt like it was the right spot. With some wandering around and trying on different places for size, we were all able to place our Mission Statement with some degree of certainty. We knew when we had found the right space because it just felt right. Mine was on the window of the stained glass front door. I knew almost immediately, just as David had predicted, as my eyes were drawn to that spot. My Mission Statement was simply "Serenity and Harmony" and I had previously decided on a metaphor of two swans swimming side by side as my representation of it. The window on the front door had two coloured flowers slightly adjoined… different, but somehow the same as my image. I was very drawn to the colours as well, which made more sense as I got further into my exploration.

Did I discover anything interesting about my chosen words? Well, when I first wrote down the word "Serenity" I misspelled it to begin with, and the word I might have been writing was "Senility"! *Does that mean I have to get Alzheimer's before I find some peace,* I wondered? Interestingly, I made the same mistake as I wrote the word in this piece just now!

When we had completed the first part of the process David gave us further instructions:

> "Step 2 – If your Mission Statement is "B" – where is "A"? Where are you now spatially in terms of where you have placed your Mission Statement? Pay particular attention to the angle!"

Again, I found this easy, and saw the spot straight away, in the kitchen quite near to where I sat. A small oval mirror with a candle holder built into its frame caught my eye. *I am right there*, I thought, *right up close to that mirror, but there is no illumination from the candle. And I'm so close to the mirror I can't see much else.* As I stood in the spot to see how it felt, I realised I couldn't even see myself because my eyes were shut... so the experience was metaphorical even at this early stage in the process!

> "Step 3 – What's in the space between A and B? Call this "C". Write down your first brain dump. Any tangible real bits of furniture etc. that might have somehow, coincidently ended up in the path between your A and B. Also the logical bits – what stops you getting there?"

Further thoughts David advised us to pay attention to were whether the space between A and B had a shape or a size, and whether it could be represented as a metaphor, by asking *"What kind of space is that space?"* or *"It is a space like what?"*

David gave some good advice here: *"Don't spend too long on this part of the process. Presumably something is stopping you from reaching "B", otherwise you wouldn't still be at "A", and you have probably already spent much time exploring 'that something' without success. So maybe the job of that 'something' is to stop you knowing what it is!"*

David explained that maybe the best way to get to "B" might be from a different angle, or start point, which was what we would be exploring. *If you want to get there, I wouldn't start from here!* as the Irish joke goes!

Step 4 was in several parts:

a. *"From where you are now, identify in which direction is your past, and your future."*
b. *"Where were you born? Spatially, in this house, garden or local surroundings?"*
c. *"Plot any significant life changing events / defining moments in your life… stand in each spot. Ask yourself if you decided on a particular life mission at this stage."*
d. *"At what age were you 'pristine' ie. totally pure, at peace, and 'at one with the world'?"*
e. *"Is there a shape to the spots you have plotted?"*
f. *"Look up any significant words as before."*

Again, David suggested we work through this as best we could, and that if nothing came up for a question, we were not to worry, just move on.

I saw very specifically my life-changing event 'spots', although my problem was that the past is lower down.

So, the spot I was born was metaphorically in the cellar. Just my luck I spent most of my time stuck down in the cold!

Events up to aged twelve were also in the cellar. Other significant events were outside, in the cloakroom area under the stairs, in front of the radiator (thankfully) and the spot for 'being pregnant' was a nice comfortable chair in the front room. I couldn't find a 'pristine' age.

"Step 5: Look for coincidences – in the space around you, objects, items, pictures, what is the space trying to tell you? These are co-inspiring elements."

I was unable to find any, but another participant had been exploring metaphors around 'Brazil' and 'Brazilian people', and he noticed a salt container attached to the wall in the kitchen – every home in Brazil has one of those, he explained. I'd never seen one in this country before.

> "Step 6 – Stand on the spot where you were born." (Back to the cellar for me). "Turn around 90 degrees. Lean towards the space that is just before you were born. Notice if you feel any boundary or resistance. Describe what that is like. Then ask yourself 'Where did I come from before I was born?'" As well as a possible direction to our parents' lineage, David was looking for a story, or the 'genesis' of who we are.

Then David said, "Step over into that space before you were born. Look towards your life from this spot. Then ask yourself 'What was my mission before I was born?' Write it down and compare it to the Mission Statement you wrote down earlier."

"Then," David said, "You'll be ready to work with me."

His starting point now was to take us back to the "A", "B" and "C" spot and ask at each place "*What do you know from here?*" Then he had us turn around. Then he asked "*What does this space know about (another space)*" and "*What kind of space is around that space?*" I never really got that far. My time was spent exploring the time before I was born, and all the 'before's' before that.

I stood on the spot where I was born and pushed gently towards the space before it. Surprisingly I felt a strong force push back and nearly knock me over!

I struggled for some time stepping into the space before I was born. When I did, I stepped into the beam of the single light bulb hanging from the cellar ceiling and felt the warmth of the light on my face. This felt pristine! But I didn't have a 'life mission'. In fact, as I looked towards my life, I felt a distinct reluctance to go in that direction: I didn't even want to be born. I was pushed! Against my will… not a very nice start to life.

At this point David worked with me personally, starting at my "A" spot in front of the mirror. He asked me what I knew from that space, and it wasn't a lot. He told me to step even closer to the mirror. I replied that I could not see anything with my eyes shut. He asked, *"At what age were 'eyes' open?"* This got me quickly back down to the cellar again, back in the space before I was born. David's questions encouraged me to notice that when in this space, in my mind's eye I saw lots of twinkly blue lights.

"These are aspects of you that didn't come with you when you were born" he said. *"They were so reluctant to be born that you left them behind. Now you've found them, you can gather them up and re-integrate them into yourself."*

"OK," I said yawning. By now, all I wanted to do was sleep. I felt quite disappointed with my pre-start to life as I had hoped for some profound insight.

David replied that I did need to sleep, and that during my sleep these separate parts would have the opportunity to reintegrate and come back to me. I sat back in the 'pregnancy chair' for a while, taking in all I'd experienced. Then I went home and slept soundly.

On day two I was not keen to go back to the cellar. However David said I needed to check out what, if anything had changed. I said I still felt I wanted to 'find' a life mission and to go back further.

I began this on my own and, when I stood again in the place before I was born, although I still felt the same sense of peace the blue twinkly lights had gone. I could not find where the space was before this one for a long time, but eventually was moved to bring down a little table from the front room and sit on it. 'Before' was lower down, and by sitting I got a sense of 'before the before'. I saw a bright iridescent blue, deep and dense.

That makes sense, I thought, *I came "out of the blue!"*

I sat there for a long time, turning and twisting around, trying out other 'adjacent' spaces to find any new insight or understanding, but nothing else came to me.

By the time our host Phillip came to check on me I was back in the pregnancy chair, looking up words and feeling quite lost.

Phillip got me back into the process by asking, *"And where are you drawn to?"*

I noticed a stained glass window in the hall that had a bright blue panel. The blue had the same deep iridescence as the twinkly lights. David joined us and asked me to turn around, getting me back to the same spot as the deep blue 'before'. *"And what's before that blue?"* he asked.

I got an impression of the beginning of the universe, the 'big bang', and saw my 'blue' as starting out as a very dense ball of super-charged energy.

David asked, *"What's on the other side of that blue ball?"*

I couldn't answer the question. *"There is no other side,"* I said.

Further questioning around what was outside of that space got me back into the flow of being in the light with the blue twinkly lights, then being born as before in the cellar. It seemed as if David was helping me find another way into the world.

Eventually, after repeatedly asking me what was on the 'other side' of the blue dense ball, I began to think of the ball as a hole in a tunnel, and the 'other side' would be through the tunnel and out again. This felt like progress.

I made my way through the tunnel, which in reality was along the hall, down some steps and back into the room with the kitchen area. The 'other side' was in the middle of this room, my new 'place of birth'.

The next step was to re-examine all the previous life events. *"Where are they now?"* David asked. *"Have they changed at all?"*

And finally David asked us all to review our previous "A" and "B" spots. I, like most others, could not find a sense of where most of my previous life events had gone. The "A" and "B" spots seemed uncertain too.

David explained that by coming into the world from a different angle, I had gathered up the lost parts of me, so could no longer sense events as separate 'spots'. They had all integrated within me now. And maybe even the elusive "B" is with me too.

The final review session with David gave us more information about the differences between the afflictions acquired through our natural life and those that were already embedded in the "*shadow world of our psychological DNA gifted from whence we came*", as he expressed it.

David said it might take a week or so for the full impact of changes to be noticed. After three days, I felt that something had shifted in me. I did not feel as stuck as before, and my "B" mission now seemed achievable. I still felt I had further to go, but now had a clearer sense that I would get there.

Clean Language Session Transcript
by Angela Dunbar, facilitating Christine Compton

AD:	When you're facilitating at your best, that's like what?
CC:	It's magical and effortless.
AD:	It's magical and effortless. And when it's effortless, is there anything else about effortless?
CC	I feel valuable. I feel… gosh, 'vindicated' is the word that comes to mind. I feel my belief that when you are doing things perfectly it is effortless.
AD:	And when you are doing things perfectly, it's effortless. And you feel valuable, and when you feel valuable, what kind of valuable is that valuable?
CC:	I feel my whole life has purpose. It has meaning. It's what I was made for.
AD:	And you feel your life has purpose and meaning. And when you feel valuable, whereabouts do you feel valuable?
CC:	I'm putting my hand on my heart, right in the middle there.
AD:	And you feel valuable right in the middle there, with your hand on your heart. And when you feel valuable, right in the middle, whereabouts right in the middle?
CC:	Right at the core of my being. Right at my very centre. Right at my heart.
AD:	It's right at the core of your being. And when it's right at that core of your being, is there anything else about that core?
CC:	I'm blossoming. I'm opening to my potential. I'm… gosh this isn't easy… it's exactly I guess my whole life has meaning. It's what I was made for. It's my purpose. It's my reason for being.

AD:	It's your purpose. Your reason for being. And it's blossoming and opening to your potential. And when it's blossoming and opening to your potential, then what happens?
CC:	Then I just grow, I relax. I become who I am. I feel safe and confident.
AD:	You grow and relax and you feel safe and confident. And is there anything else about that confidence when you grow and relax?
CC:	I'm connected to something beyond. I'm connected to something bigger than me. Gosh, this is making me feel very emotional, I'm really surprised. I am connected to the whole. I'm part of the whole. I'm part of everything. I'm not alone. I'm not isolated.
AD:	And you're not isolated. And this is making you feel quite emotional. And you're connected to something beyond. And when you're connected to something beyond, is there anything else about that connection?
CC:	It's like it's everything that there is, it's everything I yearn for. It's everything I want.
AD:	It's everything you want. And it's a connection to something beyond. And when it's a connection to something beyond, whereabouts is that something beyond?
CC:	It's everywhere, it's everything. It's close to me and it's way, way out there as well. It's… to me it is the universe, it's everything that's a part of the universe. The whole.
AD:	It's the whole. And it's everywhere. And you're not alone. And that's confidence. And that comes when you grow and relax, blossoming and opening to your potential. And what happens just before you blossom and open to your potential?

AD:	I feel a sense of opening. I feel real excitement. I feel, again validated because it's what I've always believed in my head but I'm feeling it.
CC:	You feel a sense of opening and a sense of excitement and again validated. And when you feel a sense of opening, whereabouts is that sense of opening?
AD:	Again in my heart and the centre of my chest.
CC:	And what happens just before you feel that sense of opening in your heart?
AD:	I can feel something like a star burst. A huge firework going off.
CC:	You feel a sense of a huge firework going off. And is there anything else about that firework?
AD:	It's one of those huge ones that bursts and showers all those gorgeous sparkling lights. There's something about it being very momentary but everyone's witnessed it. It's like they've seen it and they know it can happen. They know that those fireworks are possible
CC:	Everyone's witnessed it. And it's a huge firework that bursts and when there's a huge firework like that, where could that huge firework have come from?
AD:	My logical mind keeps imagining people making them, but it's something… it's the magical thing again. There's something absolutely magical about what can be created and the thrill that it can give. It's almost like it's… yes I know it's made by men but the end result is just pure magic
AD:	Yes made by men but the end result is pure magic. And I'd love to explore this further with you, however would that be an OK place to bring this to a close?
CC:	It would be fine, and I'm absolutely bowled over…

Angela Dunbar – angeladunbar@cleancoaching.com

ADRIAN GOODALL
Clean Space Workshop

Adrian Goodall combines Constellation techniques with Clean Space/ Network to provide insights for a team in a corporate environment. Below he provides an account of this work.

I was working recently with a team at a large multinational corporate client which wanted more collaboration and engagement within a group of fourteen senior managers and specialist staff. This is a team that operates in a virtual way, with every member also involved in several other product and organisational teams. Normally, they have a highly logical way of working (scientists, project managers etc). It seemed an ideal opportunity to bring together a 'constellation' systems approach with Clean Space questions to introduce a different way of 'conceptualising' their team – and hopefully connecting with each other.

Halfway through the first morning, the team was invited to stand up and "find a space in the room which best represents your sense of involvement in this team". (The tables had all been moved to the sides of the room so there was a good 'space' available.) There was some initial reluctance and confusion, but simply repeating the invitation resulted in movement and exploration of the space they were all in, 'assessing' each others' moves and positioning, and quickly coalescing into a much more tightly packed arrangement than I expected.

I then asked a series of questions to the group, including:

"And what's happening here?" (resulting in creating additional movement);

"And are you facing in the right direction?" (resulting in turning and a recognition of a dynamic of continuing to turn);

"What are you noticing?" (a need for different relative positions for different aspects of the team's work);

At this point, the group was again invited to "find the right space" around 'speeding up the delivery of a key product development milestone' – a strategic imperative for the business.

"And what is happening now?" (three specific people in the 'middle')

"And are you facing in the right direction?" (central trio facing out, others facing in);

"What do you know now about this team?" (more awareness of who is involved);

"What's happening for you, out here?" (to one specific member)

"Are there any other voices from this system?" (his work – the previous person – is fundamental to what we are doing now so he could be much more central)

"What do you want the other teams in which you are involved to know about this team?" (focus, delivery).

"And what's different now?" (greater awareness of who is involved, what our focus should be on, greater confidence in being able to achieve that).

This was only one of a number of activities over two days of working. Specific feedback about this exercise from one participant a week later was that it had helped them to think very differently about their role, and how central they were to this challenge, and how the rest of the team were both looking to them and valuing them to a far greater degree than they had previously realised. They now felt much clearer and more engaged. For me it was good to witness such a positive engagement from this team which had no prior knowledge, experience of (or introduction to) either Constellation or Clean Space approaches, and served to build my confidence that these are approaches which can be used effectively in a very broad range of situations.

Adrian Goodall, 14th Dec 2009
http://www.adriangoodall.co.uk, adrian@adriangoodall.co.uk

PART FIVE

TRANSCRIPTS OF DAVID GROVE'S SESSIONS AND WORKSHOPS

In this section, transcripts of a number of David Grove's sessions and workshops are provided to demonstrate the techniques described in the rest of the book. All the sessions were either recorded or transcribed live.

I have occasionally added explanatory notes marked [-CW].

Summary

SESSION WITH PRIVATE CLIENT 28 MAY 2005
CLEAN PRONOUNS WORKSHOP AT THE THATCHED
 COTTAGE 2005
CLEAN HIEROGLYPHICS SESSION WITH DEBORAH HENLEY
GROUP SESSION BY PHONE 15 MARCH 2006 FEATURING
 CLEAN START AND CLEAN NETWORKS
SESSION WITH ANGELA DUNBAR: "I'M GETTING FITTER"
 FEATURING CLEAN BOUNDARIES
SESSION WITH PRIVATE CLIENT FEATURING
 CLEAN SPINNING 2005
SESSION WITH LYNN BULLOCK DECEMBER 2007

GROUP SESSION BY PHONE OCTOBER 2006 FEATURING CLEAN NETWORKS

SESSION WITH PRIVATE CLIENT 28 MAY 2005

This session took place with a private female client at my house. The client gave her permission for me to be present, to transcribe the session to laptop as it took place and to publish the transcript.

David introduced the session by saying: "I am working on a 20/20/20 rule – 20 minutes each phase. *[i.e. 20 minutes, Clean Start, 20 minutes Emergent Knowledge process, 20 minutes Clean Finish – CW].*"

1. **20 minutes to set up:**

David followed the Clean Start process set out on page 61.

2. **20 minutes Clean process (which David described as the "Epistemological section"):**

David:	So what do you know from that space?
Client:	That this space is really beautiful and I feel quite emotional, a sense of awe, beautiful. Quite strong about that feeling of beauty.
David:	So how old is that feeling of beauty?
Client:	[Long pause then shaking head]. Can't seem to… I think maybe three years [shaking head].
David:	And what kind of three years is that three years of beauty?

Client:	I think I'm only just appreciating, like it's always been there, but I was not appreciating in the same way as now.
David:	And is that three years in time or three years old?
Client:	three years in time
David:	So what kind of space is the space around you?
Client:	It's confusing
David:	And how big is it?
Client:	It's directly here to here [indicating].
David:	So what kind of shape is that space? [indicating]
Client:	Like a channel.
David:	What kind of channel?
Client:	Quite a smooth channel, like it should be really easy.
David:	And what kind of sides does that smooth channel have?
Client:	Kind of tubular, smooth, kind of plastic-y, perspex-y.
David:	And what's on the outside of that smooth tube?
Client:	I've just seen cows.
David:	And what kind of cows?
Client:	Friesian. Fields and buttercups.
David:	And what else?
Client:	Sun shining.
David:	So what kind of sun shining?
Client:	Really warming
David:	A warmth. And is there anything else about the warmth of that sun on those fields?
Client:	It's just a very peaceful, happy scene. It's just like a beautiful day in nature, the cows, the grass is growing. The sun goes out at the end of the day. It just all happens.
David:	So what kind of nature is that nature?
Client:	Nature as it should be.
David:	And how far does that "nature as it should be" go and where does that "nature as it should be" end?

Client:	[Pause, stretching arms out] It goes quite a way out and then it goes into more like dusty rubble.
David:	So what kind of rubble is that rubble that's at the end of that nature?
Client:	It's like soil going on into the distance as well and it's dry and it's dusty and there's ants. I've been seeing ants all day actually, scurrying little ants. [The client was referring to real ants as we were working in the garden].
David:	But how far does that soil go into the difference and what kind of edge is there to that soil after the dry and dusty soil?
Client:	[Pause] I can't seem to see it very clearly in my mind's eye. It's maybe… it goes on quite a long way.
David:	So how old could your mind's eye be?
Client:	Sort of three or four
David:	And what could the three or four be wearing, in your mind's eye?
Client:	I don't know. I can't see.
David:	And what kind of three or four could three or four be?
Client:	A spirited four
David:	So what could a spirited three or four be wearing?
Client:	A pretty dress and boy's shoes.
David:	And is there anything else about three or four who is spirited and had a pretty dress and boy's shoes?
Client:	She's got this pretty dress on. She kind of quite likes the pretty dress but she might also come back with it torn or dust all up her legs or completely dusty and muddy (hand gestures) because she's been playing about. She's got a real zest for life and adventure.
David:	So she's spirited and has a zest for life and adventure?

| Client: | Maybe a bit mischievous but in a way that she wants to do what she wants to do rather than be naughty for the sake of it |

David broke off here to explain his processes to the client:

"What I've done here is this is A, the space of A, which has come out three spaces. What I'm looking for is, who owns these strangely scaled worlds around the space of A? I got the clue a bit earlier and I took the "mind's eye" – that gave me the three or four, but when I pulled it back I got her with the boy's shoes and the dust.

[To client] What was lost, because it's several worlds removed from you, was the spirited zest and doing what you want to do, and so you lost that between three and four. So what happened is you escaped into this other world which is the one we're looking at.

So we've just expanded that space around the space of A and that way now I have an observant position – instead of just relying on you – because all you have is a smooth plastic tube to look through. Now we have here a spirited and zest for life three year old who hasn't had to have this mind's eye. So something happened between three and four: you acquired this mind's eye which led you to your beautiful world today. What I've done is pulled you back out so I can find out how were you before.

A cosmological change occurred – you have been operating out of a cosmology which originated out of that three or four mind's eye. My mistake was to ask 'What could that three or four with a mind's eye be wearing?' But if you are in "mind's eye" you have disappeared out of your body into the mind's eye. I want to go back and find her because rather than rely on you to tell me all this detail I can go back and ask her. She's what you gave up to be who you are. She's going to have a very different view. The double bind for you is you can't argue with her because she precedes you."

David Grove session with client 28 May 2005

David:	Now go over to B
David:	So what does that section know? [client had at some point divided the landscape around her into sections but I do not have a record of this in the transcript]
Client:	I don't know any more.
David:	So what kind of section is that section?
Client:	It's a confused section. It represents health.
David:	So what kind of shape does that section have when it represents health?
Client:	I don't know.
David:	So what kind of shape does it have?
Client:	It's pink and it's [pause] smooth and supple, and it's got give, and then it bounces back.
David:	So what kind of space is a space that's outside of that represents health?
Client:	It's a confused space.
David:	And how big is the confused space that's outside the represents health space?
Client:	It feels like it's been narrowing down over recent years
David:	So how many recent years has it been narrowing down?
Client:	About five
David:	So what kind of a space is that space which is outside those five years?
Client:	It's a frustrated space
David:	And how big is that frustrated space?
Client:	It's like chasms
David:	And how many chasms?
Client:	I can't even tell you because you go into one and there's another one and another one

David:	So how far does that maze of chasms go that's like chasms and represents health?
Client:	It's – I don't' even know because it's so confusing. It could go anywhere. I just feel I could quite happily take a big mallet to it and smash them all up
David:	So how old could you be before you take that mallet? (On that question I put the before in to expand time the same way we've been expanding space.) [During this session David added occasional explanations of his process as both the client and I were studying with him at the time – CW].
Client:	[Long pause]. Maybe one or two
David:	And maybe one or two. And is there anything else about maybe one or two before one or two takes a mallet?
Client:	I can't see that far. I can only see when I took the mallet.
David:	So what kind of mallet could that mallet be?
Client:	A big mallet, wooden handle, big metal bit here.
David:	And is there anything else about that mallet and where did you take that mallet from?
Client:	Pause. I can't see where I took it from – I don't know.
David:	And is there anything else that the mallet knows?
Client:	That although I might have taken it at that age I could have used it for a number of years throughout a lot of my childhood.
David:	(I'm asking her what she knows but she doesn't know anything – since she vividly describes the mallet I know the mallet has knowledge.) And is there anything else about that mallet?
Client:	The mallet knows it could have done a lot more damage but it held back, didn't go for it.
David:	So what kind of space is outside the space of that mallet?

David Grove session with client 28 May 2005

Client:	Angry space.
David:	And what kind of space is outside that space?
Client:	It's kind of like it's propped up in the corner of a garage, in the corner away.
David:	And what kind of garage is that garage?
Client:	It's like, quite a square, cleanish, non-cluttered. It's almost like I can go and get it if I want to.
David:	And how old could you be when that mallet is propped up in that garage?
Client:	I don't know when it was first propped up in the garage, but certainly 8, 9, 10, 11, 12, 13, 14, maybe more.
David:	So what kind of space is outside that garage?
Client:	I'm not sure. I can't see the space.
David:	And how far does that space that you can't see go?
Client:	[Shakes head] I can't see.
David:	And how far does that can't see go?
Client:	Thick.
David:	And what kind of thick when it's a can't see thick?
Client:	It's quite sludgy.
David:	Sludgy.
Client:	Thick sludgy and ...
David:	So what kind of edge or boundary does that second sludgy have when you can't see?
Client:	It's like it changes as you try to get through it and the shape changes. It might change your mood to obscure view.
David:	And how far does it go when it changes like that?
Client:	I don't think it goes too far but it changes.
David:	And what kind of edge or boundary is there between when it doesn't go too far?
Client:	It's kind of like the tunnel, the channel.

David:	So what's outside of that sludge that changes, that doesn't go too far, that's like the channel?
Client:	It's like the tunnel. It's like if I can get through the sludge, the tunnels slightly smooth, like you can go whoooo when you go to a water park and go down those chutes. I just can't get through it.
David:	And what kind of space is the space outside the tunnel?
Client:	Like the Friesian cows. The sludge is here.
David:	So what's outside the space of the Friesian cows?
Client:	Dirt and ants.
David:	And what's outside dirt and ants?
Client:	The sea.
David:	And what kind of sea? (I've gone out of space of space of space again now we have a different thing like sea.) What kind of sea is it that's outside the Friesian cows and the ants?
Client:	It's like a sea as it should be.
David:	So how far does that sea as it should be go?
Client:	Sometimes its smooth and beautiful sometimes it's angry and choppy. And that's just infinite.
David:	So where does that infinite go to and what kind of boundary or edge?
Client:	Like the world.
David:	And what kind of edge does that world have? (This is the world as it should be outside the rocks — before it was inside the rocks.)
Client:	It's a world where I want things to be.
David:	(This will be another strangely scaled world here. What I'm doing as I'm coming out [of the session – CW] is I want to end up with an owner of like size – I've got to keep pulling the girl out of this world and find out who she was before she disappeared in here.)
Client:	It's like a world where I want things to be nice.

David:	So how far does that world go? (I have a choice either expanding the world or taking the "I" that wants to be nice.) So how far does that world go and what's outside that world?
Client:	It feels like our world, planet Earth.
David:	So what kind of planet is that planet Earth?
Client:	Cyclical.
David:	Cyclical.
Client:	It's like cyclical in terms of nature, seas, tides, war. It's like it all ebbs and flows to – you do something somewhere, there's a reaction somewhere else.
David:	And what's outside of that world that's cyclical?
Client:	A blockage.
David:	So what kind of blockage?
Client:	Quite – it's like in the other world something – the other world is cause and effect – this world the blockage is quite impacted.
David:	And what's outside of the world with a blockage? (These are all strangely scaled worlds – doesn't have a knock on effect.)
Client:	Well it's like the planet earth where things ebb and flow and things happen, cause and effect. Whereas that other part is all blocked.
David:	So what s outside of that?
Client:	Don't know.
David:	So how far does that don't know go?
Client:	Quite a long way I think.
David:	And when it goes quite a long way, what kind of edge or boundary does that quite a long way have?
Client:	It's like a circle here that goes like that. [Client gestures a circle]
David:	So what kind of edge does that circle have?

Client:	Quite straight lines exactly like a section of a circle from the middle of a circle.
David:	So what kind of circle is that circle that has a section? (Again another strangely scaled world here and here's the use of the word section again that was part of the shape of B.)
Client:	It's a smooth, simple, very straight kind of a perfectly formed section.
David:	And what kind of circle is the circle that that section's in? (I'm going to the circle because by definition it must be outside of the section in the circle.)
Client:	It turned into a rotating sphere – like the world.
David:	So what kind of Earth is that Earth? [I think David may have misheard client's 'world' as 'earth'. Note how she challenges this, staying true to her own metaphor – CW]
Client:	I don't know whether it's an earth. It's like a ball and I suddenly want to kick it. [Client gestures kicking.]
David:	How old could that foot be that wants to kick that ball?
Client:	Three.
David:	(What I've got now is the zestful three again and I've got three's foot. Before I got three's head. Again this is all the strangely scaled part of what three's constructed.) And what could three be wearing?
Client:	Three is wearing whatever she's just dragged on.
David:	(Three's different now – not wearing boys shoes or a dress.) And is there anything else about three?
Client:	She's got her hair pulled back like this but she wants to take it out. It's tight.
David:	So where did the tight of her hair come from?
Client:	Her mum dragging it back into a pony tail.

David Grove session with client 28 May 2005

David:	(This is part of three's differentiation from her mother and three disappeared – the age old struggle, 'the terrible twos'. That's why I pulled back pulling back of the hair.) So what kind of three could three be before her hair was pulled back?
Client:	She's like off with the wind in her hair running around the top of a box and leaping off it.
David:	And what kind of box is that?
Client:	A big box. She just jumps anyway.
David:	(It's the same shape as… she's been pulled back into her mother. If you could do it you could leave her behind. She's not in your space and she doesn't view life through a plastic tube. That's the view you had to take mind's eye foot. The key to that was where did the pulling of that hair come from – we got the mum then we can pull the mum away from her, move time back, then she is released by it. One little act of that pony tail is what made the little girl lose herself. All I've done is space of the spaces of B. I've pulled them all back until I've got a normally scaled world. This one I got out of her foot and the other one out of her mindset. Now I am not relying on what she purports as A or what she says is over here [indicating B]. She is way out here. There is nothing you could say in this world that she won't say pooh pooh to because she has a completely different mindset. Now we'll go to C.) So what kind of space is the space between you and that section?
Client:	It's like a place I want to kick out of the way.
David:	And how big is that space and what kind of shape or size?
Client:	Like a cube.
David:	So what kind of cube?

Client:	I've just got this overwhelming… I want to trample all over it.
David:	And what's that cube made of? How big is it? (Now we have a three year old who wants to kick the cube – but the cube has information.)
Client:	I'm finding it very difficult to concentrate on it.
David:	So what kind of space is the space that is outside of that cube?
Client:	I think I'm more in my emotions than seeing.
David:	So how far can't you see anything and what kind of space is the space that's outside the cube?
Client:	It's like I feel like if I really concentrated maybe I could see something but I'd rather go and get my mallet and go at it.
David:	And is there anything else about that cube?
Client:	It think it's like – things are changing – it's like a space and it's like – imagine concrete and jagged bits of things stuck up like that, all different shapes and size. It would be difficult to work on because you might break your ankle. Now it's more like a flat with cubular shapes sticking up.
David:	So what kind of space is inside that cube?
Client:	It's like a pavement with lots of little cubes all over it. Quite solid.
David:	And is there anything else inside that solid?
Client:	It's like steel.
David:	So what kind of steel?
Client:	It's like keeping it – because the shape's quite odd, you need steel inside so when people do walk on it, it keeps it solid.
David:	And is there anything else about steel?

David Grove session with client 28 May 2005

Client:	I still want to take my mallet to it. It has been constructed to last.
David:	And is there anything else inside that steel that's been constructed to last?
Client:	I can break it if I want to. It's in my head.
David:	So what's inside that steel that has been constructed to last? (Now I'm pulling the time back of that last.) So where did the construction of that steel to last come from?
Client:	From my family.
David:	So what kind of family is your family that constructs steel to last?
Client:	It's the kind of family where we do things along certain lines in a certain way and if a job's worth doing it's worth doing well and proper.
David:	So where did those lines come from before they came into your family? Proper lines?
Client:	From a feeling of caring what people think, feeling like you have to be something to a certain rule that potentially society may or may not.
David:	So where did those rules come from before they came into your family?
Client:	I think they are potential society rules but you don't have to take them. My family chose to.
David:	And what kind of family was your family before they chose those rules? (Taking it back to the pristine.)
Client:	Well, I don't know. They always had those rules.
David:	So what kind of family was it then before they always had those rules?
Client:	Too concerned about what people think.
David:	And what kind of family were they before they were too concerned?

Client:	They were a good old laugh.
David:	So what kind of laugh is a good old laugh and what kind of family is a family that can have a good old laugh?
Client:	A good old laugh – they really enjoy each other, appreciate each other.
David:	And what kind of shape is a shape that that family could be in?
Client:	A heart, a big heart too bloody heart.
David:	So what kind of heart could that too bloody heart?
Client:	Like a soft cushiony one with arms that wrap round.
David:	So what could happen to a three year old in a family like that?
Client:	That if she sticks to the rules she gets the beautiful loving arms and she sacrifices a bit of mischievousness for the arms.
David:	So what kind of legs would a three year old have?
Client:	They're kind of like this and off on adventures and they probably jump first and think later. They maybe get into trouble, they maybe come back dirty. Like 'don't get snow on your coat because it's snowing because it's a new coat'.
David:	And is there anything else about that cube and the steel? (Come back to the cube.)
Client:	It kind of wants to bend.
David:	And what kind of space is a space outside of the cube?
Client:	The concrete's changed a bit now. It's like the steel can bend and it's like the concrete is more like that rubbery stuff at children's play centres. Still quite firm rubber but a bit more give in it. Not so treacherous. If you walk over it you could have grazed skin or broken ankle.
David:	So how far does that rubber go and what shape is it?
Client:	It's just here – over to the flowers.

David:	And what's on the other side of the edge?
Client:	I'm finding it amazing how my emotions are blocking me from seeing things. Angry hand now.
David:	Angry hand on this side? And what's on that side?
Client:	It's a bit sad.
David:	And what's above it?
Client:	The heart with the arms.
David:	And what's below?
Client:	The rubbery concrete-y.
David:	And what's below that?
Client:	All the chasms.
David:	And what kind of space is the space around all of that?
Client:	It's a peaceful wide space.
David:	And how wide is it?
Client:	Easygoing. Quite vast, as far as the eye can see.
David:	And what's on the other side of what that eye can't see?
Client:	Of what it can't?
David:	Mm.
Client:	It's darker.
David:	Darker.
Client:	And I remember — I don't know if this is a real memory — I remember something about being in a cot and crying. It's morning. Feeling 'get me out of this cot' — I remember a harness with a rabbit, being put in pens, like a playpen. I was always shaking, strapped into the cot and feeling so angry to get out, but strapped in to stay there longer. Maybe eighteen months old.
David:	(That's where the anger's from.)
Client:	Also very angry at my brother later on, but in this cot.
David:	(Probably like the steel of the bars of the cot made the concrete.) So what kind of you were you before you got into that cot?

Client:	Just wanting out – to go and explore – wanting to be out exploring having a chat with people.
David:	So what could you be wearing when you were out exploring chatting?
Client:	Just some sort of – it doesn't matter what I'm wearing, it's what I'm doing that is important.
David:	So what kind of doing is your doing?
Client:	Wanting to go out look at people talk to people tease laugh have a bit of a joke run around.
David:	And where does your want come from?
Client:	Feels like me.
David:	And what kind of me is the me where the want comes from?
Client:	A really healthy me.
David:	So where did your health come from when you had a healthy me?
Client:	From my spirit.
David:	And what kind of spirit is your spirit when it gives you a healthy me?
Client:	It's adventurous; it's exploring and seeing new things and really being with people and enjoying people's company; and not feeling fear, just going for things and not worrying about them in a kind of 'just going for it' rather than worrying about doing something and then not doing it because the worry stops – anxiety.
David:	So where did your spirit come from?
Client:	Mum's got a really beautiful sprit. Hers is suppressed in a lot of ways but she has given me that spirit.
David:	So where did your mum get it from before she gave it to you?
Client:	It's like a real female spirit.
David:	So where did that real female spirit come from?

Client:	It feels to me like what's good and what's right.
David:	And is there anything else about that female spirit?
Client:	It's really lovely and empowering.
David:	And what kind of form does that spirit take when it's lovely and empowering?
Client:	I've just seen a bloody snake again! I had a snake on another metaphor trip. I don't know whether…
David:	And what kind of snake is this snake?
Client:	This is like a really loving snake, like it's a snake that's got purpose and it gets on with things and goes about things and at the same point it's like 'don't take the piss!'
David:	And is there anything else about that snake?
Client:	It's having a good time. Wagging its tail which it can do to music. And it's got a hat on – it's on holiday. It's not scary but it's like 'don't take the piss because I can be scary if I need to be'. It's got a bit of that as well. It's doing that ' de de de de de de de' – snake dance – the conga on the floor. [Client sang the tune to the conga, a British dance where many people form a line and snake around the room – CW]
David:	So which floor?
Client:	Like a wooden dance floor.
David:	And what happens to a wooden dance floor when a snake?
Client:	It has to take a lot of weight because everybody's fallen over. Snake has given everybody a jab in their tummy with its tail. It has to take that weight. Snake wants to wrap around with another snake then it's off again, then it comes back and wraps around again then it's off again. It's just a fun loving easy going snake that just wants to get out there and do things and make a big song and dance and drama over things. Just enjoy life. Explore.

David:	(Now we're going to start moving on the snake.) So is there a space that you could go to that knows about that snake?
Client:	I feel like I know about the snake from here.
David:	And is there a space that that snake would like you to go to?
Client:	I'm going to walk and see if something happens. [Walks] Snake likes looking out over there.
David:	So what do you know from the looking out over there space?
Client:	That life's an adventure. [Turns to face opposite way].
David:	And what do you know from that direction?
Client:	That's safe – pretty and beautiful and safe.
David:	And what else?
Client:	That it's seductive. [Returns to first space.] Snake wants to take the mallet to it in a cheeky way.
David:	So find a space that knows how to do that. [Client moves to another space]. So what do you know from that space about that being seductive? (The irony – this is the very thing she wants and the snake wants to smash it)
Client:	Now I can see how seductive it is.
David:	(At A she only knows she wants B. Now at B, she wants to smash it.) And is there anything else you know from there?
Client:	That the mallet won't smash it I need a chain saw. But it is so pretty.
David:	And is there another space that knows that it is so pretty and that you need a chainsaw?
Client:	[Moves]This isn't so seductive.
David:	So what do you know from that space?
Client:	I could just chain saw along and if I keep my eyes down I don't look at that seductive space.

David Grove session with client 28 May 2005

David:	And is there a space that knows about keeping your eyes down?
Client:	It's like I don't need to move to know that it's hard to destroy it when I look at it because it is so beautiful. I could destroy it with my eyes down but actually I want to destroy it looking it at it.
David:	So where's a space that knows about that? (A recapitulation – she's going through different ages, all the sadness, anger, kick, mallet, will have out – this will be a dance as we go round to different space – until denouement, until these knots will loosen. She wants to keep the tension there right through.) What do you know from that space (indicating the first space)?
Client:	It's so beautiful.
David:	And is there anything else?
Client:	It doesn't seem fair that really beautiful things can be so seductive and they are not necessarily good.
David:	And is there anything else?
Client:	I feel like my three year old could destroy it quite easily.
David:	Which one – the kicking, mallet or mind's eye one?
Client:	Any of them.
David:	And is there anything else you know from that space?
Client:	I feel like I've just got to get on and do it.
David:	So where's a space that knows you've got to get on and do it?
Client:	[Moves around near first space – backs away ten feet, facing the space.] Here.
David:	And what do you know from there?
Client:	There's a bigger picture.
David:	Ah, so how big is that picture?
Client:	There's life beyond.

David:	(Keep the conundrum going until you get another solution – the bigger picture.) And is there anything else you know about a bigger picture?
Client:	Why put your focus here (first space) when there's a 360?
David:	Ah, so what's in the 360?
Client:	Who knows?
David:	And what does who know?
Client:	That it's just every possibility to be everything or do anything. [Turning 360 degrees] That's a seduction that section.
David:	So how many sections are there?
Client:	There's still these 2. That section is particularly seductive but it's so narrow and this [indicating behind] makes me feel like 'whooo!' when I look at all this.
David:	And what else do you know when you look at all this?
Client:	That my three year old has jumped in the water and is swimming.
David:	And what do you know now?
Client:	I'm bored with that now [turning her back on space one].
David:	And what do you know now?
Client:	Just yeah yeah.
David:	So what's the first yeah and what's the second yeah?
Client:	The first is like a 'yeah it's over'. The second is more determined – it needs that kind of. I'm trying to put myself into my three years old because for her it's easy.
David:	So where's a space that knows about that?
Client:	Down there [indicating the landing stage on the river next to which we are working, ten feet below]. I won't be able hear you

David:	(She doesn't need to hear because I don't need to ask questions, because this is the three year old being given the freedom to roam. Knots are untangled now – the whole conundrum is now loosed after the 'yeah yeah' – if I follow her she won't go away. Freedom – she goes away and does something and comes back.)
Client:	[Comes back smiling]
David:	So what do you know now?
Client:	That it's different now from when I was three. Maybe it will feel a bit scary but that doesn't mean I can't go for it.
David:	So do you know that from this space, or is there another space you could go to?
Client:	I've got some sadness. I don't know what that is [indicating her diaphragm].
David:	(Now we've got more information we can just follow through with it.) [Client kneels near space 1.] So what do you know from there?
Client:	It's like I don't like hurting people. Maybe this will hurt people. I know this is not the right reason not to do things but I feel sat at hurting people.
David:	And is there another space that knows about feeling sad at hurting people? [Client moves her chair 45 degrees.]
David:	So what do you know from there about the need for chocolate? [Client must have mentioned chocolate but there is nothing in the transcript – CW]
Client:	That I love chocolate and maybe it's something about being sad eating chocolate, I don't know.
David:	And is there another space that knows about eating chocolate and feeling sad?

Client:	I feel like I don't want to talk about the chocolate. When there's a heart with arms there to wrap round you and make you feel good, then you might do something to hurt those arms that can be so loving and giving. That's why I don't want to hurt. It's like the disapproval. That's where that comes from, having a family that gives so much love as long as you are abiding by the rules
David:	So how similar is that to the seductive over there?
Client:	Very similar.
David:	(This is a difficult question – a cleaner way of drawing association. Now she's looking on a 45 degree angle from it.)
Client:	The question is, how can you have both?
David:	So where's the space that knows that question?
Client:	I wish you had one of those swinging hammock things – sitting here swinging [on the fence with her back to the landing stage]. It's kind of you can have both, you've just got to... maybe it's my own prison that tells me I can't have both. But that doesn't have to be the case, that's just my own perception. A self-imposed cage.
David:	So where's the space that knows about your own self imposed cage?
Client:	I'm sitting on it, swinging on one of those things (swinging movements)
David:	(Normally here I would turn person round here but there is movement, swinging.)
Client:	There's something comforting about the swinging It's not locked this door – it's not like it's a locked cage. All I have to do is get off the swing, open the door and walk out. It's quite seductive, this cage. It's got a lovely swing on it. Again it's not helpful. It's just comfort. Think I'll go out [moving forward]. I don't feel sad any more.

David Grove session with client 28 May 2005

David:	So where's a space that knows about after you've come out and not feeing sad any more? [Client moves her chair into a position bisecting the angle between where she started and sadness.]
David:	And what do you know from that space there?
Client:	It's time for new things. I don't know what that looks like though. Maybe that's all right.
David:	And what else do you know when you don't know what it looks like?
Client:	Just to take my three year old with me.
David:	So where's a space that knows about taking your three year old with you?
Client:	In fact my eighteen month year old, she's the same.
David:	So where's a space that knows about taking the three year old and eighteen month year old?
Client:	I know from here – I've got them in mind – what would they do.
David:	(We want to keep finding enough spaces so that they will integrate – at the moment they are still separate. This part is very experiential – we're just waiting for the three year old and eighteen month year old to figure how they can join up. We're undoing the stuff they don't want – seductive, guilt, sadness. Until we've done those they won't integrate.)
Client	It's a bit embarrassing to let them come in fully because [laughing] they're quite silly and they might want us all running round the garden. They're silly. See my three year old might get your hat and throw it into the water – that's the trouble with bringing the three year old in. But that's all right to leave that part behind, because that's the three year old doing that. The three year old's behaviour is different from the three year old's essence.

:	What I want to take is the three year old's essence. I guess it's more that female essence that I talked about [stands up and walks forward, sits down]. I need to go over here now. Now she'd be telling your foot off (David's foot is kicking). It's like 'what a lot of nonsense! What a lot of angst over nonsense!'
David:	Well it's your nonsense and it has affected your life.
Client:	Isn't that ridiculous!
David:	It's the power of the bits you left behind not wanting to be left behind. If you can set up what you've had to do to avoid that – the effect it's had on your life and the amount of energy it's taken – you get some measure of the contribution the eighteen month and three year old spirit can make, and with what ease your life can move from here because you are not moving without them and you are not in a round cubular world, which is what your view was when you came here and sat down, because that is all you knew. Now you know a lot more because of the contribution of eighteen months and three. So it's a lot of nonsense in the sense that it stopped you doing all the things you can possibly do and the degree to which they limit you is also the degree to which they can add. And they can inform your life instead of de-forming it.
Client:	[Sighs, shakes head.] It is extraordinary – you think about what people go through in their life and for what? Anyway, no more nonsense, I don't want to talk about nonsense anymore.
David:	So what do you want to talk about?
Client:	It's just going forth now.
David:	So what kind of forth?
Client:	I'm conga-ing off into the future. Into the unknown. Spring in step.

David Grove session with client 28 May 2005

David:	That's different than a kick and attacking with a mallet.
Client:	You don't need a mallet when the floor underneath is spongier. It's much more rubbery now, all rubbery.
David:	So what could that rubbery be instead of being a floor?
Client:	Like a landscape.
David:	And what kind of landscape?
Client:	A rolling landscape.
David:	(I'm trying to get perspective, to get things life-size. Questions now are going to A, B and C.) And is there anything else about that landscape?
Client:	Just here – there in front of us – before it was too dangerous, you would get hurt too easily. Now it's just spongy grass.
David:	(Now transforming – softness can take away a lot of the fear in the landscape. Now going to A – that was C.) And is there anything else you know from that?
Client:	You can run about and take different turns and it doesn't matter if you fall because you can just go into a safety roll on the grass, whereas you couldn't do any of that on the concrete. You might graze your knee, but hey.
David:	So are we going to see a safety roll?
Client:	No. It just feels freer.
David:	So where's eighteen months and three?
Client:	The first thing I saw was the heart with the arms, and they are in the arms wrapped around.
David:	And the snake?
Client:	The snake's always with me I think.
David:	Whereabouts?
Client:	I can't tell you where the snake is from here.

David:	(I'm looking to integrate these things so that she can't tell where they are and where she is, and the landscape doesn't have any strange scaling elements.)
Client:	It's round my shoulders like a scarf thing.
David:	And eighteen months?
Client:	In the arms of the heart.
David:	(Not necessarily her arms.)
Client:	Those are wrapped round me. They were always wrapped around me. It's like they're in the arms somehow.
David:	Where's a space that knows about them in the arms? (They are still not in her.)
Client:	[She walks over to landing boundary again, turns back and walks towards space one, rests between last chair and seductive, then back to the river boundary.] The arms have become my arms.
David:	So what do you know now from that space? Now what do you know?
Client:	I'm holding my family's love so I've got them here [gesturing within arms].
David:	So find another space that knows about holding your family's love.
Client:	I kind of know here. It's like I'm holding all that love in here and they can feel that I am different but they also recognise that different because they have known me since I was born. It's kind of nice for them too. Dad might feel a bit challenged at times but hey. Yeah, it feels like… [smiling, sitting down].
David:	And is there a space that you'd like to place that chair in that knows what it feels like?

David Grove session with client 28 May 2005

Client:	[Moves chair forwards, turns it 15%.] Feels good – time for a cup of tea and a Mars Bar. [Client is referring to our usual afternoon break.]
David:	So how are you doing?
Client:	Yeah good. Feels kind of different. I'm getting used to that.
David:	(Referring to 'Cup of tea' and 'Mars Bar' is scaling back to this time. When something is healed it ought to be very natural – the ending kind of meanders, it's not big and explosive – an experience that feels natural; you have nothing more to measure it against so nothing is explosive – those are the qualities I'm looking for.) So what do you know?
Client	I feel like I'm done. I feel like [shrugs nonchalantly], feel like – I don't know what else to say. Why am I sat here? Let's have a chat now.
David:	(It's scaled now.)

243

CLEAN PRONOUNS WORKSHOP AT THE THATCHED COTTAGE 31 JULY 2005

David introduced this session:

When you ask a person, "Could you to think about *this*", where is that information going? Will your question evoke a considered thoughtful response, or is it going to go to some feeling in their body and they can't find words for it? It's good to be able to identify where your words are going to go into the person. So we need to make a map of your pronouns, of a person's" I", their "me" and their "you". Then you can also do their "myself".

For example, someone might say, "Well I was just beside myself". You know that there's an "I".

And this: "I left and went over here, and left myself somewhere else." So there is always a clue that is embedded and encoded into people's speech patterns that give you a clue as to how people operate in this inner space, this inner world that they have.

What we're doing here is going into the space of A *[explained on page 49 – CW]* and then we ask questions, and inside the space of A we need to know what the age and what the nature of these pronouns are, so when you use the word "you", you have some idea of where it's going.

Session at a Workshop at The Thatched Cottage 31 July 2005

The Demonstration

David explained to the group what he was doing as he went along. His words to the group in general are in brackets; his words to the client are not.

David:	So when you say I, whereabouts is your I, when you say I? is it in your head? Is it in your body? Is it outside of you? Whereabouts is your I?
Client:	In my head.
David:	And whereabouts in your head?
Client:	The front of my head, here.
David:	And does it have a shape or a size when it's in the front of your head?
Client:	I'm kind of getting skipping.
David:	(I'm asking to see if we've got a metaphor and we get "skipping", so it's anthropomorphic, so there must be someone in there doing the skipping.) So how old could a "skipping" be?
Client:	Three [wriggles her toes].
David:	(You can see it's in the toes – it's probably three's toes that are wriggling there.) And what could three be wearing when three is skipping?
Client:	A boy's shoes.
David:	And is there anything else?
Client:	And a dress.
David:	(What that means is from that pronoun the cosmology – the world of "I"ness – was first conceived, or the genesis of it was from that three year old in that moment in time and that has lasted all the way up to her age today.) [Client was about forty years old – CW].

	So when you say me, whereabouts could your me be? Is your me in your head, in your body, or outside? Whereabouts is your me?
Client:	It's in my stomach.
David:	And whereabouts in your stomach?
Client:	Here [indicating with hand].
David:	(We know from the hand movement that this me is fairly young, because there may not be many words, particularly if it's coming from the stomach.) And how old could your me be when it's coming from here [indicating with same hand movement as client]?
Client:	I don't know.
David:	And is there anything else about your me?
Client:	Me's a bit more butterfly-y.
David:	And what kind of butterfly-y could that me be?
Client:	A bit more anxious-y butterfly.
David:	And is there anything else about an anxious-y butterfly?
Client:	I can manage it though.
David:	(So there's an I and we know where that I is because that belongs to three, and the 'I can manage an anxious-y butterfly' of the me. We're going to leave that me for the moment, and the reason for that is the nature of the me-ness is anxiety. So I am just lightly touching me and that me-ness can be encoded in the butterfly. This pronoun "you" is a bit different. We hear phrases like "You stupid boy!" You is usually defined by events or people outside of us.) And when you hear the word you, where does the word you go to? And whereabouts could your you be? Is your you in your head, is it in your body, or is it outside?

Session at a Workshop at The Thatched Cottage 31 July 2005

Client:	Here I think [indicating in front of the face].
David:	(So now we wrap words around that here to give it a form.) So does that here have a shape or a size when it's about here? [indicating the same place].
Client:	It's like a hand, but I think that's my hand just going like that.
David:	That's a left hand moving backwards. And how old could that hand be?
Client:	I think it's something like eight.
David:	And what could eight be wearing when a hand is going like that?
Client:	It doesn't seem to matter.
David:	And is there anything else about a hand?
Client:	It's like yeah, yeah, whatever, to the hand. Mm. [laughing]
David:	(So we can see the hand and attached to it is a "yeah yeah whatever". So those are the words that are encoded in that movement and that hand. Whatever is there can emerge out of that question.) And when you say myself, whereabouts could your myself be?
Client:	Here [Indicates shoulders and front arms].
David:	And is there anything else about a myself? [Indicating with same movement].
Client:	[It is not clear from the transcript whether client patted herself or said she was patting herself].
David:	Is there anything else about a patting myself?
Client:	It feels very caring, looking after.
David:	(So that's some of the qualities of patting myself.) And how old could that myself be that's very caring and looking after?
Client:	I think it's much older.

David:	Much older than you?
Client:	No, more thirties, mid-thirties
David:	And is there anything else about mid-thirties?
Client:	Yes, more looking after myself.
David:	And what could myself be wearing when it's a "more looking after myself" myself?
Client:	Wrapped in my big blanket on the sofa.
David:	And is there anything else about that big blanket?
Client:	It's cosy and safe and looking after.
David:	(So that myself, then, is actually outside, but it's still fairly close. So also is the you which is outside in that hand wave.) If you would like to make a little map of where those are, and perhaps draw it here, so we can have a visual cue about what those experiences are.

In conclusion David said:

"So this is some of the interior-scape that is going to lie inside the body of the person in the space of A. Her pronouns are in quite different places: two are inside and two are outside.

I am going to coach your "me". You as the coach would then go into this "me" metaphor that's in the stomach, and you would then coach the anxiety out. And that way, you can then grow the "me" up that is encased in this anxiety so that that "me" can be integrated into who she is today. So that's how you might make that decision, in terms of, "I heard that "me" so I know that "me" is different than if she said "I".

CLEAN HIEROGLYPHICS SESSION WITH DEBORAH HENLEY

This is a transcript of a session I witnessed between Grove and Deborah Henley in July 2005. We were at The Thatched Cottage in Laleham, Surrey, a house of mine where David stayed during that year. Deborah is a passionate advocate of Clean work and spent a considerable amount of time studying and practising with David and other Clean practitioners.

She first met him at a residential workshop in 2001 and he later mentored her during a time when she was working with hundreds of people suffering from addictions. She would work with large groups of twenty people and learned a lot from David about working with groups. There would be emergence within the group, a group mind, and David helped with that. It transformed the way she worked, using imagery and art. He once told her that the psychologist RD. Laing had suggested that he take his trauma clients off to a beautiful place and let them go as mad as they wanted. That was when he bought his ranch. People could allow themselves to fully express their own missions and aspects of themselves, some through the presence of the horses that were there, some through the river. Deborah said that Laing was something of a mentor to David and they met on lecture circuits.

Part One: Set Up

David:	Write down your goal. *[Pause as Deb writes her goal on a post-it]*. Find a space for you and for your goal. *[She moves to a space and puts the post it in another space.]* What would you like to call your goal?
Deb:	That's 'what I want'.
David:	And is that the right space for 'What I want'?
Deb:	I'm going to move it up a bit.
David:	Are you in the right space?
Deb:	*[Moves forward]* – my feet are over the edge *[standing on a step]*. It's a diving board. I'm about to dive in.
David:	And is 'What I want' at the right height? *[She moves it down]*. And are you at the right height?
Deb:	No I'm probably here *[sitting down[*.
David:	And are you in the right space?
Deb:	I'm actually like this. I can see it.
David:	And are you at the right height?
Deb:	Yes.
David:	And are you at the right angle?
Deb:	I'm like that *[hands out to the side]*.
David:	And are you facing the right direction?
Deb:	Yes.
David:	And is that statement facing the right direction?
Deb:	Yes.
David:	And are your arms in the right place?
Deb:	Yes.
David:	And are your legs in the right place?
Deb:	Yes.

David:	And are your feet in the right place?
Deb:	Yes.
David:	And is the 'What I want' in the right place?
Deb:	I'm going to make a tiny adjustment – moves it slightly. It's really tiring staying in this position which is…
David:	All part of the deal.
Deb:	Yes, irritating and frustrating. *[She stands, bending over, arms out to the side.]* Even when I stand up to get more comfortable I am no longer engaging in 'What I want'. When I crouch down in the uncomfortable place I am engaging again.
David:	Now we're coaching B rather than A.

Part Two: Hieroglyphics

David:	So what do you notice about the letters of the words that are on goal?
Deb:	They are in a thick marker so they are not very clear or neat.
David:	And is there any letter that looks different?
Deb:	The letter C is almost becoming an O or an A. It's a nice open, spacious letter.
David:	So what does that letter C know?
Deb:	From where it's positioned it can see me more than I can see it.
David:	And what else does it know?
Deb:	It's comfortable and it's creativity.
David:	And how old is that letter?
Deb:	It's an adult.
David:	And are there any other interesting letters?

Deb:	The A is quite sharp and pointed like an arrow. The A is pointing up. It looks like an arrow pointing towards that C, or it could be a four. It says 'as' but it could say 'fours' or it could that bit of a male symbol, the kind of penis bit pointing up in that direction. I'm also noticing the colour of bright yellow, which is slightly falser than the flowers that it's behind. It's a false green.
David:	So what does that letter 'A' know?
Deb:	The letter 'A' is very sure of its direction. Very confident. It knows where it's going. It's going that way [gestures up]. I guess it's a kind of assertive male thing. It just knows where it's going.
David:	And what does the yellow space know?
Deb:	Around the post it? The yellow space is false and not a true colour of nature. Not natural. Slightly toxic. It's doing its best to try to emulate the colour of nature, these yellow flowers, but it's trying too hard.
David:	And is there anything else interesting about the letters or the spaces between the letters?
Deb:	The 'and' seems quite interesting, a kind of cross. It's like a little t and it also looks like this cross up here which is kind of like a very relaxed, comfortable, Christian cross, like a child who's very comfortable with God and crosses and those kinds of symbols.
David:	And how old is that child?
Deb:	About four.
David:	And is there anything else about four?
Deb:	It's like the four in the A that knows its direction. That little cross has four ends to it as well. There's an ant playing around on the four, squiggling around.
David:	So what does the ant know?

Deb:	The ant is just comfortable exploring. The ant has gone off the paper, on the paper, exploring, it is comfortable on the bricks or the flowers. There isn't that discrimination. There are quite a few ants crawling around just being and enjoying.
David:	And is there any other interesting or unusual information that is in those letters between them or in that space?
Deb:	This isn't in that space but I have just noticed two other ants. They are all doing their own thing. If they come across another one they make contact. There is another ant on the yellow thing, on the word 'pooh'. It's just walked off so it is totally okay. It's just exploring the edges of the piece of paper so it is aware that the paper is not the same as the true environment. It's just been stuck on. It looks really horrible. I saw the word creative written but it looks ugly, not like the ants doodling in their own way. A sort of forced thing. It's not even written neatly.
David:	So what does that know?
Deb:	It reminds me of things being written neatly when you're learning hand writing.
David:	And how old is that hand writing?
Deb:	Maybe five, six, four. It's sort of learning to write and use a pen or a pencil and it looks really messy and there's a kind of…
David:	So how old is a 'learning to write'?
Deb:	I think it's four, five or six, I'm not sure. All those times with a pen when even drawing it doesn't' look as good as it should. It's really frustrating, you can't make what you want, you can't do what you want to do because these stupid hands don't know how to do it properly and don't know how to get that out there.

David:	(Note that letters 'A' and 'C' have quite a lot of information in them and they are showing different ages, suggesting two different disassociated parts of her. She has reached a negative space which she doesn't know how to get out of, so I am now going to question around the space of B to move her forward.) so what kind of space is the space that is around that 'want'?
Deb:	The want itself is hidden from view from there, which is not hidden from view from me from all people. I was expecting it to be hidden from me most of all but I am the only one that can see it because that's the position I was wanting to get to and it thought when I get to that position I'll know that. So the position I want to get to is not the right one.
David:	So how big is the space around that?
Deb:	The thing I want is hidden by the flowers and there is this plane which is here, this place which I wanted to enter into. I thought I wanted to get to there. So it's that and that and there's also another space here which I am slightly closer to and I'm closer to this one, it's not hidden.
David:	And what kind of space is the space that is around that statement?
Deb:	Kind of elliptical thing there.
David:	And is there anything else about it when its elliptical?
Deb:	It's like an I.
David:	And what kind of an I?
Deb:	Like an eye.
David:	And is there anything else about that eye?
Deb:	It's a right eye.
David:	And is there anything else about that right eye?
Deb:	The right eye is beautiful – those flowers – the left eye is ugly, not attractive.

Session with Deborah Henley on Clean Hieroglyphics

David:	So what kind of space is a space that's on the other side of that right eye?
Deb:	There's this space which is kind of like the space behind the eye. That bit I don't know. I'm not sure about that path where things can come down – my left eye. Whereas this *[indicates right eye]* – things emerge in a different way because there are flowers growing.
David:	And how far does the space go on the other side of that eye?
Deb:	The length of the lawn. It's interesting there's a well there as well. This is part of the space which is really mysterious at the end of the path. I don't know what's at the end of the path.
David:	So what kind of space is the space outside of that edge? *[Deb must have mentioned a hedge – it is not in the transcript]*
Deb:	Hedge – outside that hedge.
David:	And what kind of space is on the other side of the hedge?
Deb:	It's life, other people, the whole of the rest of the world.
David:	And what kind of world is the rest of the world that's on the other side of that hedge?
Deb:	It starts off pleasant, green especially in that direction and over there, the river, really pleasant. That's a little bit dark and spooky *[indicating left side]* almost pitch black in there.
David:	(We are now in the space of B).

Deb:	I can't see at all. It's really nice there but is pitch black in there in that ominous looking tree. It's got flowers which have fallen over and been trampled on carelessly. What's really strange is that bunch of plants there suddenly looks like a huge field in somewhere like the Philippines or it could be the big field – I'm not sure where it would be – it looks like a place where people would have wars in a tropical place – Philippines or India, that used to have lots of wars going on but now it's all grown up and it looks like a nice field where people are growing crops.
David:	So how far does that world go to and what's on the other side of that world?
Deb:	Really dark black space. I'm beginning to see two little leaves in that pitch black place.
David:	And what's on the other side of pitch black?
Deb:	It might be a gate or a fence. I can't tell whether I'm hallucinating.
David:	And what's on the other side of that gate or fence?
Deb:	I expect some more dark plants but then it might get light again like a mirror version of this part.
David:	And what kind of a light?
Deb:	It's like a mirror thing, a parallel universe.
David:	And what's on the other side of that parallel universe?
Deb:	It will be another right eye but it will be a left eye because it's been flipped around. It could have different colours. The colours in that garden would all be the reciprocal ones to this so the grass would be magenta. That would be fuchsia like a sunset.
David:	And what's on the other side of that parallel universe?
Deb:	It goes on garden after garden swapping like that.

David:	And when does that swapping end?
Deb:	When it suddenly becomes brick. Concrete-y structures when there are brick buildings.
David:	And what's on the other side of those brick buildings?
Deb:	It seems like wasteland. Nothing growing.
David:	And how far does that wasteland go to?
Deb:	To the edge of the country.
David:	And what's on the other side of that edge?
Deb:	The sea.
David:	And how far does the sea go and what's on the edge of the sea?
Deb:	The sea goes all around the whole world.
David:	And what kind of world is a world that the sea goes all around?
Deb:	It's held and contained by water pulled together by gravity, otherwise it would all just fall apart. All the land would float off, the sea would float away.
David:	And what kind of world is a world outside that world?
Deb:	Like in hitchhiker galaxy, strange planets and interesting people, different ways of experiencing life. A creative world.
David:	And what kind of world is the world that's outside of that creative world?
Deb:	It's the edges of the universe.
David:	And what's outside the edges of the universe?
Deb:	I imagine it held in by a skein, like what holds the water in.
David:	And what kind of world is a world outside of that skein?
Deb:	Sandy coloured.

David:	And is there anything else about sandy coloured?
Deb:	Like sandpaper. The whole experience is dry and sandy. There is no fluidity. It makes that sound –not white noise, more yellowy, dirty grey.
David:	And what kind of edge or boundary does that world have and what's on the other side of that?
Deb:	It turns into sand dunes which go down to water again with waves. It's on both sides and above it it's sky again but there's no life. Maybe the odd little crab. Like the beginnings of time.
David:	So what kind of time was the time before this time began?
Deb:	The little crabs weren't there. My mum's a Cancer and I think my dad is as well. They weren't there. It goes deep, has dunes, like an old fashioned moustache.
David:	And what's on the other side of that old fashioned moustache?
Deb:	There are two ways of going here – one into a Hercule Poirot type person's brain, or on other side of that moustache it goes sand all the way down to the bottom of a well.
David:	And how far does that sand go to and what's on the other side of the sand?
Deb:	All round this thin layer of sea and it seems to be quite flat, not a rounded well, quite square, rectangular, in a fish tank.
David:	And what's outside of that fish tank?
Deb:	The person looking at the fish tank.
David:	And what kind of a person is a person looking at the fish tank?
Deb:	Me when I was a little girl.
David:	And how old you could be when you were a little girl looking at the fish tank?

Session with Deborah Henley on Clean Hieroglyphics

Deb:	6 or 7.
David:	And what could you be wearing when you were a little girl looking at the fish?
Deb:	A skirt with an elasticated waist.
David:	And where did you come from just before you looked at the fish?
Deb:	We'd been down the stairs and bought some horrible red squiggly wiggly worms to feed the fish.
David:	And where did you come from before you bought those worms?
Deb:	We might have been sailing.
David:	And what kind of you were you that had been sailing?
Deb:	I've got bare feet and just had fun messing around with ropes, jumping up and down on boat, sitting with legs over side.
David:	And is there anything else that you know?
Deb:	This place here is quite like being on a boat maybe holding onto something or just leaning against things. Slightly uncomfortable but okay because a nice place to be.

David stopped here and said to the group:

"Here's a reality check. We are now in scale and have an observer. The plane of bisection – the distance between F and A is probably the distance there was between her and the fish tank.

[To Deb] You've positioned yourself in that way, so what we've done from that, I think, has gone through a whole series of cosmologies, in which your mind has strangely scaled all of that stuff and your statement is part of that goal to get that back. So we have arrived there by starting with the letters, going in, then expanding out to edge of the 'I' and got the plane, all the fractured worlds, mirrors, edges and other terrains. With every question I am just expanding out the space and going out to the edge of every bit of information. Until we followed the sand, which went out to the edge and it became an aquarium. That was actually life-size. I wanted to get an observing position that is not strangely scaled. What happened is the moment after looking in that aquarium you went into it: this part of you that has left that statement went into it; this part of you has been encoded into the water and the sand; the scaling that went up from there; your mind when you went to the aquarium – when you turned around and left it you were not the same person. That is who informs that goal. Part of why that goal is written by that, and why you are strangely drawn to it, is to try to get that part of you back. Now we have found that and we know who you were before you changed. Just by finding it and pulling you away from the aquarium, we get your mind before you went into the aquarium. The mind you had before would not have had this goal. You have reclaimed that part of you. The mind that you have at 'A' is the aquarium mind – all the other stuff is strangely scaled.

[To the group] Once she described the rectangular well, she was in the fish tank. I wanted to get the person looking at the fish tank in scale. Until now, the rest of the world has always been constrained in that view. Looking at the world through glass or water gives you a distorted vision. That will be the 'right eye' thing. Now you have a mind back with two eyes which are looking in the right direction.

Deb said, "Now I feel like I am pre that time – now I'm sitting in here on the floor instead of outside on the steps."

David replied, "Your toes hanging over the edge is the equivalent of the right eye only seeing that stuff.

[To the group] We will need a side bar about scale. The cycle is a content free zone: let the content download into the space, but coach doesn't take the content, just explores the spaces. The client is engaging with her information – you know what you know here at A. B has information in it. When we have coached it out of that space you will know more. Start out with:

- Nothing
- Noise
- Data
- Information
- Knowledge
- Experience

[To Deb] Now you're in two minds – you have come out of water and the refractive index of your eyes is probably going to change as well. Now we have to unpack everything out until we have a world that includes the fish tank world and the rest of it – at the moment you are in two minds, in both. The goal is to get you into a mindset or a state of mind in which the bit of you that didn't go into the fish tank (the one on the boat) can also participate. It's like the fish tank mind plus the one before it and maybe plus the one before that. Now we want to put all those together into a landscape or a psychescape. One thing we could have you do is write up all the drivers and attractors which made you do strange things. For instance the artificial colours, which are often in fish tanks. The garden on the left was the dark side of the fish tank. The left eye never went in – only the right eye went in. the room is dark but the fish tank is lit in the middle of the night, still full of colour.

Part Three: History of B

David:	And is that the right place for you to be?
Deb:	It's different from the last place, is that okay?
David:	Yes, because something has changed.
Deb:	And is that the right height for you to be?
Deb:	I think so.
David:	And is B in the right place?
Deb:	I don't know if this is the right place for me to be particularly.

David:	And is that the right place for B to be?
Deb:	Either I go somewhere else or it goes somewhere else.
David:	So where would that statement like to be?
Deb:	If I'm going to stay in that place, I might put this somewhere where it belongs better than a garden which might be on a board (pins to flipchart).
David:	So is that the right place for that? The right height?
Deb:	It's a bit crowded for this. I am going to put it on a clean sheet of paper. *[Deb moves around to different places.]*
David:	(There is now an interaction between A and B. information is starting to exchange.)
Deb:	I'll put that there.
David:	(On the left hand side of the page and put up with the left hand. My guess it is probably there in that place because both eyes can see it.)
Deb:	What I am going to do is move this whole board outside.
David	Are you?
Deb:	Yes. I want to get it right in the middle. I'm doing that because then it gets more light on it. It's tilted back a bit which is quite like a sailing-y thing in boats, tipping over the sail. I'm on the windward side. When you're sailing along on the windward side there is always a bit of a blind spot. You can't see what's coming. I feel like getting something down the side here *[points to right side of page. Places orange post-its all the way down]*. A lot of ropes are these colours now on boats. Then it was old greyish stuff *[draws a curved line down the flip chart – post-its make the mast, curved line the sail, statement is top left outside the sail.]*
David:	(We now know we're dealing with part of her that was on the boat. This orangey colour was a bit like those wiggly worms that fed the fish.) So where's your position?
Deb:	Here in the cockpit.

Session with Deborah Henley on Clean Hieroglyphics

David:	And is that the right space for you?
Deb:	I can stroll up and down quite easily.
David:	(A major difference – she is now perpendicular to the edge *[of the steps]* and opposite where B was.)
Deb:	The mast is opposite where A was. It's almost like we've tacked. They're on the leeward side. Everything's is on the other side.
David:	(Now there is no edge – before she was facing the edge. Often people are facing the wrong way – they have been turned around – their goal is to get back from whence they came.)
Deb:	It's interesting to have tacked because even if you are trying to get into a direction on the boat you often can't head straight for it. I don't know if that's where I'm wanting to go, this is as close as I can get. I'm going as close to the wind as I can. We're not leaning over too much. It's still uncomfortable to go down to the leeward side and you can see everything. *[She bends down and goes backwards and forwards under the flipchart.]*
David:	(She is picking up the physicality of the child – we got the child's mind now she is picking up the child's body.)
Deb:	*[Looks at the door]* – maybe this could be another sail at the front, but it's in the wrong place for a gib.
David:	And is that the right space for you?
Deb:	About here.
David:	And is that the right space for that statement to be?
Deb:	It doesn't really seem relevant that statement particularly.

David:	(The goal of a lifetime is now no longer relevant – it's hanging off the back of the sail on the boat. The sad thing is, this has often been the driver and the goal for years and years and years and has marked a person's life that has driven them thematically to do all sorts of things that they actually don't have to do any more.)
Deb:	It seems to me as I'm sitting here cruising along [*she has seated herself at an angle to the flipchart and both eyes are looking past the mast – the other way only one eye could look one way and the other went the other way*]. It's just a nice breezy day, a little bit cloudy. What I would do if we had sellotape is make this a proper size [*indicating the flipchart*].
David:	And is that the right space for you to be in?
Deb:	I'm cruising at the back with my foot on the tiller or the wheel.
David:	You have to have a tiller or a wheel, one or the other.
Deb:	I think I prefer a wheel. In this kind of world I'm not really worried about what my clients want – this is just not a worried place.
David:	(The reason for that is this particular goal was constructed out of that aquarium world. Now we've pulled back and we're into the world before it, that goal is meaningless from this position because it's not necessary to have that, so her mindset that she has today is obsolete, or didn't exist in this new position that she is in now.)
Deb:	I can't even contemplate why you'd want to worry about that.

Session with Deborah Henley on Clean Hieroglyphics

David:	(Her body is stretched out in the chair relaxed, not crouched over uncomfortably like before. The remarkable thing is that her neurology is being changed in real time, so all the long term memory aspects are changing and reorganising which is why you start getting different insights, all because we now have her pre-aquarium mind or the state of mind before the current one.) So is that statement in the right place?
Deb:	It's fine for there to be some tell tales at the back of the sail.
David:	So what kind of goal was your goal before it was that one? What was the one on the tell tale?
Deb:	To just get in the flow. I don't understand the question. Am I doing the goal directly before that one? That was an adult goal; I just made it up today.
David:	And what was your goal before you had that one?
Deb:	It must have been a goal I reached.
David:	(That's what she is probably on now – a broad reach – she eased off the sails, she was close hauled before – on a broad reach it's all downwind sailing.)
Deb:	Where I am now feels like where I aspired to be at one time. Just to cruise along and enjoy it. But I actually want more now than to just be where I am now.
David:	So what kind of goal was your goal before that one?
Deb:	Shall I write it down?
David:	Write it down and place it.
Deb:	I know what it is but I can't get it to this position.
David:	So is there an object that represents it?
Deb:	That pot of flowers but it's not in the right position. *[She moves the pot]*. I don't think that's a good example *[she moves it back]*. I can see it it's just there *[pointing at flowers]*. It's flowers.
David:	So how old could that goal be?

Deb:	I don't know how old that is. It could either be a very recent one or it's something I've always wanted. I think I've had it for years.
David:	(Now I'm going to pull back and do a little development of that.) So what kind of space is the space around that goal?
Deb:	It's got a good structure behind it. There are lots of other nice yellow flowers around. It's all part of the garden. But it's particularly beautiful.
David:	So what kind of space is the space outside the garden space?
Deb:	On that one side it's a structured brick-y place and on the other side it's that fairy dell dark place.
David:	(Are we in a normally scaled world or a strangely scaled world? It started out seeming normal.) How old could that goal be?
Deb:	It could be since I was – I don't know – two or three – it seems like it's all my life really, that's what I've always been wanting to do.
David:	So how old could you be when you always wanted to do that?
Deb:	About three or four.
David:	And what could three or four be wearing?
Deb:	Maybe some blue pyjama-y all in one thing.
David:	So what's outside of three or four with blue pyjama-y thing?
Deb:	It's a sort of garden in a place called Chiswick Staithe where we lived before we went to Hong Kong.
David:	And what kind of garden was that garden?
Deb:	A communal garden with a tree with mud that we played in. I am not sure I was aware that that's what I wanted to do at that time. It was a bit dirty and muddy so that's quite nice and pretty.

Session with Deborah Henley on Clean Hieroglyphics

David:	(Now I'm pulling back.) And what kind of you were you before you went into that garden?
Deb:	I was nice and clean in my pyjamas ready to go to bed. That garden was all messy and dirty.
David:	And is there anything else about being ready to go to bed and nice and clean before that garden?
Deb:	I can just remember each person had their own little garden and there was a tortoise in one called Molly.
David:	(I'm getting the state of mind before she went into the garden, equivalent to the state of mind that existed before the aquarium. When your goals change, your cosmology, or view of the world also changes. Now I have to find out what this world is. We're in B–2.) So what kind of goal did you have when you were clean?
Deb:	I think it is easier to be asked what I wanted.
David:	Okay. So what did you want when you were clean?
Deb:	I wanted to stay nice and clean, my hair brushed, just looking on at tortoises and things, maybe touching them.
David:	(We're now in B-2). So could you either find an object that represents that or write it down?
Deb:	There's a nice clean plate *[fetching a plate and clearing the space around the plate and around the table it is resting on, and the magazines under the table.]*
David:	And is that the right space for you?
Deb:	Yes.
David:	And is that the right space for what you want?
Deb:	Yes this feels a bit more like the ants who didn't discriminate between anything that they saw – things could be interesting or curious. The table is just an interesting surface, and the plate – they don't have to mean a lot.
David:	And is the plate in the right place?

267

Deb:	Yes.
David:	And is it at the right height?
Deb:	Yes.
David:	And is it at the right distance?
Deb:	Yes. There's a stain on the table [wiping off the stain].
David:	And are you in the right space? [Deb makes small adjustments at each question.] And are you at the right height? And are you at the right distance? And are you at the right angle?
Deb:	I am a bit too big, that's the trouble. I feel like I'm standing [kneeling].
David:	And is that plate in the right space?
Deb:	Yes [moving plate with her hands].
David:	And is it at the right distance?
Deb:	These look like carrots (markings on the plate). I thought they were arrows. Tommy Tiddlemouse or something. No, Peter Rabbit, Mr McGreggar. Reminds me of those three carrots [staring at plate and touching it].
David:	And is that plate facing the right direction? And are you in the right space?
Deb:	I don't like that those carrots look a bit too sharp. Apart from that it's okay. I can't do anything about that.
David:	So what kind of space is the space that's around that clean plate?
Deb:	It's a nice clean table [she has her chin on table looking at plate with alternate eyes].
David:	(She has gone into the plate, the clean world, the B-2 world. We have to pull her out of that). So what did you want before you wanted to be clean?
Deb:	I wanted to look over a shoulder.
David:	And what did you want before you wanted to look over a shoulder?

Session with Deborah Henley on Clean Hieroglyphics

Deb:	I wanted people to look at me.
David:	And is there something that represents wanting people to look at you?
Deb:	The leaves on that tree.
David:	So what space would you be in and what space would the leaves of the tree be in? And what did you want before you wanted people to look at you. (This is B-4.)
Deb:	I want to be nice and warm in bed.
David:	(This is B-5.) and is that blanket in the right place? And are you in the right place?
Deb:	I'm a bit worried that everyone has forgotten about me?
David:	So what did you want before you wanted to be nice and warm?
Deb:	I wanted to be loved and be nice and warm and people to hug me.
David:	And is there something that represents your wanting that?
Deb:	Yes, being in this room represents me wanting it but I haven't got it.
David:	So what did you want before you wanted this?
Deb:	I didn't get this.
David:	And what did you want before you wanted this and you didn't get this?
Deb:	I wanted to find out what it was like to be alive.
David:	And is there something that represents that?
Deb:	Maybe the bud on a flower.
David:	So is there a space that you could go to and where would the bud on the flower be? (B-6 – this may be the demarcation of before she was born.)

Deb:	This feels like before I was born. About as babyish as I can get. This feels like just before the bud on the flower.
David:	Okay so where's your space? So where would you be and where would the bud on the flower be?
Deb:	It feels like the chance to search for which kind of flower I wanted to be.
David:	So where is the space that you could be in and where is that want?
Deb:	*[She is in the middle of the lawn walking around.]* It's here because I found it.
David:	So are you in the right space?
Deb:	Probably something like this *[crouching over on the pond like she did at the beginning on the steps]*.
David:	And is that bud in the right place?
Deb:	Yes. I found it.
David:	And are you in the right place? And are you at the right distance?
Deb:	More like this.
David:	(She's leaning sideways – another plane of bisection. This is the bit that never came here – often people's goals are to go back whence they came and it's all obscured.) So what did you want before you wanted that?
Deb:	To enjoy being here *[running around the garden with her arms stretched out]*. A bit like running around.
David:	So find a space where you can run around and where you can enjoy being here. So whereabouts is a space that has wanting to be free in and whereabouts are you?
Deb:	This space is where I want to be free but I've found what I wanted before that.
David:	So whereabouts is what you wanted before you wanted to be free?

Session with Deborah Henley on Clean Hieroglyphics

Deb:	It was to grow and learn. An unknown place.
David:	And where would you be?
Deb:	On the edge of the unknown place and I want to know what that's all about.
David:	So go to that place and when you've found out what you wanted to know ... [*She runs to the end of the garden.*] What did you want before you wanted to know that? (Now we're beginning to unwind with just a very simple little thing, but huge complexities are coming out. All I'm doing is repeating the same pattern – the history of what her goals and wants and desires have been.)
Deb:	I wanted to know whether there are real warpings and senseless pain.
David:	And is there something that represents that? Where is that?
Deb:	At the gateway there.
David:	And where would your space be if that is at the gateway?
Deb:	There crouching down next to it.
David:	So crouch down next to it. And what did you want before you wanted to know that about warpings and senseless pain? (Part of this is what you bring with you as a narrative since before you were born – it is the narrative that ends up driving the goals that you want today.)
Deb:	I wanted to know what real love was.
David:	(What is the nature of the goal and how it can change – this is all to do with Bs – your A changes according to what this is. That whole notion is an earth shattering notion – you don't ask the person to describe or define because it's an information system.) So where is a space that knows about real love and where would you be?

Deb:	Looking at the sky.
David:	And where is a space where you would be?
Deb:	It wouldn't be raining – standing in the middle of the lawn looking at a clear blue sky.
David:	And is that the space where you should be?
Deb:	Yes.
David:	And is that the right space the question should be in?
Deb:	Maybe it's something closer to me, a flower.
David:	And is that the right space for you?
Deb:	No I've got to be inside and warm. I'm going to bring this flower in. Somewhere quite low [sitting on the floor].
David:	And is that the right place for you to be in?
Deb:	Yes.
David:	And is that the right space for that flower to be in?
Deb:	Yes.
David:	And is that the right distance? And is that the right angle?
Deb:	Yes. It's not really about the space. As long as I'm comfortable temperature wise and not getting rained on. It's more just communing with the flower.
David:	Okay. So what kind of space is the space around that flower?
Deb:	It's held in my hands so it's me around it.
David:	So how old could those hands be that hold that flower?
Deb:	It could even be my grandmother's hands.
David:	And what kind of grandmother was your grandmother that had hands like those hands?
Deb:	One that could have been a flower but did not dare show it.
David:	And is there anything else about a grandmother?

Session with Deborah Henley on Clean Hieroglyphics

Deb:	Untrusting. Guarded. There's some stems inside here, tiny little seedlings like they have the potential to create more life, like ovaries. Sort of like the rest of the world is a womb and this is a tiny little place. Or if it were fertilised it could bring in all sorts of new life.
David:	(That's still an ABC type world so I'm going to pull back again.) So what did you want before you wanted to know the answer to that question?
Deb:	It's something about bringing forth life and if it's okay for me to do that or when it's the right time.
David:	Okay. So is there something that can represent that or is there a space where that could be?
Deb:	The garden is a place which represents that, looking out at the garden from inside.
David:	So whereabouts in the garden?
Deb:	The whole garden.
David:	So where's the space that you could be?
Deb:	In the middle between you, looking out into the garden. [Moves onto sofa looking towards garden].
David:	(Is this scaling life size?) And are you in the right place? And are you at the right angle? And are you at the right distance? And is outside the right place?
Deb:	The board's not in the right place [she moves the flipchart out of the view of the garden]. It's interrupting the view.
David:	And are you at the right angle? And is the distance right between you and outside?
Deb:	The only thing that's not right is that spring is the right time to be thinking of this. [We are in July and it is raining.]
David:	[This is a time thing because outside is frozen in time – somebody's mind has frozen outside to only be in spring. It is strangely scaled temporally, not spatially. So there is another world here that makes time stand still.) So what's outside of this outside and how far does this outside go?

Deb:	Outside this garden in spring is other gardens at other times of year.
David:	And what's outside those other gardens?
Deb:	There's a whole sky full of birds and oceans full of fish.
David:	(This is still strangely scaled because we've reached the fish.) So what did you want before you wanted the garden in spring?
Deb:	I wanted a garden in spring and to know it was the right time to bring a life into the world.
David:	And what did you want before you wanted that?
Deb:	I wanted to express or create something.
David:	So where is something that represents that want?
Deb:	It is actually that painting there [*indicating a painting on the wall*].
David:	And where is a space for you to be when the painting is over there?
Deb:	Standing before it and wanting to paint a painting (*moves to another painting*).
David:	And is that painting in the right place?
Deb:	It can be any painting.
David:	And which is the right space for that painting?
Deb:	I think it would be over – let's use this painting (*picking up a painting and carrying it – holds it half way up a rubber plant stationed in one corner*) I think it's about here.
David:	And is that the right space for that painting? And is that the right height for that painting? And is that the right angle for that painting? And are you in the right space?
Deb:	Yes except my hand should not be holding it.
David:	And are you at the right height? And are you in the right space? And is the painting in the right space? And are you the right distance from the painting? And what kind of space is the space around that painting?

Deb:	There's a tatty old frame.
David:	And what's outside of the tatty old frame?
Deb:	What's happening to me is that Tatty was a friend who was at art school the same time as me, and we were at school together when we were kids, and he came from the Virgin Islands, and I came from Hong Kong. We had both come from a hot wonderful place, so that's the frame in which the wanting to express myself and create was in.
David:	And what kind of a space is a space outside of a tatty framed space?
Deb:	The rest of the world with all its pain and disappointment.
David:	So how big is the space of that world?
Deb:	It's like this house here is the dark rooms and the pain and the garden outside is the happy times.
David:	And how far does that happy world go?
Deb:	The world is full of gardens and outdoor bits and houses and buildings and a mixture of both.
David:	(Note that this is not so strangely scaled any more.) So what did you want before you wanted that?
Deb:	I wanted to be an actress before that.
David:	(Note we have cycled back so this is like a spiral. As we are pulling back it is not going back in a straight line.)
Deb:	I wanted to be an actress.
David:	And where's a space that knows where that want is?
Deb:	It's behind the sofa.
David:	And is there something that represents that want?
Deb:	This space here, cut off from where you are. It's actually my dad's bed.
David:	And is that the right space for your dad's bed to be in? And are you in the right space?

Deb:	Yes I can see the alarm clock and I want to be an actress.
David:	And are you in the right space? And are you at the right angle? And are you at the right height?
Deb:	I should maybe be lower (*sitting down*).
David:	And are you at the right distance? And wanting to be an actress – is that in the right space?
Deb:	It seems to be represented in the alarm clock.
David:	And is that the right distance from you? And is that the right height? And what kind of space is the space that's outside of that alarm clock?
Deb:	The rest of the bedroom.
David:	(Defining parameters of bedroom) And what is outside the rest of the bedroom?
Deb:	It's Strawberry Hill in Hong Kong.
David:	And is there anything else about Strawberry Hill in Hong Kong?
Deb:	It's free and hot and fun and warm, but not in the bedroom
David:	(We're in another world now – B.) So what kind of want was your want before you wanted to be an actress?
Deb:	I wanted to be a vet.
David:	And is there something that represents wanting to be a vet and is there a space that represents that?
Deb:	It might be here with a dog. My dog Hannah [*she picks up a cushion*).
David:	And is that the right space for you? And is that the right space for the dog? And is that the right distance from the dog? And is your body in the right place? So what kind of space is a space that's outside for that dog?
Deb:	The room that I'm in.
David:	And what kind of room is a room that you're in?
Deb:	A normal room with a carpet like this.

David:	And what's outside of that room?
Deb:	The rest of the house.
David:	And what's outside the rest of the house?
Deb:	The garden and the rest of the world.
David:	And what kind of world is the world?
Deb:	A normal world.
David:	(Is it scaling right now? back to B?) So what kind of want was your want before you wanted to be a vet?
Deb:	I didn't really think about it before.
David:	And where is a space that knows you didn't really think about what you wanted, and is there something that represents that?
Deb:	It's just a space of being.
David:	So where is something that represents the space of being and where would you be?
Deb:	I could really be anywhere. Could be… *[she moves to doors looking out at garden)* I could be out here.
David:	And is that the space where you can be? And where is the just being? Is there something that represents that?
Deb:	I am just being here.
David:	(I am trying to force a B in place. What's happening now is that each time we started getting Bs they were getting closer and closer to her, then the actress was close to the alarm clock and the dog was right next to her. Now she's at not wanting anything and she is right where B started, not where A started.) So is that the right space for you? And is there anything that represents being and where would a space be where that would be?
Deb:	This represents being right there and even these flowers represent being too.

David:	(Those were the flowers at the very beginning. Now I can get where A is and I can't get a B. there is a sense of being and the separateness between A, and B is not there anymore.) So what kind of space is the space around you?
Deb:	Ah well, quite normal really.
David:	(She said 'ah well' at the beginning. Things are starting to scale to life size.) So how big is the space that's around the space that you're in?
Deb:	Well, there's the space that my body is in, which is this big, then there's the space of the garden, the space of the garden, the house, the size of Laleham *[the village where this took place – CW]*.
David:	(It's all perfectly scaled, 1:1 – there is no psycho-active space any more that has stuff in it that's not with her. What we've done by pulling back through all the 'Bs' and the 'wants', we've got her in a space where all those lost bits have been accounted for. So we've now gone back through the history of her goals and wants and all that history is what informed the first statement at B. And so in a strange way by going back on the history of B, it's changed the nature of A. Now we'll start the exit of this pulling back exercise.) So what do you know from that space there?
Deb:	That my original quest to discover what people here want has ended in me being in this place and realising it's about being just as we are without any distortion. So that's what I know.
David:	So what does the space around you know? (Hopefully this is a dumb question – if it is scaling right there won't be much.)
Deb:	Everything seems to be being its own thing and is at it is.

David:	(I predicted that is what I was looking for – she has individuated from the ground – she is now separate and independent – parts of her were all over the landscape and now she is just who she is. What that means is we have collected up, and all those bits are integrated in her. Each of the 'wants' is now in here, and they can all now participate in creating a new goal. How we know that is because I can't get any Bs and she is insistent that she is just who she is, and the ground is completely separate. This is the old gestalt thing – the ground fades in and out. And that's what it was at the beginning. There is nothing of her that's out of any of the ground.)
Deb:	Does that mean I can never do this exercise again? If I'm not separating myself out?
David:	This was referring to what you want, so the nature of what you want is not going to create this fracture. So is there anything else you know from that space?
Deb:	That there is beauty in all living things and non-living things – not all of them and not in all living things either – I take that statement back. What else do I know from here? Nothing really. I feel fine.
David:	(This is my exit.) And as we begin to finish this exercise is there any space you would like to go to?
Deb:	To the original A place out of curiosity [*she tries to take original position*].
David:	(I wouldn't be surprised if she cannot get back into it – if she can't she does not have those young kid's legs any more.)
Deb:	[*She assumes the original position.*] I can't really – there doesn't seem to be anything to get from this. It doesn't give me anything.

David:	Okay. And is there any other space you would like to get to?
Deb:	I thought I wanted to get to this place facilitating both this and this, because my original want was to find out about these two client groups, to find out about facilitating both. There doesn't seem to be much information to get from those places. It's not doing anything. It's nice to look at the garden but there doesn't seem to be anything particularly…
David:	(Exit back for reality check.) And where's the space you could be in this room now?
Deb:	I can come and sit there [back on the sofa between us]. I like your luminescent toes [I think this refers to David's socks – CW.] The socks are orange like the post its on the mast).
David:	(Part of reality check. We have to come back to the beginning for the reality check.) What would your goal or objective be now?
Deb:	My goal now would be to… it's all unfolding as it should, but it's the next thing for me to do rather than a goal.
David:	And is there something that represents what the next thing for you to do is and is there a space for you to put it in? Could you write that down?
Deb:	Yes I could put it on the flip chart.
David:	So write it on the flip chart and put it in a space where you would be to that.
Deb:	[Draws a diagram on the flipchart.]

Conclusion

David added: "Theoretically, what I'm going for with this is do the exercises on each goal – for each one we come out and do a reality check. We have come out and challenged the goal. Whatever this goal turns out to be, then you have a much better chance of achieving this, because it is not burdened with all the strange drivers from her past. That means that all of her past history of goals is now encoded in her being and present with her as she writes this one. We have done hieroglyphics, space of B and history of Bs.

GROUP SESSION BY PHONE 15 MARCH 2006 FEATURING CLEAN START AND CLEAN NETWORKS

David conducted this group session by phone without any input from the participants. He paused between each of the instructions or questions below to give people time to write down their answers.

Locate yourself in a space that seems to reflect who you are today.
This could be exactly where you are now or you might want to move around.

Think of what you want to have happen – from a short-term goal to your mission statement in life. Whatever change or outcome you would like to see in your life.

What kind of goal might you have from the space that you are in now?
Now write that statement down, or draw a picture that represents it, or choose an object you can see which represents it. A symbol of your goal.
Whereabouts would you place that goal with respect to the space that you are in now?
Would it be behind, in front, above, below, the other side of the room, in another room?

Group session by phone featuring clean start and clean networks

And is your goal in the right place? Adjust the position if necessary.
And are you in the right place in relation to your goal?
And is the goal at the right height?
And are you at the right height in relation to the goal?
And is the goal facing the right direction?
And are you facing the right direction in relation to your goal?

1. And what do you know about your goal from that… space… there? Write it down. And is there anything else about that? 'That' being what you have just written down. Move within the room or outside it.

2. Is there a space you could move to that knows about what you have written? Move!
And what do you know from that space there?
And does what you know have a size or a shape?
And where is what you know located? Is it in your head, your body or outside you?
Draw a body map and draw the size or shape in its correct position, or write down your answer.

3. And find a space that knows about that. Move!
And what do you know from that space?
And is there anything else about that?
And is there anything else about that?
Write or draw it.

4. And find a space that knows about that.
And what do you know from that space there?
And does it have a size or a shape?
And where is it located?
And is there anything else about it?
Write or draw it.

5. And is there a space that you could move to from that space? Move!
And what do you know from that space?
And is there anything else about that?
Write or draw it.

6. And, as this session draws to a close, is there a space that would like you to move to it?
And what do you know about your goal from that space there?
And what does that space know about you?
And what does your goal know about you?
And what do you know now about yourself and your goal?
And is there anything else you know now?
And what action would you like to take? Be specific – when, where, who – and write it down.
Is there any other space you would like to move to in order to comfortably close this session?

I want to leave everyone in a comfortable space. I can continue with one to one questions now or after this call. Has anyone been left in a place they feel unhappy in?

SESSION WITH ANGELA DUNBAR "I'M GETTING FITTER" FEATURING CLEAN BOUNDARIES

A group telephone session with David Grove on 9th Oct 2006 by Angela Dunbar, narrated by Angela:

In this session, I was working with David Grove as part of a group, this was the first distance-learning version of the Clean Coaching training, and there were six of us in total participating.

Although I have the recording to this call, some of the participants did not want the recording to be passed on to those outside of the training group, so I have transcribed just David's explanations and questions, and my own responses.

The demo was done with all of us as a group, so for much of the time, we just went through the process without feeding back any comments.

[The 'A' and 'B' referred to are explained on page 49]

David:	Write down on that paper a particular goal, or specific issue or problem that you would like to use as your experience as we go through this. You could either write down the words, illustrate it or find an object that is in the room around you that seems to represent the problem. This will be called 'B' your goal which we will coach today. Place the paper or object somewhere in the room that's away from you at a certain distance, and find out where you want to be in respect to the problem. How far is your paper away from you?
Angela:	At the moment, I've placed mine on me. It's on my tummy.
David:	The Clean Start question set will go either to you at A or to the statement at B. So I'll ask these questions, and as you hear them where you feel you need to change something, please go ahead, you don't need to answer: **To B:** So is the statement at the right height? If not, please adjust it. And is the statement at the right angle? And is the statement facing the right direction? And is that the right space for the statement? Take your time to make any changes you need to make. **To A:** And are you in the right space with respect to that statement? If not, then change where you are. And are you at the right height? And are you facing the right direction?

	And are you at the right angle with respect to that statement? And is that the right distance between you and that statement? Do you need to be closer or further away? **To B:** So now that you have changed, is that statement in the right space? If not, then readjust it. And is the statement at the right height? And is the statement at the right angle? And is it at the right distance? So that is a Clean Start. What was your experience?
Angela:	I had to change a couple of things. I had scribbled some words on A4 paper and balanced it on my tummy. But it didn't feel right, it had to be attached in a different way so I wrote it on a yellow sticky. Now it is a little flap tucked into my trousers 90 degrees from my body. My issue is I am getting fatter, so if I stick my stomach out I can see that even more clearly!
David:	You can see the types of coincidences that occur. The circumstances of where you place the statement are often very indicative of the issue you are addressing. How you can begin with almost any client and any issue is by making this simple Clean Start and allowing 10-20 minutes for the person to set it up. Let's make sure:

	To B:
	And is that statement still in the right place? And is it at the right height and is it facing the right direction? If there is anything you need to adjust, then please go ahead and adjust that statement. To A: And are you in the right space? Are you facing the right angle? And are you at the right height? And are your legs and arms facing the right direction and in the right place? Make any adjustments to your body, legs, arms, head. Did anyone have to make any other adjustments?
Angela:	I had to put my hand on my tummy.
David:	Now we will coach the space of B. All the questions will be directed towards the space of B. Then we will find out how that progresses towards the space of D that has other information in it. First we will add what else needs to go in there. And what else could also go on that paper? And are there any other words that also need to be on that paper as well as the ones that you have? And if there are then put those on. And what other words or phrases could there be before the words or phrases you have on that paper? And what words or phrases could there be before these words or phrases?

	And if there are other words or phrases then put them on before the sentence you have got up there. How many were there? And you might also like to put on what other words or phrases can go on the end. And what might the next sentence or paragraph be? And what changes were made in your statement? And are any of the words and sentences going to the edge of the page? If you have any writings or drawings that are really close to the edge, put a piece of paper there. Place a piece of paper there and keep adding what should be on that paper. Sometimes the paper is not big enough to contain all the information. The problem will be limited by the paper, so new information will occur at the top, the bottom or two sides of the paper, and that gets us into the information supplied by D.
Angela:	My piece of paper is quite small because it needs to be portable and attached to me. The statement of the problem 'I'm getting fatter' did not need any more words, as that really says it all. What came before was another 'I'm getting fatter' and I think there are probably about six but I haven't written them out in full.
David:	You will need to write them out in full.
Angela:	I'll need a bigger piece of paper.

David:	Put all those words down in full and follow the angle at which they go up and put the age that is connected with each of those statements. I am expanding the domain of the statement by finding out what are the words before and what are the words after. It helps to set the context of the nature of those words. We are still on coaching the words on the page. Now for the next part we are going to look at the source of those words. Where did those words come from before they were on that paper? And where did those words come from that are on that paper? Did those words come from you and if they did, how old were you when you first had those words? And if they came from someone else, what kind of someone else gave you those words? And who were they? And where did they get those words from? So where did those words come from before you wrote them in that statement? And did they come from you? Or did they come from someone else? Whatever the answer is, either place or draw yourself, or that person, on the same piece of paper or add another piece of paper that's around that.
Angela:	At this point, I drew myself in the words of "I'M GETTING FATTER" I drew me on the "A" of 'FATTER' giving it a head and arms and turning it into a tiny fat person.

David:	As I am coaching where the words come from in the source, I am taking those phrases and asking her to place them on the statement. This then becomes like a very living document. The fact that you repeat something is crucial. What is means is that one of those phrases is not enough.
Angela:	The words came from me. About a year ago. It was going back in two month intervals. I think they are just getting louder.
David:	And where was the original one from?
Angela:	The original was just over a year ago and that was I am in good shape.
David:	So we have coached the words on the page by expanding the context – the words before, the words after, and what was the source of the words before they appeared on the page. Often the goal you have now may not be the goal you had before. The origin of where those words are stored gives you a greater context for the meaning of those words. Now we are going to look at the space around those words or around the statement you have made. In the same way you have a frame round a picture it gives the picture a different perspective And what kind of boundary or edge does that statement and those words have? And as you answer that question, place that boundary or edge on that statement.

And when you have that boundary or edge around that statement:
What kind of space is the space that is around that boundary of that statement?
And what kind of space is the space around the edge of that statement?

And what kind of space is the space that is around the boundary of that statement?
And how big is that space and what are the qualities of that space?
And how far does that space go?
And what kind of boundary or edge does it have?

If you need to redraw or rescale your original statement, please do so. You will have the boundary around the statement, the space and the next boundary.

Now we are going to download information from B. It is similar to visiting an internet site – what does each of those different kinds of spaces know? As you answer, place the answer in each of these spaces. I am going to work from the furthest out boundary to the space in between to the boundary around your words, then the words themselves.

So what does the boundary that is outside of the space that is around your statement know?
And what does that outer edge know?
Place the answer to that question on that page.
And what does the space between those two boundaries know?
And what does that space know?
Place whatever answer seems to be there in that space.

	Now to the boundary around the statement: And what does that edge or boundary know that is around that statement? And what does that boundary know? And what does that statement know now? And what do all those words know now? Place that answer on that statement. And when you have done that, return to your position A and adjust the space between you and the statement so that it feels you are in the right place and the statement is in the right place. Now I am going to download to you at A. For the first time I am going to ask a question with the pronoun you. So what do you know now?
Angela:	All I know now is that it is all a matter of scale. The problem does not seem very big at all now. It seems quite small and so do I.
David:	Place that on the statement. If you need to rewrite it then do so.

Conclusion by Angela:

What I then did was change my little drawing of me to look like a thin person, so scribbled over my "A" until it looked like an "I".

It wasn't until later that I realised my overall statement had changed from "I'M GETTING FATTER" to "I'M GETTING FITTER" which was an absolutely amazing realisation, it was like the letters decided to change the words, and so change my reality.

I lost about two and a half stone over the next year and a half, and started to swim twice a week. This was a totally different behaviour / result for me and one I didn't really feel I had to work on much consciously, the "I'M GETTING FITTER" had a life of its own and just got on with it!

SESSION WITH CLIENT FEATURING CLEAN SPINNING

This is a transcript of a recorded session which took place in August 2005 during a workshop facilitated by David Grove in the garden of the Thatched Cottage. The participants were executive coaches, including the client of this session. David's words are in standard script and the participant's words are in italics. Some of the words were indistinguishable on the recording and where this happened it is stated. David frequently addresses the group rather than the participant, and this shown in brackets.

David:	(Your standard question as coaches would be "What would you like this session to be about today?") So what would you like the session to be about today?
Client:	I've got a pain in my shoulder and around my neck that goes round here and I would like to have an understanding of what that pain is and to be free of it.
David:	So do you have a statement that you can write down about that or have an object that represents that pain?
Client:	I have a statement.

David:	So find a place that seems to be the right place to place that statement and then where might you be with respect to where that statement is? (So she has put it up with a post it note so it actually covers it and as you can see it points right to the t of the pain there. So since we're working with space, we have got to make sure that the space is pretty unclutterable. She does this.) Do you still want that post it note up there? *[Client's response inaudible.]* (So there's a green post it note that's over the top of a piece of paper and the statement is to be free of the pain and have an understanding of what it is. I'm going to move my position so I'm not directly in front of the spaces.) So are you in the right place? And is that statement in the right place?
Client:	It could be bigger but I can work with it like that.
David:	Okay so make it bigger. *[Participant complies.]* So now the writing is bigger. And is that the right size? And is it at the right angle? And is it at the right height? And are you in the right space? And is it at the right height? And is it facing the right direction? And is that the right space for you? And that is the right space for the statement? So what do you know from that space there?
Client:	It makes it real.

Session with Client Featuring Clean Spinning

David:	So what kind of you are you in that space there? [*Client's reply inaudible.*] And how old could that me be that's an anticipatory me? [*Client's reply inaudible.*] And what do you know from that space there as you are now?
Client:	I know that I've got the answers.
David:	Is there anything else you know when you know that you've got the answers?
Client:	I know that I've got the answers but I don't know what they are.
David:	So what kind of space is the space around you when you are as you are now and you know that you've got the answer?
Client:	A fuzzy space.
David:	And it's a fuzzy space. And how big is that fuzzy space that's around you and how far does that fuzzy space go?
Client:	It's a fuzzy space that can change according to what mood I'm in.
David:	And how far does that fuzzy space go when it can change? What kind of boundary or edge does that fuzzy space have depending what kind of mood you're in?
Client:	It can go right out, right to the boundaries of the garden.
David:	And is there anything else about that fuzzy space that can go right out to the boundaries of the garden? [*Client's response inaudible.*] And how old could the I be that's in that fuzzy space depending on whatever mood you're in?
Client:	It's my current age.
David:	Your current age. So what kind of space could this space be that's on the other side of that boundary?

Client:	Older and wiser.
David:	How big is that older and wiser space that is on the other side of the fuzzy space that's on the other side of that boundary?
Client:	That is an infinite space.
David:	And that is an infinite space, and how far does that space go when it's older and wiser?
Client:	There is no boundary on it.
David:	And is there anything else about that older and wiser space that's on the outside of the fuzzy space that depends on whatever mood you're in?
Client:	That there is a lot of unknown-ness about it.
David:	And is there anything else about the unknown-ness?
Client:	That it can be tapped into by different people and at different points in somebody's life.
David:	And what kind of statement is that statement?
Client:	Its' a releasing statement.
David:	And is there anything else about that releasing statement?
Client:	It can be comforting.
David:	And what kind of space is the space that's around that releasing and can be comforting space?
Client:	It's quite a confined space.
David:	And how big is the confined space that is around that comforting statement?
Client:	It's kind of like a bubble.
David:	And what kind of bubble could that bubble be?
Client:	A floaty bubble.
David:	And it's a floaty bubble. And when that's a floaty bubble what kind of space is the space that's outside that floaty bubble?
Client:	It's in between the fuzzy space of me and the wisdom space outside.

Session with Client Featuring Clean Spinning

David:	And how big is that in between space?
Client:	It's a bubble that's on the border.
David:	And what kind of border is that border? And what could that border be made of?
Client:	It's like when two energies meet so it's an energy border.
David:	And is there anything else about that energy border when two energies meet?
Client:	That it can be very strong or it has its weak points.
David:	And what kind of a space is a space that's on the other side of that energy border?
Client:	That's the infinite wisdom space.
David:	And how far does that infinite wisdom space go? What kind of infinity is the infinity that that wisdom space goes to?
Client:	Just a wisdom.
David:	And what kind of wisdom is that wisdom?
Client:	It's unknown.
David:	And that's an unknown wisdom. And what kind of space could the space be that's on the other side of that unknown wisdom?
Client:	It's kind of like molecular space.
David:	And what kind of molecular space could that molecular space be that's on the other side of that unknown wisdom?
Client:	[Client's reply inaudible.]
David:	And is there anything else about that too far away molecular space?
Client:	Curiosity.
David:	And is there anything else about curiosity about that molecular space?
Client:	It's kind of there, but too far away to focus on.

David:	And is there anything else about the too far way to focus on?
Client:	I can't connect to it.
David:	And how far does that molecular space go when you can't connect to it and you can't focus?
Client:	Further and beyond I don't know.
David:	And how far does your I don't know go when it's further and beyond?
Client:	Too far for me to comprehend.
David:	And when it's too far for you to comprehend, what kind of space could the space be that's on the other side of the too far for you to comprehend?
Client:	It's black.
David:	And what kind of black could that black be?
Client:	A soft black.
David:	And that's a soft black. And is there anything else about that soft black?
Client:	There's something in it.
David:	And what kind of something could be in something that is in that soft black?
Client:	Something creative.
David:	And is there anything else about the creative that's in that soft black?
Client:	It's very old or very young.
David:	And is there anything else about that very old or very young that's in that soft black?
Client:	No one's got there yet.
David:	And what kind of space is a space that's on the other side of that?
Client:	It's very light.
David:	And that's very light. And what kind of light?
Client:	Just a shimmering light.

David:	And is there anything else about the shimmering light?
Client:	It's got an energy.
David:	And it's got energy. What kind of energy does that shimmering light have?
Client:	A powerful energy.
David:	And it's a powerful energy. And what does that powerful energy know?
Client:	That everything's for a reason.
David:	And what do you know from that space there now?
Client:	That I need to have this statement there.
David:	And is there a space that you could go to that knows that you need to know about this statement? And what space could you go to that knows also that you need to know that?
Client:	[Client goes to flip chart.] Actually I can't turn this round because of my arm and I need to turn this round.
David:	(That exactly states the problem.) So can you find a space without turning it around or do you need to turn it around? So is there another space you could go to that knows you can't turn that around because of your arm?
Client:	I guess behind [names another participant].
David:	So what do you know from that space there? [She is now about 20 ft back from the statement.]
Client:	That I need to get it sorted.
David:	And is there anything else you know from that space when you need to get it sorted?
Client:	That it's not going to be as hard as I think it is.
David:	And is there anything else you know from that space when you need to get it?
Client:	That I'll have great relief.

David:	Okay. So just turn around a little bit in that space to a different direction. And find out what you know from that direction. *[Client turns.]* Okay. Keep turning around. So what do you know from that direction there?
Client:	It might not matter if I know.
David:	And is there anything else you know from that direction that it might not matter if you know?
Client:	That it would be nice to know.
David:	Okay. And turn around a little further. And what do you know from that direction there? (The angle now is about 45 degrees from the statement and her shoulder is now aligned with the statement.)
Client:	That I'll be able to do more.
David:	And there anything else you know from that direction?
Client:	No.
David:	Okay. Keep turning. (So now we're about 200 degrees all the way around.) So what do you know from that direction there?
Client:	I'm frustrated.
David:	And is there anything else you know when you're frustrated?
Client:	That I'll procrastinate.
David:	Okay. Keep turning. And what do you know from that direction?
Client:	That if I get it sorted, medically or whether *[inaudible]* that I'll have that understanding of what it was.
David:	Keep turning. (It is now about 364 degrees.) What do you know from that direction?
Client:	That I need to do it.
David:	Keep turning. (She is face on now.) And what do you know from that direction there?

Session with Client Featuring Clean Spinning

Client:	That if I get it sorted it will help me in lots of ways.
David:	Okay keep turning. (So that's a first full revolution.) And what do you know from that direction?
Client:	I need to take action.
David:	Okay. And is there anything else you know from that direction?
Client:	Sooner rather than later.
David:	Okay keep turning. And what do you know now from that direction there?
Client:	That I should make an appointment…
David:	(She is back to a 45 degree angle.) Keep turning. (So her face is always directed towards the statement which means there is a lot of space behind her which is uninvolved.)
David:	So what do you know from that direction there?
Client:	That there is a fear whether or not it is going to work.
David:	Okay keep turning. So what do you know from that direction?
Client:	That it could get worse.
David:	Okay keep turning. So what do you know from that direction there?
Client:	That if it does I just need to manage that.
David:	Okay. Keep turning. (Her body is not quite looking at the statement.) So what do you know from that direction there? *[Client's response inaudible.]* Okay keep turning. (Two turns and three quarters.) So what do you know from this direction? *[Client's response inaudible.]* And is there anything else about that fighting? *[Client's response inaudible.]* And is there anything else you know from there in that direction?

Client:	Plants grow and they might be damaged but they still grow.
David	Okay. Keep turning. (She is now about 350 degrees on our third turn.) And what do you know from that direction there [Client's response inaudible.] And life is renewable. Okay. And anything else you know from that direction?
Client:	It needs nurturing.
David:	Okay. Keep turning. And what do you know from that direction there?
Client:	That things have many purposes.
David:	Okay. Keep turning. (So this is about a three and a quarter and a bit turn.) And what do you know from that direction?
Client:	I just need to do it.
David:	Okay keep turning. (Three and three quarters is the first time she's had a position and not looked back at the statement.) And what do you know from that direction there?
Client:	You have to be in the right environment to thrive.
David:	Okay. Keep turning. And what do you know from this direction?
Client:	When you don't have a choice, you feel as though you don't have a choice sometimes, there are still choices there.
David:	(Her body is aligned.) And what do you know from this direction here?
Client:	That you can heal yourself.
David:	Okay. And keep turning. And what do you know from that direction there? (four and a quarter)
Client:	You can put unnecessary barriers up.

David:	And that you can put unnecessary barriers up. (Four and a half turns. For the first time her body is aligned and her head is looking directly opposite the initial statement.) And what do you know from that direction there?
Client:	To have faith.
David:	(Four and a quarter) And what do you know from this direction?
Client:	To trust others.
David:	Okay. Keep turning. (Her body is facing into our first turn, her eyes are looking) *[inaudible]*.
David:	And what do you know from this direction? *[Participant makes a big breath. Her statement is inaudible.]*
David:	Okay. Keep turning. (Four and a quarter) And what do you know from this direction(This is the first time she has looked directly out there and her body is aligned head and shoulders… a little twist to the right.)
Client:	That there's lots of information out there.
David:	Okay. Keep turning. (Four and a half.)
Client:	And what do you know from that direction?
David:	That it's a good feeling to be free.
Client:	Okay. Keep turning. And what do you know from this direction? (Four and three quarters)
David:	That everything has a reason.
Client:	Okay. Keep turning. (Not quite the full turn yet.)
David:	And what do you know from this direction? *[Client's response inaudible.]* Okay. Keep turning. (Starting our sixth turn.) And what do you know from this direction?
Client:	That the sun's a great healer.
David:	Okay. Keep turning. (Six and a quarter.) And what do you know from that direction?

Client:	That there's an awful lot of suffering in this world.
David:	Okay. Keep turning. (Six and a half) And what do you know from this direction there?
Client:	That I'm being stupid.
David:	Okay. Keep turning. (Six and three quarters.) And what do you know from that direction there?
Client:	*[inaudible]* Wide world.
David:	Okay. Keep turning. (She's looking at the statement now.) And what do you know from this direction now?
Client:	I should go and see somebody and just get it sorted and it's no big deal.
David:	So just turn again. (Six+.) So what do you know in this direction? *[Client's response inaudible.]* Okay. Keep turning. And what do you know from that direction there?
Client:	I am sure there are other things I could do.
David:	Okay. Keep turning. And what do you know from that direction? (Six and a half)
Client:	That I need to generally take more action.
David:	(Six and three quarters) And what do you know from this direction? (Her eyes are looking in the foreshortened distance now not the long distance.)
Client:	That I miss travelling.
David:	Okay. Keep turning. (We've done six full turns.) And what do you know now from this direction?
Client:	Travelling used to ground me.
David:	And is there anything else you know?
Client:	*[inaudible]* is quite significant now.

David:	(We've done our Six Degrees of Freedom *[See page 53 for an explanation of the Six Degrees of Freedom – CW]*. One more round.) Keep turning. And what do you know from that direction now?
Client:	That life's too short.
David:	And what do you know from that direction?
Client:	That I can be better than I am at the moment.
David:	Okay. Keep turning. And what do you know from that direction?
Client:	*[Inaudible]* lots of opportunities.
David:	Okay. Keep turning. (We've done seven turns now.) So what do you know from that space there?
Client:	*[Inaudible]* Can be over complicated.
David:	And is there anything else you know?
Client:	That there's nothing to *[inaudible]*.
David:	So what does that statement know in that space now?
Client:	That it doesn't need to be as big as it is and it can just be an action rather than a statement.
David:	So could you re-write that statement? *[Client rewrites the statement]*. The statement now says 'make an appointment to get my arm sorted'. So is there a place you could go to *[inaudible]*. So what do you know now from that space there?
Client:	I just need to do it.
David:	Okay, and is there anything else you know?
Client:	That I have the knowledge.
David:	And what does that new statement know?
Client:	That it's no big deal.

David:	Okay. So is there another space that you would like to go to or another space that would like you to go to it as we begin to finish this part of the session?
Client:	Over there.
David:	('Over there' refers to a direction which is past the chair by about ten feet and lined up with that statement.) So what do you know from that space there?
Client:	That was quite an interesting process.
David:	Is there anything else?
Client:	It has put lots of things into perspective.
David:	Is there any other space you would like to go to?
Client:	No.
David:	So is there a space you could go to, to begin making an action plan or is it the one you're in now?
Client:	[Client's response inaudible.]
David:	So you can do it from wherever.
Client:	The action plan is I need to phone a couple of people that I know who are seeing physios and get their recommendations and make an appointment and get it sorted.
David:	So do you know which people they would be?
Client:	[Client's response inaudible.]
David:	And is there any other action you could do?
Client:	Go back and tell my partner I am doing something about it.
David:	That's a second action. And is there a third?
Client:	To say thank you to David for getting me to this space.
David:	Okay. And is there any other action you could do?
Client:	Just to make time for the appointment.
David:	Okay, so that's four actions. Is there a fifth?

Session with Client Featuring Clean Spinning

Client:	Just to be careful of my arm in the meantime.
David:	Okay. And is there a sixth?
Client:	No.

SESSION WITH LYNN BULLOCK DECEMBER 2007

David:	So what I'm interested in exploring is what I would call 'Visionscapes'. It's a little bit on the 'Perceptualscape' side of things as well, which is how and where you store information on memories and stuff like that, and actually mapping out where these different boundaries are of what you sort of see that's right here, and the sort of real estate that's got taken up through different experiences. One of the common ones is that instead of your past being behind you, some segments of it don't go behind your normal history but they come flying forward and they sit out at awkward angles. They're usually defining moments and so you end up living out the same thing all the time. So I thought what we'd do is look at your sight path and probably just do a 'Bodyscape' of your eyes and where you see around this way, and then we'll just look at what the boundary conditions are. It's mostly a little similar to what you are doing first, except that it's just usually these different lines of sight where you know that there's something there and we can interrogate and get the something. So I think that with a lot of different traumas or experiences your eyes end up holding the information.
Lynn:	OK.

David:	So the conventional path is that either the vision goes or you just don't see stuff, like when you were saying you didn't see [xxx]. So you either fall short or lengthen your vision in order to avoid seeing stuff. So if something bad happened to you and it was three feet away, it's likely that you'll keep that experience stored there and then, of course, as you get more and more stuff stored there then your eyes are less able to function as eyes. But I think there's also this function that we talked about, a symptom called blind sight, when you know something is there but you can't actually see it, but it's like you can... you can see it there. There's all that sort of interesting phenomena.
Lynn:	So you relate it to memory?
David:	Well not to begin with, because it's just related, but if we ask the questions then we often find that there's very, very specific memory, so then we can interrogate these memories and then they drop out and then, all of a sudden, it's not there anymore. So it's the picking up stuff that's out on these. Did you see the session this morning with [xxx]? Well that was the same. She went like this *[gesture]*, then she stood up and went where her daughters were. She had one of the daughters in one spot and her weight was collapsing underneath her, it just drove her to the floor! So she ended up having to sit on the floor and, of course, that changed her sight. Her experience of her daughter was encoded with being on the floor.

	If you're reading at school, and you're told you're stupid or something like that, it goes right back to a specific page of a book when those letters started doing strange stuff. And you try to escape from going out there and you end up going in between the letters, in the holes in the "e"s and just stupid things like that, or inside a period. So I go inside; it's part of a hieroglyphics thing if I'm doing it on what they write down, and then all of a sudden you go in through a full stop and there's a world in there on the other side, you can just travel through it, flow down. Then I have to get them back out of that dissociative world that's inside of that stop, so every time you see a dot, that dot's not just a dot on a page there's a bit of you that's stuck in there, in that little mark and then you're going to get some funny feelings, so it's uncomfortable looking at text and you don't know why it is, but there's something that's warning you about it. I'm also intrigued by the possibility of doing the sorts of things that you're doing, which is to get the stuff that's blighted and then get the stuff that isn't, and then see what can be entrained from the stuff that's working ok, and then educate the other that isn't. Ok so let's start with you. Choose a place in the room and then I'm just going to just take your line of sight and then you can make a map of it. Find the most comfortable place where you're standing or sitting.
Lynn:	In the room?

Session with Lynn Bullock December 2007

David:	Yes, anywhere.
Lynn:	I already found it.
David:	That's great.
David:	So when you look out here, whereabouts do your eyes go?
Lynn:	Over there (points to right and up, corner of ceiling).
David:	How far?
Lynn:	Just as far as the corner.
David:	Ok and what's on the other side of the corner in this direction? Oh gee, that's the damn drawing you just did!! It's wild!!
Lynn:	What drawing?
David:	The eye that you did today was that eye looking up at that angle! I was sitting over there, and I saw the eye looking at me, so that was the eye you drew, the right eye looking up this way, I was at the table this side and when I looked I saw it looking at me.
Lynn:	I don't remember.
David:	Do you not remember playing with the words "Eye see you"?
Lynn:	Yes.
David:	Well you drew an actual eye on the page.
Lynn:	Really? Oh, I don't remember.
David:	Alright. So what's on the boundary between, on that side of the corner and then on this side of the corner?
Lynn:	What's on the boundary?
David:	Yeah what marks out?
Lynn:	There's a little dot (shows a small black mark in the corner of the ceiling).
David:	Ok and what's the difference between the space on that side of the dot and on this side?
Lynn:	This side is darker than the other side.

David:	Now how far around this way do your eyes go? [Points to the opposite direction.]
Lynn:	How far?
David:	Yes.
Lynn:	They go to about here, about arms length [shows to the left and out to the side of herself].
David:	So what's there? How far does it go that way?
Lynn:	I think just about here, now it can go just about to this wall.
David:	It goes from there, and when you come all around this way does it go out the window or just to the wall?
Lynn:	To the wall?
David:	Yes. So if you sweep an arc all the way here, do your eyes freely go all the way through from back there all the way around?
Lynn:	No they kind of go like that [shows the arc]. I can make them go all the way around, but if I don't think about it then they'll go that way.
David:	What is that shape?
Lynn:	What is that shape?
David:	Yes.
Lynn:	A curve.
David:	So what's the curve made of?
Lynn:	What's the curve made of? I don't know.
David:	Ok, So what's on the top of the curve and what's on the bottom?
Lynn:	On the top of the curve there's that dot (points to mark on ceiling).
David:	Yeah.
Lynn:	On the bottom of the curve, there's this foot.
David:	And then this way, past your foot? Or does the curve end at your foot?

Lynn:	No it curves down, and then it goes up.
David:	So where does it go up to?
Lynn:	There [shows on wall to left and slightly behind her].
David:	Up to there. So what's the difference…
Lynn:	[Interrupts] I think it goes to that knob there.
David:	So what's the difference in the curve from that knob to your foot and then from your foot up to that corner?
Lynn:	The distance.
David:	And is there any other differences?
Lynn:	The shape.
David:	Any other?
Lynn:	Ehm… it's as if this is what I can do with my right eye and this is what I can do with my left eye.
David:	[Laughs] I wasn't asking that question.
Lynn:	Yes, and this is itching [points to inside corner of left eye], this is where I had muscle…
David:	[Interrupts] So let's take the itch. What's the first itch?
Lynn:	Itch? Ah! The first itch is a reminder that I had that muscle cut there.
David:	What's the second itch?
Lynn:	Ehm, I think it's the same as the first one.
David:	And what's the third itch?
Lynn:	The third is noticing that if I move my hair out of the way it might not itch.
David:	And what's the fourth itch?
Lynn:	Hmm, a bit of regret.
David:	Ok, the fifth itch?
Lynn:	It's another doubt.
David:	And the sixth itch?
Lynn:	Ehmm… I don't want that doubt (smiles)
David:	Ok rest your eyes for a moment. Then I'd like you to look at the two different curves again.

Lynn:	*[Laughs]* I felt that move down there… look at the two curves again! *[Laughs.]*
David:	Is there any difference between the two curves?
Lynn:	Yeah, it's funny that *[talking of curve on her left side]* can go up to that top knob there now.
David:	What about this other one?
Lynn:	I don't know… it doesn't seem any… maybe it's wider, like I was more thinking of a line.
David:	Yeah.
Lynn:	Now it's more a wider line.
David:	Ok and then this goes up like that… so what about your foot?
Lynn:	My foot?
David:	What's your right foot doing now?
Lynn:	*[Sighs.]*
David:	The curve was at your left foot.
Lynn:	Yes, the low part was at the left foot.
David:	So what's the right foot doing? Put the right foot in *[sings]* it's doing something.
Lynn:	Yeah, it's twitching.
David:	And what's the first thing it knows?
Lynn:	It's twitching.
David:	Ah it's twitching is it? The first twitch?
Lynn:	"Tsch" *[sighing/tutting sound]*.
David:	The second twitch?
Lynn:	*[Chuckles.]*
David:	That's the second one, the third one?
Lynn:	*[Carries on laughing then silence.]*
David:	So what's that?
Lynn:	Ehm, this is the first time that I remember that most of the time when I injured myself it was on the left side, most of the time.

Session with Lynn Bullock December 2007

David:	So what's this now?
Lynn:	I don't know…
David:	Just keep it tapping [talking about the foot].
Lynn:	…some kind of impatience.
David:	So what is it now?
Lynn:	Impatience still.
David:	More impatience?
Lynn:	[Acknowledging sound.]
David:	Ok keep doing it. What's that?
Lynn:	That was the pain.
David:	So what's your foot doing now?
Lynn:	[Pause] I don't really know how to keep still, I think.
David:	No, keep moving, keep the foot going, I'll ask different questions, if it's got more in it then I'll check.
Lynn:	[Continues movement of foot.]
David:	Now keep the foot moving and then is there any difference now between these two curves?
Lynn:	Between the two…?
David:	The two curves… this curve got wider last time [points to curve going up and to the right of Lynn].
Lynn:	No it's like as if this curve doesn't start here anymore it starts here now, then it goes kind of like out… it goes out then it still gets to that point but I don't know how.
David:	That's alright. And what about the curve going up to the top knob there?
Lynn:	[Laughs.] That one there [points but doesn't look].
David:	The one that you're not going to look at.
Lynn:	[Laughs again.]
David:	So I know it's there, but you don't have to look at it.
Lynn:	I don't have to look at it… OK!
David:	Yeah, so just keep looking this way, but keep that right foot moving.

Lynn:	[Acknowledges.]
David:	I'm going to go with that [talking of right foot]. So what's this now? What tapping is this?
Lynn:	It's keep moving.
David:	So keep moving And your fingers?
Lynn:	That's the music.
David:	Ok. So what music is that tapping to?
Lynn:	Well it coordinates and then I get a song in my head.
David:	Ok so what's your song?
Lynn:	It's like a marching band song.
David:	Ok, keep it going, keep your fingers going.
Lynn:	[Laughs.] I don't know where that came from.
David:	So as your feet are going, your fingers are going and there's a marching song, what's happening to that curve?
Lynn:	It's getting wider and wider.
David:	Is it still connected to that foot?
Lynn:	Yes. [Silence.]
David:	Getting wider?
Lynn:	[Acknowledges.]
David:	Just keep the hand moving, the song going, is it the same marching song or different?
Lynn:	Different.
David:	Yeah [laughs] it's syncopated, this ain't no marching band! I can tell when it's marching and when it's not (laughs more). It's fantastic because it's just so emblematic of you be-bopping around, you know, with your music on, and that's what's encoded in it, it's pleasing to see this is a direct relationship between your psyche and music. Now the other foot's going.
Lynn:	Yeah.
David:	So can you yet see the other curve or is it still just as…

Lynn:	Well there's like another curve opening up, like a sideways curve.
David:	Ok, and is the original one still there or not there?
Lynn:	Yeah *[Laughs and chuckles]*.
David:	We'll just take the "yeah" I know a glance and that's enough.
Lynn:	*[Laughs more.]*
David:	So just keep looking away, just keep that going… So if you have to change positions or you need to move, you know then just get the movement, keep going…
Lynn:	Yeah.
David:	…and yeah the movement, it's fine to move from the couch or whatever intuitively you think your eye wants to do then just go there and tell me when the music changes.
Lynn:	It changed.
David:	So now what is it?
Lynn:	Bom bom tada bom, bom bom tada bom, bom bom tada bom… *[Silence.]*
David:	So what happened then?
Lynn:	I saw something new.
David:	Ok, so where are our curves? Is the something new related to any of the curves?
Lynn:	No it's like this curve's come round here, but then when I look at the lines on that chair then I get double vision back.
David:	Double vision?
Lynn:	Yes.
David:	Ok, So what's the first vision of the double vision?
Lynn:	Well it's either or.
David:	Ok and what's the second vision of the double vision?

Lynn:	The same…without going to touch, I don't know which is the real one and which is the double one.
David:	Ok, so does that finger want to go and touch it?
Lynn:	*[Small laugh]* No.
David:	So what does the either or want to do?
Lynn:	I don't know.
David:	So what's it doing now?
Lynn:	It's pushing me away.
David:	Ok, which direction does it want to push you?
Lynn:	That way.
David:	So how far that way does it want to push you?
Lynn:	I don't know.
David:	Ok we'll find out.
Lynn:	I don't know whether I want it to let me be pushed.
David:	It's too late now, you're already being pushed.
Lynn:	No it wants to push me.
David:	You said it is pushing me.
Lynn:	Ah.
David:	I know the difference. It's debatable as to whether that it's going to be able to continue pushing you but the fact that that's pushed you is not debatable.
Lynn:	I won't allow it to push me.
David:	Anymore.
Lynn:	Anymore.
David:	So how far does it want to push you and where does it want to push you to?
Lynn:	Ehmm… it does need to push me… it doesn't need to push me because now when I look this way I see double also *[laughs]*.
David:	So now what does it want to do now you can see double?

Session with Lynn Bullock December 2007

Lynn:	Ehmm, it's like… I feel as if I'm going round in circles it's as if it's, it wants to remind me that I forget, and at the moment everything is like reminding me that I forget.
David:	So that's the first thing that it wants, what's the second?
Lynn:	Ehmm… I don't know.
David:	What's the third?
Lynn:	*[Silence.]*
David:	What's the fourth?
Lynn:	*[Gestures and moves.]* Hang on I'm going to take its… and it doesn't have to… any more.
David:	Where are the hands going to go? You crossed your hands over… no they want to go this way.
Lynn:	They can't do that, that's really not a good idea.
David:	So where does that go to? Have you got it?
Lynn:	Yeah, yeah OK.
David:	So what space do you need to be in now?
Lynn:	Yeah, I'd better get a look from a different direction *[moves]* before it gets intense.
David:	It's going to get you in, but there is also a way out.
Lynn:	Yep.
David:	So that's why I'm not on your side, I'm on that side, and that and that, so you see at the moment we are distal shaking the proximal. *[This is a reference to involuntary movement of muscle groups.]*
Lynn:	It's like there's a compulsion to go there, so I get rid of it so I don't see it, but as soon as I get here I want to go there, but as soon as I'm there then there is no way I'm staying there.
David:	That's alright; we'll go there and not stay there.
Lynn:	It's really weird.
David:	That's why I crossed your hands over because I saw them go and you saw the reactions. So you can go there in six steps or you can go there any other way.

321

Lynn:	Yeah, well if I sit on it then I don't have to see it [*moves*].
David:	I don't care if you see; I'm just watching your hands, keep doing that.
Lynn:	That? [*Gesture of moving the arms to cross the hands over in front of body.*]
David:	No Stand up, and just keep your hands crossing over, that's it, they look like they might be cross over behind too.
Lynn:	Yeah.
David:	So let your hands do this thing.
Lynn:	This is bad memory.
David:	That's alright just keep moving.
Lynn:	This is hard work, you know?
David:	Just step out of it… as long as you keep that moving you can just step right out and rest, just keep your hands moving, alright?
Lynn:	Yes.
David:	Yeah, just let them cross over, that's the movement that's going to do it.
Lynn:	This movement?
David:	Yeah, or any crossing over, that's what your eyes were doing.
Lynn:	Or not doing.
David:	Yeah well before…
Lynn:	Ok.
David:	Do you want a rest space?
Lynn:	No
David:	So where else do you not want to go?
Lynn:	Where do I not want to go?
David:	Yeah.
Lynn:	I don't want to go over there.
David:	Alright, anywhere else you don't want to go?

Lynn:	Further back than you.
David:	Ok that's the second, the third place you don't want to go?
Lynn:	[Looks somewhere.]
David:	That's a different place, that's three there isn't it?
Lynn:	Yeah, behind.
David:	It's behind. OK any other place you don't want to go?
Lynn:	I wouldn't go under there.
David:	Ok the fourth, anywhere else?
Lynn:	I wouldn't go anywhere near there, that green thing there.
David:	Ok so what position is this?
Lynn:	Dunno.
David:	Is it different sitting more forward than sitting back?
Lynn:	Yeah.
David:	This is more back?
Lynn:	No ehm Yeah.
David:	So what do you know from here now?
Lynn:	[Silence.]
David:	Let's take that right foot, what does that right foot know now?
Lynn:	It knows that I've just got a little bit of pain here right now and if it moves a little bit then maybe the pain will go and…
David:	So what do the hands know? That one that's not pointing there [laughs loudly].
Lynn:	[Laughs] I thought this was a Clean process! This one is reminding me "ah ho!"
David:	[Laughs more and more.] Absolutely and I know that it's reminding you, that's why I said, "What is it not reminding you that's not over there?"

Lynn:	It's like no matter how much you try not be yourself you end up being yourself.
David:	Yeah. So what do your feet know about that…? Move your feet again like that, on your toes and swing your heels again, move that one to here and back this way, keep that moving. So what do your eyes know now? What does your left eye know?
Lynn:	The left eye, it knows something but… it knows… ah… it what it doesn't know that's more.
David:	What does the right eye know?
Lynn:	[Yawns.]
David:	Ok, so what's the difference between the curves now?
Lynn:	Curves… curves…? Something with the curves… yes, this one doesn't go so far.
David:	OK, What about the one that went up the top there?
Lynn:	Gone.
David:	It's not there? And this one here is it still there?
Lynn:	It's still there.
David:	What quality is it now?
Lynn:	It's faster.
David:	As wide?
Lynn:	No.
David:	OK, What can you say is over there?
Lynn:	There? [Chuckles.]
David:	Yeah, that's how it started; it knows that that's there [laughs] we're just pretending that you don't know that that's there.
Lynn:	I can pretend well, OK.
David:	There's two of us pretending, OK?
Lynn:	Yeah, can we pretend a long time?

David:	Well I am, I'm pretending, it's pretending but it's not pretending as much as we are…
Lynn:	No it's not pretending.
David:	No it's not.
Lynn:	I know what I'm going to do, I don't know whether this is allowed.
David:	Just follow that finger.
Lynn:	[Moves things around.]
David:	You go over there and stand in the place of the chair and see what's in that place.
Lynn:	[Laughs.]
David:	What's there? And turn around, it'll be very interesting which way you choose to turn… it's like I'm getting all my revenge, this is fantastic, if I look like I'm enjoying it, I am exceedingly enjoying it.
Lynn:	How many times have I turned round, about three?
David:	It looks like you are until you stop.
Lynn:	[Carries on turning around.]
David:	Just keep going until you stop in a direction. So what do you know from that position, that direction?
Lynn:	I'm still not looking that way [laughs].
David:	And your finger's still pointing where you're not looking [loud laughs] only this time, let me tell you why you're in trouble, both fingers are pointing, just in case you didn't realise it with one, the other finger has joined in [laughs and laughs]. It's just so fantastic! So what do you know now?
Lynn:	I still know where I don't look.
David:	You what?
Lynn:	I still know where I don't look.
David:	Yeah, that's alright, keep turning.
Lynn:	[Turns.]

David:	Yeah, keep turning at any moment you want to, any moment that you want to turn around.
Lynn:	*[Turns.]*
David:	What's that doing a larger circle like that? Just let your feet keep taking you until they stop.
Lynn:	*[Keeps turning then stops.]*
David:	So what do your feet know now?
Lynn:	*[Silence then smiles and laughs.]*
David:	What do your thumbs know?
Lynn:	They're holding the fingers *[laughs]*.
David:	*[Loud laughing.]* The fingers are still pointing, I could see they're bent like this they weren't just crossing over and going the other way.
Lynn:	I can't even do it again like that.
David:	Yeah , I know, that's why I looked this is going like this, but underneath I could see this finger, it's not doing that but it's pointing this way, so one's going this way one's going that way (laughs). So your feet have brought you here, what do you know from here?
Lynn:	This is an angle where I can look at it.
David:	And what's on the other side of the other angle?
Lynn:	What angle?
David:	Well there's an angle here and over here or back there, so I'm wanting to contrast the twp of them.
Lynn:	That's an easy range, I can see it from here too, I can see it from the back (looks around herself to the right and can see from her right what was previously on the left).
David:	Oh my goodness, yeah.
Lynn:	So I don't have to go this way, I can go here.
David:	And what's the first thing you see this other way?

Session with Lynn Bullock December 2007

Lynn:	The first thing I see this way…? This *[points to something in the room]*.
David:	And the second thing?
Lynn:	I see the mat.
David:	And the third thing?
Lynn:	This that's just behind the chair.
David:	And the fourth thing?
Lynn:	I see you… that's a wobble!!!
David:	Yeah that's right… and the fifth thing?
Lynn:	Well I still see the chair and I see you through the chair.
David:	Well yeah to see me you had to see through the chair And the sixth?
Lynn:	I see you and I see the table and I see the chair and I see the mat.
David:	That's quadruple vision there then isn't it? There are four things. So what do you know now?
Lynn:	I turn better this way, than before.
David:	First turn better?
Lynn:	*[Mutters something.]*
David:	What's the second turn that's better?
Lynn:	Ah, it's the looking.
David:	And what's the third turn that's better?
Lynn:	*[Sighs.]*
David:	And the fourth turn?
Lynn:	I go back this way…
David:	Yeah.
Lynn:	It's as if I have to go this way so I can go that way.
David:	That's your fifth.
Lynn:	If I keep going this way then I get stuck.
David:	Ok… I learned some of that stuff, I can't remember where now And what's the sixth turn that's better?

Lynn:	The what? I don't have to go down, I can stay up.
David:	So what do your eyes know now?
Lynn:	The preference is that way.
David:	And your right eye?
Lynn:	It's as if ehm…
David:	So keep that finger going.
Lynn:	It's as if this thinks, this eye thinks it holds the whole picture but it doesn't want to let the other eye in.
David:	Yep, keep that finger going, the next thing?
Lynn:	I surprise myself sometimes by actually seeing more with the other eye.
David:	The next thing? And keep the finger going.
Lynn:	That's all.
David:	So what does your left eye know now?
Lynn:	I don't know.
David:	So just for the moment what would be a good Feldenkrais thing to do, just with your eyes or with your eye help some kind of integration, would you sit down or lie down or stay standing and… I don't know.
Lynn:	[Sits down and palms eyes with hands.]
David:	So just stay there and rest for a while. [After a few minutes.] So what's there now?
Lynn:	[Tone of voice very different, calm and smooth.] I'm remembering some of the strategies I used to start to be able to coordinate the movements of the eyes and one of them is using imagining the eyes elsewhere, like rocking the heels it's like the eyes moving and if you can really and if I can get that co-ordinately then I thought then one day that will tell the eyes what to do, same for the elbows and the knees and the hip joints, so all that is very present now.
David:	So what are your eyes doing now?

Session with Lynn Bullock December 2007

Lynn:	They're beginning to coordinate again.
David:	So what's the first thing they're beginning to coordinate?
Lynn:	Hmm it's like hmm it's like it takes so little for the coordination not to be there so I use other resources and that's ok and... hmm... you know, any kind of awareness of not being completely in the present moment like fucks it all up.
David:	Well part of what we're doing is perturbing the system again because we're going in and taking away that which you had to adapt to, so it will mess up your adaptive process.
Lynn:	Yes.
David:	But it will also mean that then what you have to readapt to will be much simpler than what you had to as we unload all this other stuff that your eyes had kept, so for example, how far can you look now to the left?
Lynn:	About there.
David:	So where can you look and where can't you?
Lynn:	I can look from here.
David:	So you can look from here and past, so you can look at the chair?
Lynn:	Yep.
David:	So that's ok and you can look all the way past the foot?
Lynn:	Yes, though, you see, as soon as I do that, when I come back to it, it doesn't come back, it opens out.
David:	A little bit further?
Lynn:	Yes.
David:	So just keep going back that way. Does it open further out to your left or to your right?
Lynn:	It opens out further to the left.

David:	And what does it do with the right?
Lynn:	It opens.
David:	So what happens when you keep doing it?
Lynn:	I get my peripheral vision back this side.
David:	And can you keep looking further round to the right rather than…? Just take your time to see which way you'll get further around there, going to the right or going to the left and then if you wouldn't mind just turning yourself upside down. If you lay on the floor or you can lie on the couch, I just want you to put your head so you're looking around. Flip yourself, put your feet up. Lay here, put your feet up and come down here then drop your head.
Lynn:	[Turns with head upside down, feet up.]
David:	Ok? I want you to see the same scene… if I had my gyroscope… So see what your eyes do with the boundary condition left or right. So just keep rotating around and see how it goes.
Lynn:	Can I have a cushion?
David:	Yes.
Lynn:	It would be so much easier to just be upside down.
David:	Why do you think I have a gyroscope? Just do the same thing, how could you realise the depth that way, so you've got to decide which way is it now? Is that stuff that was over there, is it still over there that way or is it actually over there now so you've got to let your eyes kind of figure that out?

At this point Silvie de Clerck comes in and asks "Ca va?" Lynn replies, "Yes, it's Clean Yoga!" Then the phone rings and David leaves the room.

Lynn:	Please can I come up? I must be mad, must be mad must be really mad! [Stays lying upside down. Then David comes back with Jennifer de Gandt.]
David:	Here, have you met my Lynn it's a different version than yours [Lynn is still lying upside down]. Oh yes, here the Lynn, the upside down Lynn.
Lynn:	We would do anything for science.
Jennifer:	Yes, anything, that's right.
David:	So what's the difference? So where's the stuff you can't look at that way? Is it still that way?
Lynn:	No.
David:	Is it that way? So how much of it is it that way now compared to how it was the other way?
Lynn:	What was the question again?
David:	Which way is the stuff that you can't look at and how much is there compared to when you couldn't look at it sitting up? Is it over on that direction?
Lynn:	No it's not.
David:	So where is it then?
Lynn:	It's over there.
David:	So how much of it is over there?
Lynn:	About probably half of it.
David:	Ok and what's different with it being over here than being over the other side?
Lynn:	It's easier to ignore.
David:	What's your tummy doing now?
Lynn:	It's getting bare!

Jennifer:	Yes it is! Mind the gap.
David:	I don't mind the gap at all!
Lynn:	Well I do!
Lynn:	I've had enough of that, sits back up.
David:	So what if you go that end and put your head down [*talking about lying on the sofa in a different direction hanging the head upside down*], where does that where you can't see go? Where is what you can't see now? Over there? [*Laughs, explaining to Jennifer about the fingers pointing.*] Just take your time to let the nervous system integrate [*mocking*]. [*To Jennifer*] After all the things she's been doing to me this week I've been having my day, and I have a glee on my face I can't put away, it's a great revenge! [*To Lynn*] It's making your eye quite red, do you need a rest?
Lynn:	Can you give me my eyesight back?
David:	No that's going to be, there's going to be an adaptive phase now. So do you need to rest your eyes do you want to go and have a real lie down?
Lynn:	No.
David:	So what's there now?
Lynn:	A bit of blur.
David:	A bit of blur? Oasis. this blur?
Lynn:	No, no rock bands.
David:	[*Laughs.*] How you doing?
Lynn:	OK.

David:	OK so what's the difference between your left eye and your right eye now? Are they both equally blurred or is one more blurred than the other?
Lynn:	The right eye's more blurred than the left.
David:	The right eye's more blurred? Sure.
Lynn:	This way is much clearer than that way.
David:	Is it?
Lynn:	When I look that way, I remember the sound of like a, the wind through the trees, through the bushes, and like the sound can… comes from here, comes from here as I look there.
David:	So is the sound moving or is the look moving?
Lynn:	The sound's moving.
David:	Which direction is it moving?
Lynn:	It's coming from there and it goes wwhffff!
David:	So what happens after it arrives over there?
Lynn:	It starts again.
David:	How many times will it do that?
Lynn:	I don't know?
David:	Three times?
Lynn:	Five times.
David:	And what happens at the sixth time?
Lynn:	On the sixth time say No.
David:	Say no, so what's there now?
Lynn:	Fingers are going this way and this way.
David:	Exactly, and what are the eyes doing?
Lynn:	Still going this way and it cricks my neck when it goes.
David:	That's alright I don't care about that. So how are your eyes now?
Lynn:	Not quite so blurry.

David:	Are your fingers happy?
Lynn:	I think so.
David:	And is there anything else they want to do, the fingers?
Lynn:	[Laughs.]
David:	Are you alright? Alright?
Lynn:	Yep OK.
David:	So we'll just check a couple of things, do you want to put this chair back?
Lynn:	[Moves furniture back.]
David:	How's that up there? [points to right top corner of ceiling.]
Lynn:	I can't see the spot anymore.
David:	And that curve? [Pointing to perceptual curve that was on L's left at beginning of session.]
Lynn:	It's not there anymore.
David:	And your eyesight?
Lynn:	[Moves.]
David:	Swing all the way the other way, no rotate, keep going around.
Lynn:	[turns round and round.]
David:	So what's there now?
Lynn:	[Sighs.]
David:	Any double vision over there?
Lynn:	[Silence.]
David:	So how are you doing?
Lynn:	OK.
David:	How are your eyes?
Lynn:	A bit wobbly.
David:	In which direction? Do they want to close?
Lynn:	Hmmm. It's like they're not settled.

David:	OK so what needs to happen for them to be able to settle and how long are they going to wobble?
Lynn:	*[Silence.]*
David:	So just let them keep wobbling. Still wobbling?
Lynn:	Hmmm.
David:	Are you alright sitting there? Do you want to lie down? You see we've been and got an over compensation from the right eye for the left eye and also a download of quite a bit of stuff out of that left corner and a whole bit of curve has been put on that left side and some more on the right. So it's going to take a bit of adapting to this and the same.
Lynn:	I must look a bit like that, I think, I feel as if like. *[Shows gesture.]*
David:	I think your left eye has quite a different issue now than your right eye now so there's this funny fight that's gone on between the two, and the right one's won. And now, because we started with the left side, it's carrying all this other stuff. Now it actually has the capacity to, you know, to see, whereas before most of its capacity was not to see all those years. And this I think is where part of the crossing over of that was occurring, so we've just sort of started a little bit into this so for while. We'll have to let you into rest space, I think. So you will have to work a bit again like you did at the beginning, maybe the same. This thing here might work just to adapt a bit, but my guess is it should take a lot less to adapt as there's less to compensate for.

	So, you do what your eyes need to do, and I'll come back to check up on you. So if you just need to stay there, stay there or you can go and lie down in the bedroom if you wish, but for the moment just let them adapt.

NB: Scar tissue in L's left eye swelled up during the session and became extremely red. It took approx 24 hours for the swelling and redness to go.

Finding the way to be able to see enough for reading and getting around without help from others took a few days adaptation helped by using movement and Feldenkrais… essential follow up, I think to integrate the changes and new possibilities of perception.

Lynn Bullock
www.lynnbullock.com

GROUP SESSION BY PHONE OCTOBER 2006 FEATURING CLEAN NETWORKS

This session formed part of a distance course which David Grove was delivering by telephone with Carol Wilson and Angela Dunbar

David:	C is the space between A and B. In C are things which may stop you from achieving your goal. Either you can move towards your goal or it can move towards you. Systemically at the moment we are looking at these pieces of information, ie you at A is only one part of the system. There is information in you and the spaces around you. If I only limit my questions to address you I have the least useful information. In fact the spaces at B and around B have a lot more information than you have. Information is coming outside of you or outside of the box. If you think that there is the degree of distance between you and your goal is inhabited by the kinds of information memories or experiences which don't want you to have that goal or are saying this is the wrong goal or it is unachievable.

	On the map I call this the small World Network. D is the boundary condition of anything that is not inside A, B and C. The question is how do we get that information out? We can expand space out, find the pronouns at A. Now we will look at how to get the information out of C and D. We will do the starting conditions again, where you are at A, and placing your Mission Statement at B. Then we will do six spatial movements. If you imagine that between A and B is the egg shaped world, when you walk and move to these different spaces your intuition will guide you. When I ask the question "is there another space you can go to?" intuitively you will say no but your feet will start moving and will know when to stop. I will ask "What do you know from that space there?" and you can download the information from that space. There will be six spaces and the seventh one will be the download one, "What do you know now?" • You can either start a new starting condition, write out a new statement. • Alternatively you can use your original B statement and place that at B. • Thirdly, if you are interested in having something happen to your pronouns, the space of A, you can place your pronouns in the room and they will become B. Place your choice in the B space, and then place yourself at the right distance from B.
Steve:	I have chosen a new issue. My big challenge with this whole exercise is that I can't readily wander round the room because of the telephone and my first problem – the mess the room is in. it is not a big room.

David:	You may have to find you go out. Get a long extension cord, first of all, then move without your headset on and come back to it.
Paul:	I am about ten feet away from my statement which is on a whiteboard.
Angela:	My original problem was 'I'm getting fatter', which changed to 'I'm getting fitter'. I felt very congruent, so did 'me' and my 'you'. From exploring my other pronouns, my spiritual part was all about growing! 'Myself' was about protecting and felt I needed to contract. My mission is to explore expanding and contracting. I have written the words and put them in a place three feet in front of me.
David:	And is that statement in the right place? And is it at the right height? And is it facing the right direction? And is it at the right angle? And is the difference between you and that statement the right distance? If that needs any changing then please adjust the spatial element of the statement And are you in the right place And are you at the right height? And are you facing the right direction? And are you at the right angle? And are you at the right distance between you and the statement? And what do you know from that space there?
Paul:	B is a major priority for my future development.
Angela:	It's a cycle like breathing and both regulate the other. Both regulate each other.

David:	Write both down. Write down every word as it is said. That gives you the limit of your knowledge – that is what you know in this moment, this day, right here in that room.
Steve:	This problem is deeply embedded in me.
David:	Is there another space that you could go to from that space there? And what do you know from that space there?
Paul:	The problem is less clear from where I'm now standing
Steve:	I'm looking at it from further away. The problem feels more remote because it is physically.
Angela:	It is upside down now. It's natural and like something I've given birth to.
David:	And is there another space you could go to from that space there? And what do you know from that space there?
Paul:	The further away I get the less significant dealing with it becomes.
Steve:	I too have got further away from my issue. It's not only less significant but I am less connected with it.
Angela:	It's at the side of me now and I am viewing it as a friend. I am seeing the connection between the two words expanding and contracting and the yin and yang symbol is coming to mind
David:	That is the information downloaded from the space of two. And is there another space that you could go to from that space there? And what do you know from that space there?
Paul:	When I'm completely aligned with it, the further away I get from it it diminishes with its importance
Steve:	I have brought mine back close to me but in a different place this time. I've still got this sense of disconnection but it's um

Angela:	I'm further away from it and looking onto it. I'm getting a sense of the yin yang cycle rotating around and it feels fluid and peaceful.
David:	And is there another space that you could go to from that space there? And what do you know from that space there?
Paul:	I'm right in front of it.
Angela:	I've positioned myself so it's slightly hidden from my view. I can't see it but I recognise it is easy to be distracted and I can feel it even if I can't see it.
David:	And is there another space that you could go to from that space there? And what do you know from that space there?
Paul:	If I could hide the evidence of the problem I could ignore it temporarily.
Steve:	I am now sitting on the problem and it feels even more connected with it
Angela:	I was drawn to move to the window with the big wide world outside and realised it is not over there at all but here with me.
David:	And is there another space that you could go to from that space there? And what do you know from that space there?
Paul:	The nearer I am, the clearer it is.
Steve:	I tried putting mine in the bin this time but it can't easily be gotten rid of
Angela:	I'm right next to it now and I know it's always with me. Sometimes it moves at different speeds and sometimes I might not recognise it but it's always there.

David:	That's our six different spaces we've moved you to and downloaded the information. And what do you know now? Any information you have picked up by going to these spaces then your statement will have changed in some way. Either you need to redefine it, so when you answer this question, then I'd like you to also change what you might need to do with your B statement. Also to compare your answer to this question with your initial question you wrote down. And what do you know now?
Paul:	What I know now is that I must focus on it.
David:	Your original statement was this is a major problem for me. Make any changes you need to make
Steve:	It is not of me but with me
David:	Your original knowledge was the problem is deeply embedded. Change that statement and paste it up either in the same space or a new space.
Angela:	I know that I can trust these parts of myself and trust the cycle. What I could do is find ways to regulate the speed of this particularly cycle. Instead of the words I just want the yin yang symbol now. My original download statement was it's a cycle like breathing; both regulate the other and each other.
David:	You have come out with the yin yang which is very complementary to that statement.
Angela:	The additional understanding is that the cycle doesn't flow at the same speed all the time.

David:	Place the adjusted B statement either in the same space or where you want it. Then find your A space with respect to where you've moved the B. it might be the same or different. Make sure that B is in the right space and you're in the right space. We will do one more round with the questions. Then I will move you to the spaces but won't ask you what you know until you get to after the sixth space. Make sure you are in the right space and B is in the right space. What do you know now?
Paul:	I am much clearer about what I need to do with respect to the goal.
Steve:	I wish I knew. This is something I have to banish
Angela:	It cycles anti clockwise
David:	We will go through the six spaces again. You can answer the questions as we go through but I won't ask you for the answers out loud. And is there another space that you could go to from that space there? And what do you know from that space there? And is there another space that you could go to from that space there? And what do you know from that space there? And is there another space that you could go to from that space there? And what do you know from that space there? And is there another space that you could go to from that space there? And what do you know from that space there? And is there another space that you could go to from that space there?

	And what do you know from that space there?
	And is there another space that you could go to from that space there?
	And what do you know from that space there?
	And what do you know now?
Paul:	I need to see it clearly, keep it in perspective and work at it.
David:	Your second download was 'I'm much clearer'. Make any changes you need to make to your statement that reflects that knowledge.
Steve:	This is something I have to beat.
David:	So it hasn't changed?
Angela:	I'm finding it difficult to put into words but it is about understanding that you can develop and grow but actually stay the same.
David:	Change anything that reflects that sentiment on your B statement.
	What we have done is two rounds of a Clean Network in which you have moved around in two sets of six spaces. For complicated things you would want to get six sets of six until there is nothing more there and no other spaces they could go to. This is one of the techniques to begin with – how to deal with the information at B. Once you move outside that boundary you are picking up stuff at the space of C and D and that changes your point of view on the nature or issue. Also because you are physically moving it changes you at A because you have to move to the other spaces and relate to these points of view. You are making a system of all the types of information and letting each space inform you with the different knowledge and wisdom that each space has.

Group Session by Phone October 2006 Demonstrating Clean Networks

Paul:	At the end of each session, should we rewrite B completely?
David:	That's what you have to work out each time. If you are not sure then you leave it there. The important thing about a network is that you have to go through all the different conundrums before you arrive at somewhere where you might be sure.
Angela:	I'm more comfortable moving around but working on the two dimensions isn't enough – sometimes I wanted to be high and a long way below
David:	When you are taking a client through and you see their eyes look up, it is an indication that they need to get higher – some therapists have ladders in their offices so you can stand up that bit higher. You will see a stunning change when they get to the right height. Sometimes you need to lie on the floor to get underneath, or go to the floor below and look up that way. When you get complicated things moving spaces gives perspective. Sometimes people have to go outside the door. If it is too dangerous to let them go out to the space they want there are alternative interventions. You can get amazing results by getting the space exactly right.
Steve:	Could you do this by asking people to go to spaces in their minds, not physically?
David:	Their minds are what have constrained their view of the world. You would end up with another mind game. The difference with spatial is that your mind may not want to go there but your body does. Decisions are made in your heart, gut and joints and mouth. If you can only make decisions that go into words you can only do things that can be put into words. What instinctively wants to participate

	is the rest of your body – if you make a decision with your head and your heart can't get involved, then you're not going to reach the goal. If you allow your body to override your head your wisdom in your body makes the decision. From the pathway that you made in these moves you will see that there are spaces that want to distance you from achieving that goal.
Angela:	When I am in a situation where it is not possible to get the person to stand up and walk around, could I have them pick an object to describe their B, and pick another object to represent their A, and have them move the objects around?
David:	No. When you put two objects in the place the client will not get the experience. When your body has to move you are more associated. They won't have the neurology and whole hormone system of their body get involved. You can ask a question of a proxy space, for example: "Knowing that you want to stand on that ledge above the street, is there another space you could go to instead that can represent that space?" So the space chooses another space. People's information is not necessarily in their body – it is spread all over the place. If you leave them at A all the stuff lying around, particularly at B, C and D, will not be available to them at A. When they move away from A they are not quite the same person any more.

PART SIX

LIST OF BOOKS, VIDEOS AND WEBSITES

BOOKS AND ARTICLES ABOUT DAVID GROVE'S CLEAN WORK

Capurro, M.C., (2012), *Il Clean Coaching: Come Sfruttare il Pensiero Metaforico per Facilitare il Cliente a Trovare Risposte e Soluzioni in Modo del tutto Naturale*. Bruno Editore, Italy. (e-book)

Dunbar, A. *Using Metaphors with Coaching*. **http://cleancoaching.com/#/clean-coaching-free-articles/4514711939**

Dunbar, A. *Coaching Toolbox: Emergent Knowledge*. **http://cleancoaching.com/#/clean-coaching-free-articles/4514711939**

Dunbar, A. *Using Metaphors with Coaching*. **http://cleancoaching.com/#/clean-coaching-free-articles/4514711939**

Grove, D.J. and Panzer, B.I., (1989), *Resolving Traumatic Memories: Metaphors and Symbols in Psychotherapy*. New York: Irvington

Grove, D. & Wilson, C. (2005) *Six Degrees of Separation: the Emergent Knowledge Solutions of David Grove*. **http://cleancoaching.com/#/clean-coaching-free-articles/4514711939**

Grove, D. & Wilson, C. (2005) *Emergent Knowledge EK and Clean Coaching: The New Theories of David Grove*. **http://cleancoaching.com/#/clean-coaching-free-articles/4514711939**

Harland, P., (2009), *The Power of Six: A Six Part Guide to Self Knowledge*. London: Wayfinder Press

Harland, P., (2012), *Trust Me, I'm The Patient: Clean Language, Metaphor, and the New Psychology of Change*. London: Wayfinder Press

Lawley, J. and Tompkins, P. (2003), *'A Strange and Strong Sensation: Symbolic Modelling – Change with Metaphor'*, video accessible through **http://www.cleanlanguage.co.uk/articles/articles/176/1/DVD-Strange-and-Strong/Page1.html**

Lawley, J., and Tompkins, P., (1996), *'And, what kind of man is David Grove?'*, **www.cleanlanguage.co.uk/articles/articles/37/1/And-what-kind-of-a-man-is-David-Grove/Page1.html**

Lawley, J., and Tompkins, P., (2000), *Metaphors in Mind: Transformation through Symbolic Modelling*. The Developing Company Press

Lawley, J., and Tompkins, P., (2004), *'Clean Language Revisited'*, accessible through: **www.Cleanlanguage.co.uk/Clean-Language-Revisited.html**

Walker, C., (2014), *From Contempt to Curiosity: Creating Conditions for Groups to Collaborate using Clean Language and Systematic Modelling*. Fareham: Clean Publishing

Wilson, C. (2014) *Performance Coaching: A Complete Guide to Best Practice Coaching and Training*. Kogan Page London

Wilson, C. (2003) *Metaphor & Symbolic Modelling for Coaches*. **http://cleancoaching.com/#/clean-coaching-free-articles/4514711939**

Wilson, C. (2006) *Emergent Knowledge* **http://cleancoaching.com/#/clean-coaching-free-articles/4514711939**

Sullivan, W. and J. Rees (2008). *Clean Language: Revealing Metaphors and Opening Minds. Carmarthen*, Wales: Crown House Publishing House.

Sullivan W:
Clean Language training DVDs, Module 1: Introduction to Clean Language and Metaphor
Clean Language training DVDs, Module 2: Targeting Change
Clean Language training DVDs, Module 3: Change for Good
Clean Language training DVDs, Module 4: Space for Success
Clean Change Cards
Clean Metaphor Cards
Available from **www.cleanchange.co.uk**

David Grove talking about Emergent Knowledge from Philip Harland:
http://www.youtube.com/watch?v=jncQjaCH_lo (ΣK and the power of six)
http://www.youtube.com/watch?v=bl6hK4ZCaiE&feature=related (")
http://www.youtube.com/watch?v=Qat3_4RuRyU&feature=mfu_in_order&list=UL
http://www.youtube.com/watch?v=PaXr5aqaxuA&feature=autoplay&list=ULQat3_4RuRyU&lf=mfu_in_order&playnext=1
http://www.youtube.com/watch?v=H6bV1F73yaU&feature=autoplay&list=ULPaXr5aqaxuA&lf=mfu_in_order&playnext=2
http://www.cleanlanguage.co.uk/transcriptTapestry.html
Transcript 1989

BOOKS ABOUT THE SCIENCE OF EMERGENCE

Note that this is the science which David's work draws from: these books are not about David's work specifically or about the fields of coaching, psychology or therapy.

- *Linked: How Everything Is Connected to Everything Else and What It Means* by Albert-Laszlo Barabasi (2002)
- Strogatz, S., (2003), *Sync: The Emerging Science of Spontaneous Order* New York: Hyperion
- Watts, D.J., (1971), *Small Worlds: The Dynamics of Networks between Order and Randomness (Princeton Studies in Complexity).* Princeton, NJ: Princeton University Press
- Watts, D.J., (2004), *Six Degrees: The Emerging Science of Spontaneous Order.* New York: W. W. Norton
- Johnson, S., (2001), *Emergence: The Connected Lives of Ants, Brains, Cities, and Software.* New York: Scribner
- Rheingold, H., (2002), *Smart Mobs: The Next Social Revolution.* Cambridge, Mass.: Perseus

Popular Culture Featuring the Science of Emergence

- *Prey*, a thriller by Michael Crichton (2002)
- *The Sims*, a computer game created with Emergent software

Books about the Science of Emergence

Websites

www.cleancoaching.com
www.cleanlanguage.co.uk
www.emergentknowledge.com
www.cleanchangecompany.co.uk
www.wayfinderpress.co.uk
www.powersofsix.com
www.trainingattention.co.uk

REFERENCES

Barabasi, A-L., (2002), *Linked: How Everything Is Connected to Everything Else and What It Means*. Cambridge, Mass.: Perseus

Crichton, M., (2002), *Prey*. London: HarperCollins

Feldenkrais, M., (1991), *Awareness Through Movement*. London: Thorsons

Grove, D.J. and McGavock, R., (1998), *'Problem Domains and Non-Traumatic Resolution Through Metaphor Therapy'*, accessible through http://www.cleanlanguage.co.uk/articles/articles/4/1/Problem-Domains-And-Non-Traumatic-Resolution-Through-Metaphor-Therapy/Page1.html

Grove, D.J. and Panzer, B.I., (1989), *Resolving Traumatic Memories: Metaphors and Symbols in Psychotherapy*. New York: Irvington

Hall, E.T. (1984), *The Dance of Life: The Other Dimension of Time*. London: Anchor

Harland, P., (2012), *Trust Me, I'm The Patient: Clean Language, Metaphor, and the New Psychology of Change*. London: Wayfinder Press

Hillman, J. (1989), *The Essential James Hillman: A Blue Fire*. London: Routledge

Jung, C, (1964), *Man and His Symbols*. London: Aldus Books Ltd

References

Jung, C, (1961), *Memories, Dreams, Reflections.* London: Collins

Lawley, J., and Tompkins, P., (2000), *Metaphors in Mind: Transformation through Symbolic Modelling.* The Developing Company Press

Lawley, J., and Tompkins, P., (1995) **http://www.cleanlanguage.co.uk/articles/articles/37/1/And-what-kind-of-a-man-is-David-Grove/Page1.html**

Whitmore, Sir J. (2009) *Coaching for Performance.* London, Brealey